Ethical Judgment in Teaching

Karl D. Hostetler

UNIVERSITY OF NEBRASKA–LINCOLN

Allyn and Bacon

Boston • London • Toronto • Sydney • Tokyo • Singapore

A Viacom Company
160 Gould Street
Needham Heights, Mass. 02194

Internet: www.abacon.com
America Online: Keyword: College Outline

Senior Editor: Virginia Lanigan
Editorial Assistant: Nihad Farooq
Senior Marketing Manager: Kathy Hunter
Production Coordinator: Thomas E. Dorsaneo
Editorial Production Service: Melanie Field, Strawberry Field Publishing
Composition Buyer: Linda Cox
Manufacturing Buyer: Suzanne Lareau

Library of Congress Cataloging-in-Publication Data

Hostetler, Karl D.,
Ethical judgment in teaching / Karl D. Hostetler with Arthur Brown — [et al.].
p. cm.
Includes bibliographical references
ISBN 0-205-17408-6
1. Teachers — Professional ethics. I. Title.
LB1779.H67 1996
174'.93711 — dc20 96-25149
CIP

Printed in the United States of America

10 9 8 7 6 5 4 3 2 1 00 99 98 97 96

To the children and their teachers,
especially Jacob and Jesse

Contents

Acknowledgments

I would like to thank many people for their help with this book. Obviously, this book would not have happened had it not been for the work of those who contributed essays. I thank them for generously giving of their time and expertise. Virginia Lanigan, my editor at Allyn and Bacon, was a steady source of patient encouragement. Matt Larson and Kathryn Piller helped form a group of teachers to discuss the working manuscript with me. I thank them for their participation, along with Steve Ferris, Joe Higgins, Cathy Knight, and Steve Quiring. I shared parts of the manuscript with students in several sections of my class "Ethics and Education." I'd like to thank them for their indulgence and feedback. I am especially grateful to Jim Curtiss, Tom Deeds, and Russ Moulds, who not only gave me useful advice about this book, but have stalwartly acted as a resource for me in my other work. My appreciation to Jim Curtiss and Jacob Hostetler for offering ideas for cases. Jonas Soltis commented on part of the manuscript and has been my mentor and inspiration for much more besides. Finally, my thanks to Mary, not only for carefully reading and critiquing parts of the manuscript, but also for providing all the support without which this project could never have been completed.

I would also like to thank the following reviewers: Patrick J. Foley, University of Massachusetts, Dartmouth; Arthur Brown, Wayne State University; William E. Eaton, Southern Illinois University; Malcolm B. Campbell, Bowling Green State University; and Louise Fleming, Ashland University.

1

Introduction

CASE

It was only the first week of the new school year and already Sol Goldblum, the sixth-grade teacher, had a problem. For years he had let his students take turns running errands for him—to the principal's office, the custodian, other classrooms. This had always worked well. The students enjoyed the feeling of responsibility this experience gave them, and it helped establish the mutual trust that Sol believed was vital to a healthy classroom community.

The problem started when Billy Baker's turn to do errands came up. Billy had a reputation around school for being a "difficult" student. Billy's fifth-grade teacher had told Sol flat out that Billy was a troublemaker and could not be trusted. Sol thought about this, but he himself had not seen Billy misbehave. It was a new school year, and he thought Billy deserved a fresh start. So, in spite of the teacher's warning, he gave Billy the opportunity to take some papers to the principal's office. Well, as it turned out, Billy never made it to the principal's office. On the way, he started a fight with a fourth-grade boy who happened to be in the hallway. This boy had been taunting Billy on the playground the day before.

Now, Sol's principal had called him on the carpet for permitting Billy to go unescorted in the hallway. She told him never to let Billy go unescorted again. She was adamant about this. In the school as a whole, there had been too many incidents in the hallways. Parents were complaining, children had been hurt, and she was going to see to it that there were no more problems.

What should a teacher do in a situation like this? This book aims to show how everyday situations teachers face call for *ethical judgment* and how sound ethical judgments can be made in difficult situations like this one. The chapters that follow contain other cases about which you can exercise your ethical judgment, and there are examples of ethical judgment for you to critically examine and test your judgments against.

Later in this introduction I will say more about the plan and content of the book, but before getting to that we should ask, "Why this emphasis on ethical judgment?" This book is motivated by the belief that ethical judgment is an essential activity for teachers. It is also motivated by the belief that the nature and importance of ethical judgment are complicated matters, much more complicated than many people, both inside and outside education, are inclined to believe. If teachers are to do right by their clients, their colleagues, and themselves, and if they are to play a meaningful part in the political debate about ethics in education (much of which is quite hostile to teachers and schools), they need to understand what proper ethical reflection and action require and be able to articulate that to others. This book is to help teachers achieve that articulateness.

What is there to understand about ethical judgment in teaching? What are some of the issues involved? These will come out as you read and discuss the chapters that follow, but I'll point out a few now. This will introduce some basic controversies and concepts you will encounter throughout the book. Also, this gives me a chance to explain this book's approach to ethics. Let's think about "Trust and Safety," the case that opened the chapter, to begin our discussion.

Why Ethical *Judgment?*

Why does the situation in "Trust and Safety" call for an *ethical* response? If this is a question about why teachers should be ethical at all, there is no answer here. People who see no point in being ethical will not be convinced by this book. For millennia philosophers have looked for reasons that would persuade all people to be ethical. For instance, some have tried to show how being ethical serves people's self-interest. (In Plato's *Gorgias,* for example, Socrates tries to convince Callicles that a life of justice and virtue is happier than a life of power.) It was believed that because all people (especially those people who are inclined to act unethically) are concerned about their own interests, his argument for ethics would be convincing to everyone. But this argument breaks down: it is not clear that being ethical always serves one's self-interest, at least not in a way that appeals to selfish people.

This book is for people who already appreciate the point of ethics. But even these people could ask other forms of our question. One might go something like this: "I realize the importance of ethics, but don't teachers have to be neutral on ethical issues?" This question is informed by an important impulse. In a pluralistic democratic society such as ours teachers do need to be careful when it comes to endorsing or denying certain values or ways of life. But this does not mean that all ethical issues can or should be avoided; they are simply too ubiquitous for that.[1]

Plus, at least some of the key issues involved in "Trust and Safety"—protecting students from harm, being fair—are not the sort teachers should be neutral about. (Ethical neutrality may be more of an issue in other cases. The case "Faith and Truth" in Chapter 7 is an example.)

Our question about the need for an ethical response to the case might take another form. We could imagine someone making this statement about "Trust and Safety": "I agree that an ethical judgment is possible here. The ethical thing to do—the fair and courageous thing to do—would be to give Billy another chance. I wish we could do that, but we need to be practical. Parents are complaining, and we need to calm them down. What we need here is a practical judgment, not an ethical one." This response does not deny the relevance of ethics in teachers' lives, but it does say something about its place. Some philosophers have argued that there are times when ethical concerns cannot or should not take priority. Such reasoning may sound pretty suspicious at first blush. But *should* ethics come first all the time? People who always put ethics first might be saintly, but on the other hand they might just be moralistic, priggish, or self-righteous. They may be so concerned about keeping their hands clean that they do not do the dirty business that sometimes, unfortunately, is necessary.

However, let's not give up on ethics too quickly. The imagined "practical" statement above may be based on incorrect assumptions. It is not obvious that giving in to parental complaints is best, even best in a "practical" sense. Nor is it clear that responding to parents' complaints is merely a "practical" decision. There may also be ethical reasons for choosing that course. There is a difference between making parents happy just to make them happy and making them happy because one respects their views as concerned participants in the schooling process or because opposing their wishes would result in more harm than benefit for students. Making parents happy may not be the ethical ideal, but it still might be the right thing to do. Max Weber makes a distinction between "ethics of intention" and "ethics of responsibility."[2] The ethics of intention is concerned with sticking to one's ethical ideals, regardless of consequences. The ethics of responsibility, on the other hand, is concerned with the consequences of action based on, or aiming toward, those ideals. From this point of view, single-minded pursuit of ideals may not be a good thing; it might lead to bad consequences. For political actors (such as teachers), adhering strictly to an ethic of intention may be irresponsible. Notice, however, that Weber's distinction is not between ethics and practicalities; it is between two sorts of ethics. He does not say that we should do away with ethical ideals. He instead asserts that they need to be complemented by concern for consequences. This assertion further suggests that "no system of ethics in the world can avoid facing the fact that 'good' ends in many cases can be achieved only at the price of morally dubious or at least dangerous means and the possibility, or even the probability, of evil side-effects."[3] Ethics can be a dirty, tragic business.

Despite such possibilities, this conception does not require us to cheerfully accept evil side effects. The point is that we should be careful how we understand the ethical content of situations and our ethical responsibilities within those situations. Even if we find ourselves in a situation in which "practicalities" really do outweigh ethical concerns and are not simply a different sort of ethical concern, that does not mean ethical considerations are irrelevant. Even if we must dirty our hands, we must also recognize that we are acting in a way that is "morally dubious" and not excuse ourselves by saying that ethics does not apply to our situation. Even if we must decide to be "practical," we might also need to feel ethical guilt or regret about it.

This discussion suggests that some of the doubt about the relevance of ethics for teachers may stem from how we understand "ethics" in the first place. What is it in "Trust and Safety" that might make us think ethical judgment is needed? Surely there is something about the aspects of the situation that strike us as ethical. The decision to allow or forbid Billy to go unescorted in the hallway is not of the same sort as the decision to allow or forbid a waiter to put ground pepper on one's salad. Why is that?

Let's take one relatively clear factor—fairness. We might say that Sol has an *obligation* or *duty* to see to it that Billy is treated fairly. Correspondingly, Billy has a *right* to fair treatment. We'd be hard pressed to say that a restaurant that failed to offer ground pepper violated our rights. Rights and duties are paradigmatically ethical matters. It's pretty clear that our case involves a number of such matters.

However, problems arise when we equate ethics with duties and rights. One problem is that not all duties and rights are ethical duties and rights. For instance, one might argue that the principal had no *legal* right to make the demand she did. Even if we assume that claim is true, however, it does not settle the matter. For the principal may have an *ethical* right. While law certainly has some ethical weight, there are times when law is superseded by ethical concerns. School segregation laws may have given schools the legal right to exclude black children, but those laws were ethically wrong. The principal could appeal to her ethical right and duty to provide for the safety of the children.

Another potential problem with duties and rights is that they don't leave people room to maneuver. Duties and rights are binding, but acting in accordance with duties and rights may lead to bad consequences (which is the problem Weber points out with his distinction between intention and responsibility). Fairness might require that Billy have his turn to do errands, but shouldn't Sol have given more weight to the possibility of something unfortunate happening? And something unfortunate did in fact happen. So how can we say that Sol's fulfilling his obligation to fairness was the right thing to do? These are good questions, but again, the best response may not be to give up on ethics but rather rethink our understanding of ethics. Often, people understand ethics in *nonconsequentialist* terms. Nonconsequentialists focus on the inherent quality of an action rather than on consequences that may result from it. For a nonconsequentialist, if being fair is right, then it is right regardless of what consequences follow from it. *Consequentialists*, on the other hand, argue that actual or likely consequences of actions determine the ethical quality of those actions. While consequentialists differ in the details of their positions, we might summarize their position this way: The right action is the one that results in the greatest balance of good over evil for the greatest number of people. If the "fair" action does not meet this standard, then we have reason to set it aside. (This does not mean fairness can be set aside for just any reason. Not all consequences are ethically significant. Not getting ground pepper may be a "bad" situation, but it is trivial, ethically.)

Nonconsequentialists have a response of their own, of course. How far should we go to produce good consequences? For the sake of argument, let's say that punishing Billy severely would deter him from fighting and so keep peace in the school. A central nonconsequentialist principle is respect for persons, which means (in the interpretation Immanuel Kant gave it): People should be treated as ends in themselves, never merely as means to others' advantage. Billy should not be used merely as a means to produce peace in the school. So fairness cannot be set aside for that reason. Nonconsequentialists can respond to the "room to maneuver" and "practicality" criticisms by saying that fairness is relevant, but they may not agree that fairness requires Billy have a turn for errands. They may assert that fairness in his case requires some other course of action. For example, maybe it would be fair for Sol to find out more about Billy before letting him do errands to the principal's office. Or, on the other hand, it may be that fairness should not be the first concern, that some other duty or principle (a duty to prevent harm to Billy, for example) should take priority. Still it is duty and principle, not consequences, that are fundamental ethically. We will not try to resolve the dispute between consequentialists and nonconsequentialists in this book. First, they may not be as far apart as they seem.[4] Second, similar to Weber, we may believe that both views are essential. You will have the chance to examine the merit of that stance, for our writers often interweave aspects of both views. The point here is to avoid conceiving ethics too narrowly. "Trust and Safety" calls for an ethical response not only because of the rights and duties involved but because of a broader range of ethical goods at stake.

A focus on duty (and on consequences for that matter) may limit our understanding of ethics in a rather different way. For example, it is reasonable to argue that Sol has some kind of duty to make sure that Billy is treated fairly but that this duty does not obligate Sol to go out on a limb for Billy, say, by resisting his principal's command that Billy not go unescorted in the hallways. However, resistance might be the best thing for Sol to do, ethically.[5] Billy may not have a right to ask for Sol to oppose the principal, but it could be that is what Sol should do. Resisting might result in bad consequences for Sol, but it could show courage. We might not say that Sol has a *duty* to go the extra mile or be courageous, yet we may still esteem those qualities as admirable ethical qualities, as *virtues*.

Adding virtues to duties, rights, and consequences in our list of ethical concerns expands our view in at least two ways. First, it brings in *supererogation* (going "above and beyond the call of duty") as an ethical possibility. Second, it highlights *character* as an ethical concern. Ethically, we are not just concerned with people doing the right actions and producing good results; we are also concerned with the sort of people they are, *why* they do what they do. A selfish person may do all the right things but only for the most self-serving of reasons. Punishing Billy in this case might get him to do all the right things, but what would happen to his character? Would it help make him a better person, or would it just teach him how to avoid punishment? (Here, again, is an issue of ethical significance. A restaurateur who provides ground pepper may be doing something nice, but is that supererogatory? Is the restaurateur acting in this way to be nice or to make a buck?)

In our discussion we have covered a lot of ground quite quickly. If you feel confused, do not despair. "Ethics" is a complicated and much-contested idea.[6] Part of our task in this book is to make sense out of this complexity and determine what it means for ethical judgment. I think the contributors to this book will help you make some sense of these issues. Your task is to ponder how the writers do or do not make sense of ethics and to begin to develop an informed, well-considered understanding of ethics and its place in teaching.

Why Ethical Judgment*?*

Granting that ethics is relevant to the case "Trust and Safety," how does ethical *judgment* come in? As you considered the case, you probably focused some of your attention on the people involved. At first glance, it seems pretty obvious that Sol and Billy need to be considered. Perhaps the principal and the fourth-grade student with whom Billy fought also merit thought. But now questions begin to arise. Are we beginning to include too many people? Could it be that the matter is really between Billy and Sol only? Should we even care what the principal thinks? On the other hand, have we left relevant people out? How about Sol's fellow teachers? How about Billy's parents? How about the other students? How about the superintendent? Clearly, there are a number of people we *could* bring into our deliberations, but we must determine whom we *ought* to include. We must make judgments here.

In addition to the people in the case, perhaps you thought about the values that might be at stake. We've already touched upon some broad categories of ethical values and a few more specific ones such as fairness, courage, and safety of students. Trust is another important value, and there may be others. How about loyalty to colleagues? The principal's stand might prompt us to consider Sol's interests, his interest in getting along with his principal, for example. But once again questions arise. Are all of these concerns relevant and important for our decision? *Should* Sol's self-interest be a prominent concern for him? Shouldn't students' interests come first with teachers? Perhaps Billy's welfare is the overriding concern. If it is, what does that entail for other values and interests we have mentioned? Are trusting and being trusted vital to Billy's welfare? Perhaps at this point his welfare would be best served by punishing him.

We still may be leaving something out. Did you consider the fact that the fourth-grade boy taunted Billy in your deliberations? Perhaps besides considering things like duties, consequences, and virtues, we should also consider the ethical value of *emotions*, such as the anger Billy might have been feeling. Martha Nussbaum argues that we cannot understand such situations unless we can feel the emotions that are involved.[7] We should be disturbed by the anger that prompted Billy to fight the younger boy. Yet, should we blame Billy for lashing out? Should we expect a boy so young to be able to control his feelings? Indeed, would something be wrong if Billy *didn't* feel anger at being taunted? Shouldn't our concern for principles such as fairness and respect be backed up by ethical emotions that prompt us to act when those principles are violated with respect to ourselves and others? Emotions are sometimes considered to be hindrances to ethical judgment rather than important parts of it. Of course, emotions should not be given free rein in ethical situations. However, like the other components we have examined, emotions may have a proper place in ethical judgment.

There is still more to think about. Not only must we consider the persons, values, and emotions that might be important in the case, we must also consider *how* we ought to respond to those concerns. Does trust demand that Sol allow Billy another chance to go unescorted in the hallway? Are there better ways to show trust here? What does loyalty to colleagues require in the case? That Sol simply listen to them? That he actually do what they advise? Is the proper response to Billy's anger to eradicate it? stimulate it? control it? redirect it?

We don't have to progress far in our thinking about such things before realizing that these matters cannot be considered in isolation. It isn't just trust in Billy we're concerned about but also the safety of other children, the implications of the position taken by the principal, and a number of other things. This fact prompts some of the more difficult and anxiety-producing problems in this case, for part of what makes the case so difficult is that it seems we may be unable to do justice to all concerns; some even appear to be mutually exclusive.

We may be able to determine that this conflict is merely apparent. One might argue, for example, that both trust and safety can be satisfied by having Billy do shorter errands or do them at times of the day when other students are less likely to be in the hallways. However, is it really so easy to meld these two concerns? Perhaps trust can only really exist when risk is present. (Shirley Pendlebury says something like this in Chapter 4.) Can Sol be said to trust Billy if he arranges things so that Billy has no chance to foul up? Where is the trust in that case? It seems to be the height of *mis*trust. Maybe we have to face up to the possibility that Sol cannot have it both ways, that he has to choose—trust or safety. Judgment is needed here, for there may be no rule that cinches the decision one way or the other.

The upshot of this discussion is that we can identify at least three ways in which judgment enters into ethical deliberations: determining *what* is relevant and important in the situation in terms of people, values, or other facts about the case; determining *how* we should serve or respond to those; and determining what to do when those concerns or the responses they demand *conflict*.[8]

Emphasizing these decisions as "judgments" is meant to do two things: First, convey the need to be judgmental in ethical deliberation, and second, identify a particular sort of ethical deliberation. Let's begin with the idea of being judgmental. This is no simple "seeing" of what's right or good. We do not simply "uncover" or "discover" answers to these questions; they have to be hashed out. We should be careful here, however. We moderns tend to be too ready to discount the possibility that value may be external to us and thus something to be discovered and not just constructed by us.[9] Still, it doesn't follow that value is simply "seen." Nussbaum emphasizes "perception" in ethics. In her use of the term, "perception" is no mere naive seeing. It implies sensitivity and discernment and to that extent has some similarity to what I am trying to convey by the term "judgment." I prefer to use "judgment" because it suggests a role for explicit standards and self-conscious evaluations greater than that Nussbaum seems prepared to grant. (My choice of terms does not mean, however, that we always do or should explicitly appeal to standards or evaluate self-consciously. These are other issues this book hopes to shed light upon.)

Also, "judgment" is not the same thing as "thought" or "reflection." In their essays in this book the writers spend a good deal of time doing things like remembering (stories, old teachers, experiences) and mulling things over (the meaning of "philosophy," the meaning of "excellence"). These activities may not strike us as clear examples of judgment, particularly if we think "judgment" requires an actual decision (which is one reason why the essays are referred to as "reflections" rather than "judgments"). These sorts of thinking clearly have their place in ethical judgment. If we think of judgment as problem solving we might think of these other activities as problem finding or problem understanding, vital first steps if we are to solve the right problems or even get problem solving off the ground at all. We should also note, however, that judgment need not be separated from these sorts of thinking. Judgments suffuse these reflections: What stories are relevant to this case? Which of my old teachers were good teachers? What are the better and worse conceptions of philosophy and excellence? What distinguishes judgment from (mere) thinking and reflecting is that judgment is thought or reflection involving some *evaluation* of the objects of thought; it is a *discriminating* and *normative* form of thought or reflection. It is thought and reflection aimed at being *judgmental*. Nowadays one often sees and hears praise for reflection. The professional education literature is full of praise for reflective teaching, reflective journals, and so on. My concern here is that such reflection does not necessarily involve the vital activity of judgment. Judgment may not always be warranted, but we should not discount it.

We may feel uneasy about being judgmental. There may be good reasons for this discomfort. Getting back to "Trust and Safety," we might feel reluctant to say that Sol did the "wrong" thing, even if we might say that he did not choose the best course of action. We might be reluctant to criticize at all, believing that it isn't our place. Still, there are times when we do need to make a stronger claim and take stronger action. Even if we would go no further than saying that Sol did not do the best thing, we are passing judgment in a way that may be necessary. The case presents a problem, and ethically there is a need to think about whether there are better ways of acting.

Still, we should be cautious. The ethically appropriate response to a problem may not be "adjudication," that is, attempting to distinguish right from wrong or better from worse. In some cases it might be more appropriate to be an "arbitrator" than an adjudicator, to be more concerned with negotiation, reconciliation, and accommodation rather than with deciding who or what is right or better.[10] For instance, Nel Noddings, one of the contributors to this book, argues for an "ethic of caring" in which one's first concern is to be receptive to others, not to pass judgment on them.[11] The main point in this view is to maintain the possibility or reality of caring relationships with people. Worrying about who's right or wrong, or about what the fair action would be, may distract us from what is really important. It might actually set people against each other. Maybe in "Trust and Safety" what people really need to do is get together to mend fences and work out a plan and forget about who's right or wrong.

However, even if caring and accommodation are our prime concerns, judgment still has a place. Is accommodation *always* ethically appropriate? There may be times when one's values are too important to be compromised. (The issue of compromise will come up again.) Even if accommodation should be our aim, questions of how accommodation should be understood and with whom it should be sought still come up. Clearly, in her essay in this book (and in her other work), Noddings posits a place for such thoughtfulness and discernment.

We should not leave the matter here, however, for Noddings raises questions about how much we should emphasize even this sort of judgment. Caring persons, in aiming to be receptive to others, are less concerned with judging how to be receptive and with whom than with simply being open and receptive. This goal would seem to restrict further the role of judgment. But even if we accept this argument we should note this important distinction: Even if conscious judgment is not appropriate in the immediate situation, it may well be required in the aftermath. Even if we do not fault Sol for the judgment or lack of it he has shown in the case, he still needs to make a judgment about what to do next. What actions ought he to take now? Should he rethink his beliefs and policies about trust and his relationships to his fellow teachers and his principal? Ethical life is not just about responding to immediate crises but is also about forming an ethical character, reviewing and perhaps modifying one's goals and dispositions.

John Dewey goes so far as to say that ethical life has its "center" in this sort of reflection during "periods of suspended and postponed action" when we engage in "recollection and foresight, in severe inquiry and serious consideration of alternative aims." Thus, judgment is the most important ethical virtue, for it is "the key to the *direction* and to the *remaking* of all other habits."[12] Perhaps we should not go so far as Dewey does here. Noddings might say that caring, not judgment, is the center of ethical life and the key to the direction and remaking of ethical character. Nussbaum would give perception priority. Yet neither should we underestimate the need for judgment. Ethically, we are in a sorry state if we neglect to stop and take stock of our actions and policies, to make judgments about the ethical quality of what we do, plan, and desire.

I hope that this discussion makes clear that the aim of this book is not to claim the unqualified value of judgment. The book aims to help you develop a sense of the value, but also the possible limitations, of ethical judgment. Still, the book does stress the need for ethical judgment to the extent of pressing you to take some stands, to sort through your ethical beliefs for the sake of beginning to make some discriminations between what is ethically desirable and what is not.

However, there is more than one way to make such discriminations. Here we get to the second reason for the emphasis on judgment, which I mentioned above. By emphasizing "judgment" I wish to distinguish it as a particular sort of decision procedure. Judgments are not simple "decisions." When we exercise good judgment we are not arbitrarily choosing one or another option. Judgment implies a noncapricious process. This process, however, is not a simple, mechanical application of rules. Rules do have their place, but if judgment were strictly a matter of applying rules we would be led into an infinite regress problem. For example, what if determining relevant persons in a case were a matter of applying the rule "Students are relevant in cases in which conditions X_1, X_2, . . . , X_n exist." Supposing that we could give meaningful substance to such a rule, we would need a further rule for determining when the relevant conditions exist. For example, if condition X_1 is "Students interests are directly affected," we would need rules for deciding what counts as "student interests" and for deciding when interests are "directly affected." We could imagine those rules introducing their own sets of conditions, which would require further rules for determining their presence, and so on.

To stop the regress we need some know-how that is not itself rule-governed. This know-how is judgment. There is no algorithm or formula for judgment.[13] In this way judgment is different from calculation. It differs from calculation in its form, but also in its outcome. When we do calculations we expect determinate outcomes. We may not know what the outcome will be when we plug certain numbers into a formula, but we know that there will be some particular (though not necessarily singular) outcome. Not so in judgment. In situations that call for judgment, we expect that the assessments different people offer will differ. Although they may also utilize similar criteria in making their judgments, these criteria do not provide formulas and so do not always yield determinate conclusions. (In the language I will use later, the criteria "underdetermine" judgment.) Thus, in a gymnastics event, for example, we accept that different judges may give different marks and that all these marks may be legitimate (although we also have a sense of when scores are too high or too low).

However, ethics differs from gymnastics. Typically, we believe that there is more at stake in ethical matters—that's part of what distinguishes them *as* ethical matters. We can accept different judgments about the quality of a gymnastics performance. We're less sanguine about differences regarding justice, honesty, kindness, courage, and so on.

As uncomfortable as such differences make us, this is a situation we may have to accept. At least, one aim of this book is to explore that possibility. If we are looking for formulas and precision in ethics we are bound to be frustrated. A teacher's ethical world simply isn't precise. However, another aim of this book is to to show that such imprecision does not mean that ethical judgment is irrational, arbitrary, or merely subjective and that even if situations exist to which there is no one right response, that does not mean we cannot identify wrong responses.

The claims made above are not uncontroversial. They are offered as hypotheses that guide the inquiry presented in this book. Once you have participated in this inquiry with your colleagues and our writers, it is hoped that you will be in a position to judge whether these hypotheses embody worthwhile insights into the ethical task of teachers.

The remainder of this introduction goes into some detail as to how we will go about our inquiry into ethical judgment so that you can anticipate what is to come. The particular form our inquiry takes is itself motivated by some definite ideas that I will make explicit to help you think about them and the issues they raise.

The Plan of the Book

Chapters 2 through 7 each begin with a hypothetical school situation—similar to "Trust and Safety"—for you to think about. Each of these case studies is followed by responses to the case written by philosophers of education. (Why philosophy? That issue will also be discussed in this book.) These essays are intended to provide examples of ethical judgment for you to study. Each chapter closes with a discussion of the essays in the chapter. The discussions do not aim to be exhaustive by any means. It is likely that you will want to discuss other aspects of the cases as well. The discussions point out some main ideas, expand on some points, place the issues raised in the broader context of ethical theory, and raise some challenges to the writers' claims. Chapter 8 offers some conclusions about ethical judgment in teaching. Chapter 9 provides additional circumstances and cases to help you extend your reflections beyond the six main case studies.

I would like to say a bit more about the rationale and limitations of the book's approach. Case studies are an effective pedagogical tool for this sort of material. Cases stimulate emotion and imagination. They help bring down to earth issues that might remain too abstract otherwise. There are dangers in using case studies, however. One danger is that focusing on discrete "crisis situations" may give the impression that dealing with such situations is all that ethical judgment is about. But it is in the protracted, everyday, seemingly mundane features of classrooms and teaching that ethical judgment is most often called for. The arrangement of desks, the material on bulletin boards, the rituals schools perpetuate—all these merit ethical reflection and judgment even if their import cannot be neatly packaged in some discrete situation.[14]

Another danger is that even if we are concerned about particular situations, as surely we often are, case studies may provide a skewed view of the judgment required. Any case study in a text like this cannot do justice to all the relevant features of the situation, such as all the feelings, experiences, and history of the people involved. It is likely that when you read the cases you will sometimes think, "I don't know enough to be able to decide!" (A number of our essayists have that sort of reaction.) Maybe you reacted that way to "Trust and Safety." Such a reaction can be a legitimate response. Even so, we should be careful not to rely on this response too often. Appeal to lack of knowledge does not always justify indecision on an ethical matter. Sometimes we must judge and act, even in the face of incomplete knowledge. Some information simply may not be relevant. Also, remember that the purpose of this book is not (and cannot be) to model ethical judgment completely accurately. The case study approach has its limits, but some important and useful learning can still be gained from it.

There is something significant in the case study approach beyond its pedagogical merits. The emphasis given case studies in this book reflects particular beliefs about the nature of ethical judgment and understanding. The German philosopher Hans-Georg Gadamer argues that ethical understanding always involves application.[15] It is not that we first understand ethical ideas and then apply that understanding to particular situations; rather, we come to fully understand only *in* application.

This is so because, unlike the domain of technical knowledge, for instance (a domain that too often receives undue emphasis in teaching), ethics is concerned with determining ends. In technical tasks, we already know what the ends are—we want to put out the oil well fire, to fix the broken toaster, to get the students to spend more time on task. The technical question is how to accomplish those ends effectively and efficiently. Different contexts may present unique challenges—the oil well may be far from bases of supply, the toaster may be an unfamiliar model, the students may be a heterogeneous collection of personalities—but we can recognize experts who are able to get the job done, who "know" how to accomplish those ends. However, even if new situations present new challenges to achieving those ends, no new knowledge of the ends themselves is gained. I am not suggesting that teachers who take a technical view are unthinking or inhumane. They may search for humane ways to get their students to spend more time on task. My point is that the focus of attention still is upon the means of achieving the goal, not upon examining the goal itself. The goal is to have students on task, and the question is what will achieve that goal.

Gadamer argues that ethical action is no mere technical task. It is not simply a matter of knowing how to achieve what is right or good for students just because the ethical question concerns what is right or good in the first place. What is right, Gadamer argues, can only be known in the immediacy of the situation. Granted, we "know" that teachers should establish trust with students, protect them from harm, and get them to do their schoolwork. But as we saw in "Trust and Safety," we still need to judge whether trust and/or safety should be our guiding ends in the particular situation and determine how those ends are to be understood. Considered ethically, "time on task" becomes an issue of how we should understand the nature and value of students' "tasks" in the first place. Ethical deliberation aims at gaining new knowledge of trust, protection, and worthwhile school activities, not simply knowledge of means to achieving them.

Therefore, in stressing encounters with particular cases, this book aims to convey two related notions: how ethical understanding is only fully gained in particular applications of our ethical ideas and how different situations, with their own unique context, present new opportunities and challenges for ethical understanding and action. Reaching a defensible understanding of what trust or some other value demands in a particular situation does not mean that one is an expert on the matter; hence, Chapter 9, "Additional Circumstances and Cases." The material in Chapter 9 raises questions such as the following: What does a value such as trust demand in a different case? What if we were to have essentially the same case but some of the particulars were altered? When you finish reading a chapter, think about its case in light of some different circumstances. Try exploring the chapter's issues in the context of a different situation.

The titles of the six main case studies each suggests a theme: freedom and discipline, self and others, communities near and far, excellence and equality, unity and diversity, and faith and truth. These are basic, important, and persistent issues in teaching. Certainly, there are other themes embedded in the cases that are worth considering and that our contributors discuss. The writers were not restricted to addressing the themes proposed. Several quite explicitly resist those themes. To insist they emphasize those themes would be inconsistent with the picture of ethical thought presented above—ethically, we cannot always be sure what ends will be relevant or important. Nevertheless, we do not come to particular situations with *no* idea of what is important. Even if we find that we must modify our ideas of what is important, our understanding is not well served by simply shifting attention to other issues. There is value in explaining (as our writers do) why the initial concerns are *not* really important.

Notice that the issues in the case titles are presented in pairs. The members of these pairs might be thought of as opposites. This potential conflict is intended to emphasize the dialectic involved in understanding and living a value such as trust. A proper ethical understanding of trust is not gained by isolating it from other ethical ideas. Our understanding of trust must be worked out in conjunction with our understanding of our ethical obligation to protect students (and other ethical values). We understand our ethical values by playing them off against each other. This is not simply a learning strategy but is a statement about the nature of our ethical world. These values are inextricably bound up with one another. As we saw in "Trust and Safety," concern to meet our obligations to each value has implications for the other.

However, this relationship does not mean that judgment will always result in some combination or compromise of values. This may be the result (as some of the essays show). A prominent theme in the essays is that we should resist simple "either/or" choices when faced with conflicting values. Yet, as was suggested above, there may be times when we must choose *either* trust *or* safety. Such cases are what make our ethical world so complex, and sometimes tragic. Nevertheless, referring to trust *and* safety is appropriate because even if we must choose only one from the pair, we may not be freed of all obligations to the other. For example, even if Sol's overriding obligation is to the safety of students and he cannot satisfy his obligation to trust, we may still expect him to feel reluctant about acting against that obligation and expect him make amends to Billy.

Is it possible to learn how to deal wisely with all this complexity? Given the account of judgment already presented, perhaps you have doubts about the possibility of learning how to make good ethical judgments. It seems unlikely that we can completely formalize or systematize judgment. Perhaps we can say what judgment is *not*, that it is not "calculation," for instance, but this offers little positive guidance.

An explicit, exhaustive description of judgment may be beyond our capabilities, but this inability to articulate all that judgment is does not mean that judgment cannot be learned. Consider what Ludwig Wittgenstein said about knowledge of how to make good judgments:

> *Can one learn this knowledge? Yes; some can. Not, however, by taking a course in it, but through* 'experience'.—*Can someone else be a man's teacher in this? Certainly. From time to time he gives him the right* tip.—*This is what 'learning' and 'teaching' are like here.—What one acquires here is not a technique; one learns correct judgments. There are also rules, but they do not form a system, and only experienced people can apply them right. Unlike calculating-rules.*

What is most difficult here is to put this indefiniteness, correctly and unfalsified, into words.[16]

Perhaps we cannot present a full and accurate account of judgment in words, but judgment can still be learned. It can be learned by practicing judgment and getting "tips" from those who are accomplished at it. Hence, the chapters offer *examples* of judgment as exercised by other reflective, insightful people. Understand that these are not intended to be definitive answers to the problems in the cases. There are answers, and some answers are better than others. However, as an ethical agent it is ultimately up to you to engage with ethical issues and exercise some judgment about them. No one can do that *for* you, although other people certainly can, and often should, do it *with* you.

What the examples might do is *show* us what good judgment involves even if we cannot be *told*. Of course, our examples cannot portray all that good judgment does or should involve. Our examples of judgment are articulated, coherently composed reconstructions of a process that is actually much more involved, largely tacit, and often groping and tentative. In short, actual judgment is often rather messy. Still, our examples can model at least some of the activities of judgment, and even if real judgment is somewhat messy, perhaps our examples can also show the value and possibility of carefulness and clarity.

However, the book aims to go further than simply offering examples of judgments. It aims to offer a particular sort of example. One sort of judgment can be modeled by first sketching some broad theoretical perspectives on particular issues and then giving examples of how those ideas are utilized in judgment about particular cases.[17] A prominent problem this strategy is intended to address is to show how ethical judgment is based on reasons rather than mere whimsy.

This is a legitimate and valuable approach, but we should recognize that it highlights only one direction in the flow of ethical judgment, the "outside-in" direction. Considering first the general sorts of reasons or considerations theorists would be attuned to, these considerations are then moved into the case to see how they might apply. But there is also an "inside-out" approach.[18] In this approach, a principle or value on which one bases a judgment need not be made explicit in advance but might emerge only because a situation is appraised in such a way that the principle or value emerges as relevant and important.[19] In other words, rather than an "outside-in" movement of judgment from given principles or values to their application in particular cases, there is an "inside-out" movement from appraisal of situations to consideration of principles and values that give form and specificity to the reasons supporting one's judgment.

I cannot claim that the contributors provide clear examples of the latter approach. In fact, some of the contributors take the first approach, seemingly having pretty definite ideas of what principles or values are applicable to the case and then showing in their essays how those are applicable. But there is always some ambiguity present, for does an essay reflect the actual thought process of the author or is it a reconstruction of that process? It may be impossible to know. The structure of the book was designed to at least suggest the possibility of the "inside-out" approach.

Rather than beginning by theorizing about particular ethical ideas and binding the writers to them, the book begins from the writers' judgments. The aim is to offer a more holistic—and more accurate—picture of what ethical judgment involves. Some summation and analysis is offered, but this *follows* the examples of judgment, hence the notion of "inside-out." Taking this tack does not deny that judgment is reasoned, but it does present a different view of what it means to act on reasons. Seeing the task this way does more to characterize ethical judgment as holistic rather than atomistic, tacit rather than explicit, and particularistic rather than universalistic. This characterization does not imply that judgment is any less reasoned. That's the claim for you to think about, anyway.

The approach described above strives to present a more complete picture of the complexity of ethical judgment than would be presented if we first dictated theoretical parameters for the discussion. This method may present problems for people new to the material because a clear structure may not be obvious. Ideas may come too fast and without their relationship or point being clear. Resist this to the extent of trying to make sense of things; hopefully the discussions in the chapters will help. However, don't be too resistant to confusion; be accepting, too. Ethical judgment cannot always be neatly organized and packaged. Making sense of things is an ongoing activity. To wish otherwise is unrealistic.

Of course, to say that this approach is a good model of ethical judgment is not to say that every judgment arrived at this way is a good one. We still have the issue of how to distinguish good judgments from poor ones. This can be a difficult task. We cannot assume that just because judgments differ one or both of them must be mistaken. Nor can we assume that just because judgments coincide, they must be right. To bring out this issue, two people were asked to write on each case. Comparing essays will give you some idea of how ethical judgments may differ, how they sometimes converge, and what we might conclude from each eventuality.

Each writer wrote two essays about the case in question. The two writers wrote their first essays independently. Then these were exchanged and the writers responded to their partner's essay. The purpose of this exchange is to show that while in judgment there may be a plurality of views, we are not left merely with that plurality. Views can be criticized and refined; people who disagree can still learn from one another. This dialogue does not guarantee or presume an ultimate convergence of views. As you will see, often the writers find fault with what their partner says. Not always, though. And even when they do find fault, they are prompted to do things like refine their own views, explain themselves more, and consider new implications of their claims. To that extent we see hints of a "fusion of horizons" that enables each person to benefit from confrontation with a different perspective.[20] Such a fusion may seem like a modest benefit, but it is quite important. Fusion of horizons means that

> *whether they [participants] conclude by agreeing or disagreeing in a substantive sense, their positions are now informed by all the other positions. They are able to see the worth of different considerations, incorporate different examples and defend themselves against different criticisms. In this*

way their views acquire a greater warrant; they are less blind and one-sided and, to this extent, more rational than they previously were.[21]

I believe such a process is visible in the essays in this book.

In closing this introduction I would like to say that this book isn't just about sharpening your judgments about a set of discrete issues. A discernible "storyline" connects the chapters. (At the end of each discussion section I suggest how the chapter ties into the next part of the "story," but you need not go directly to the next chapter. You might want to review past chapters in light of what you have learned, or you may wish to go to the material in Chapter 9 in order to think more about the issues in the chapter.) As our writers address their specific issues they contribute to an unfolding story of ethical thought and action,which begins with the fact and value of teachers as free individuals and professionals embedded in a social and political context. The story proceeds as a search for the proper expression and limits of that freedom, with teachers who are concerned for themselves and the people and things close and dear to them, but who are also concerned for the communities of other people who are their clients and fellow human beings. It is a story of ethics as a political activity in which people together grapple with and toward shared values for the sake of making a better world. This activity demands sensitivity to different understandings of these values, but a major part of the story is the promise of arriving at fair, reasonable agreements about what is good in life and schooling. The story culminates in the possibility that beyond simple agreement people can join together in a search for genuine ethical understanding of what is good for human beings and the knowledge that teachers have an important role in that search.

The story is not finished, however, and I do not want to present it as such. I believe it is a story with which you can be engaged. My suggestion is that if you are to be articulate about the ethics of teaching you need to be able to do more than exercise good judgment in particular school situations, as important as that is. You need to be able to tell something of the whole story. You need not and most likely will not agree with all that is said in this book, but the contributors and I ask that you join in the debate about ethics in teaching, dialogue meaningfully with others, and keep the story going. We invite you to be part of that endeavor.

Notes

1. For an account of just how pervasive ethical considerations are in schools see Philip W. Jackson, Robert E. Boostrom, and David T. Hansen, *The Moral Life of Schools* (San Francisco: Jossey-Bass, 1993).

2. Max Weber, "Politics as a Vocation," in *Weber: Selections in Translation*, ed. W. G. Runciman (Cambridge: Cambridge University Press, 1978), pp. 212–25.

3. Ibid., p. 218.

4. To respond to criticisms that they do not give enough attention to rules, some consequentialists advocate "rule-consequentialism," the idea that we should usually follow rules (such as "be fair") because doing so tends to result in good consequences. Similarly, nonconsequentialists respond to criticisms that they are "rule-worshipers" by endorsing "act-nonconsequentialism," the belief that we need to evaluate particular acts on their own merits,

rather than simply sticking to rules. This version of nonconsequentialism still relies on rules but allows exceptions or special conditions to be built into them—rules need not be absolute. Viewed from these perspectives, it can be hard to tell the two camps apart. For the purposes of this discussion there is no need to distinguish these views definitively. The point is that each contributes something useful to our understanding of ethics.

5. Ethically, should one always do what is ethically *best*? At least at times, is it enough to do what is "good enough"? For an argument that it is, see Michael Stocker, *Plural and Conflicting Values* (Oxford: Clarendon Press, 1990).

6. In recognition of that, I use the term "ethical" judgment rather than "moral" judgment. While these terms can be used interchangeably, the "moral" is sometimes taken to represent the narrower realm of obligation and duty within the "ethical." Moral obligations are then taken to take precedence over all other considerations in all situations. Thus, with regard to moral judgment in their context, the question of what we ought to do is already answered for us—we ought to do whatever our duty is.

By using "ethical" instead of "moral" I am trying to keep open the question of what we ought to do in any particular situation. Duty may not always be the most important ethical consideration. Broadly speaking, the "ethical" is our answer(s) to the question of "How should people live?" But part of our task in ethical judgment is to decide just how that question should be answered in any particular situation. On this issue see two works by Martha Nussbaum, *The Fragility of Goodness* (Cambridge: Cambridge University Press, 1986) and *Love's Knowledge* (New York: Oxford University Press, 1990) as well as Joseph Raz, *The Morality of Freedom* (Oxford: Clarendon Press, 1986) and Bernard Williams, *Ethics and the Limits of Philosophy* (Cambridge: Harvard University Press, 1985).

7. See Nussbaum, *The Fragility of Goodness* and *Love's Knowledge*.

8. Here I adapt Charles Larmore's description of judgment given in his *Patterns of Moral Complexity* (Cambridge: Cambridge University Press, 1987), pp. 6–9.

9. On this topic see Charles Taylor, *Sources of the Self* (Cambridge: Harvard University Press, 1989).

10. David B. Wong, "Coping with Moral Conflict and Ambiguity," *Ethics* 102 (1992): 776.

11. Nel Noddings, *Caring* (Berkeley: University of California Press, 1984).

12. John Dewey and James Tufts, *Ethics* (New York: Henry Holt, 1909), p. 418. The emphasis is in the original.

13. At least in some places, Noddings suggests that her view of caring is not opposed to judgment so much as to decision by formula. See Noddings, *Caring,* p. 53, for instance.

14. Again I refer readers to Jackson et al., *The Moral Life of Schools*.

15. See Hans-Georg Gadamer, *Truth and Method*, 2nd rev. ed., trans. Joel Weinsheimer and Donald S. Marshall (New York: Crossroad, 1989), pp. 307–41.

16. Ludwig Wittgenstein, *Philosophical Investigations*, 3rd ed., trans. G. E. M. Anscombe (New York: Macmillan, 1958), 227e. The emphasis is in the original.

17. For instance, this is the principal approach taken by Kenneth Strike and Jonas Soltis in *The Ethics of Teaching*, 2nd ed. (New York: Teachers College Press, 1992).

18. To give more technical labels to these forms of judgment, we can call them, respectively, "determinative" and "reflective" judgment. For further discussion of the significance of this difference see Richard J. Bernstein, *Beyond Objectivism and Relativism* (Philadelphia: University of Pennsylvania Press, 1983).

19. See Larmore, *Patterns of Moral Complexity,* p. 8.

20. Gadamer presents the idea of a "fusion of horizons" in *Truth and Method*.

21. Georgia Warnke, *Gadamer: Hermeneutics, Tradition and Reason* (Stanford: Stanford University Press, 1987), p. 170.

2

Freedom and Discipline

CASE

"You're an idiot, Roger, and there's no point discussing this any more." With that, Scott Armstrong stomped out of Andre Taylor's office. "You see now, Andre, what I have to deal with," Roger Neal said calmly. "Really, you *must* do something about Scott." With that, Roger rose from his chair and strode out of the office.

Andre sighed. He had hoped that his attempt to mediate the dispute between Scott and Roger would meet with more success. Still, he wasn't terribly surprised. Throughout the afternoon's meeting and to the last, both Scott and Roger had been true to the form they had shown all through this episode—Scott, passionate and impulsive; Roger, composed and precise. Little wonder we didn't get anywhere, Andre thought. Now what?

Scott was a sixth-grade teacher in an elementary school that fed into the junior high where Roger taught seventh- and eighth-grade language arts. Over the past two years, tension had been building between the two teachers because of their different views on teaching language arts. Scott emphasized free expression. He wanted students to be active and passionate consumers and creators of language in reading, speaking, and writing. He had little interest in students following the "rules" of language. Great writers are the ones who break the rules, he told his students. Scott presented no formal lessons on the mechanics of spelling, punctuation, and aspects of grammar.

This pleased Roger not one bit. He had complained to Scott's principal and to his own principal that Scott's former students came to him unprepared and undisciplined. Their language was not "free"—it was chaotic and pointless. Roger agreed that students should have freedom to create. For example, every week he assigned at least one "creative writing" project. But language needed to be disciplined if it was to be more than mere spewing of meaningless, inarticulate, half-baked grunts.

Scott, of course, got wind of Roger's approach when his former students came back to visit him. He gave these students an extended polemic about the repressiveness of Roger's approach. Roger "assigned" creative writing? What sense does that make? Creation should be spontaneous and self-initiated, not imposed. Plus, Scott's students didn't have any trouble getting their messages across to each other or to him. Where there was difficulty, students themselves worked out ways to improve communication, and this approach didn't require that they conform to accepted conventions of spelling, punctuation, and so on. He didn't have to impose some program of artificial grammar exercises.

Scott had done more than vent his spleen to these students. He had also begun telling parents of his current students to request that their children not have Roger for seventh-grade language arts.

Inevitably, Roger, in his turn, heard of what Scott was doing. He once again complained to the principals and pressed them to take action. Together, the principals decided to contact Andre, who was director of language arts for the school district. After hearing their reports of the situation, Andre asked that he have first crack at the problem. He felt that this was a "disciplinary" problem in the sense that it was a dispute internal to the discipline of language arts. As professionals and specialists in their common field, Scott, Roger, and he had the responsibility and knowledge to work out the differences. Andre was somewhat annoyed that Scott and Roger had not recognized this themselves and come to him with their problem.

Andre sympathized a good deal with Scott. He had interviewed Scott when Scott had applied for the sixth-grade teaching position. At the time he had been impressed by Scott's passion and lack of inhibition. Yes, he knew there were risks there, but Andre also believed that Scott had a great deal to offer his students. And Scott did get results. His students read voraciously. They wrote books. They put on plays. On the other hand, Andre had seen some of the work these same students did for Roger. It was difficult to believe that they were the same kids. True, Roger gave them open-ended creative writing opportunities, but, on average, the students wrote only about two pages for these.

With Scott they would have written a book. Roger might have given them freedom in some sense, but it seemed that he did little to encourage or empower students to *do* something with it.

Still, Roger's students *did* learn their mechanics. Their standardized test scores in these areas were high, whereas with Scott their scores were only about average, if that. And Andre could see Roger's point about the need for discipline in language. While Scott's students did write a lot, Andre had to say that he often found the writing difficult to follow when he read it. Maybe Scott could understand it, but Scott wasn't the only person these students would ever need to write for. Even if great writers did break the rules as Scott said, didn't they first have to learn the rules so that they'd have something to break? Otherwise, their protest wouldn't be an act of freedom, it really would be, as Roger said, a meaningless grunt. When it came to that, Roger could back up his point with his success as the junior high debate coach. His teams had won many awards in competitions around the state. Roger's teams were renowned for the discipline with which they prepared their arguments and for the cogency of their presentations. Being part of Roger's debate team was considered a great honor. Roger himself had been elected by his fellow debate coaches to head their state organization.

Andre saw the tension of freedom and discipline in language. He also saw it in his authority as language arts director. He believed teachers needed freedom in order to excel. Yet, Scott really did seem to be going too far. His freedom didn't extend so far as to refuse to consider Roger's point of view and the standards of their discipline. Neither did it extend so far as to voice his complaints to students and parents. To Andre, that showed a lack of professionalism and discipline. Yet, Roger seemed just as stubborn, even if he did maintain a less passionate demeanor. In André's professional opinion, Roger had carried the notion of discipline to too great an extreme. Teachers need to submit to the best standards of their discipline and profession, Andre believed, and he had the authority to enforce those. It appeared to him that each teacher was violating some of those standards. But could he be sure of that? Even if he were, how important are those violations? How far did he really want to go to curb Scott's passion? How could he avoid alienating Roger? Would curbing their freedom cause more harm than good?

It now seemed to Andre that he'd have to take some decisive action. Apparently, his initial attempt at mediation had failed, and as far as he could tell things would only get worse. Roger and Scott appeared to be even further from reconciliation. Their dispute was becoming common knowledge in the community, and many parents were upset about it. The problem is, what should he do?

Reflections on "Freedom and Discipline"

Showdown

BY NICHOLAS C. BURBULES

My first reaction to this case is that it doesn't seem to me to be primarily a problem of different approaches to teaching the language arts. There clearly is a strong difference of opinion here, but I do not attribute the conflict to the difference itself. Nor would I want to try to base a resolution to this conflict on trying to get either Scott or Roger to fundamentally change his views. It seems to me that the rivalry here has taken on a self-perpetuating pattern in which each response engenders new resentments and further reactions. Hence it appears quite unlikely that the disagreement between these men will abate any time soon—but the problems created by their disagreement are of an immediate nature. My main initial concerns are with the way that students are being put in between them in their argument and the way that a legitimate curriculum disagreement between two teachers has spilled over into the community, undermining public confidence in the competence and professionalism of its teachers, but doing very little to inform the public by illuminating the real issues at stake.

Putting myself in Andre's position as a district curriculum specialist, I encounter disagreements about divergent curriculum theories all the time. Often these disagreements are wrapped up with larger moral, political, or ideological disputes. They are often also wrapped up with the kinds of personalities and the basic styles of teaching that different teachers bring to school—not the sorts of things that are likely to change fundamentally, and certainly not quickly. Besides, I do not see the disagreement itself as necessarily a problem; I consider it a strength of schools that there is no attempt to impose one best or correct style of teaching, and I also consider it an educational benefit for students to be exposed to different styles of teaching, different points of view, and different value systems. To my way of thinking, differences of opinion, and the disagreements that result, can be seen as problems or as opportunities; such diversity is a strength when it is encompassed by a respect for alternatives and for a sense of how different approaches can still be guided by integrity and a concern for educational quality. It can enlarge educational possibilities when students are encouraged to see the value in different approaches or in different conceptions of the educational "good."

Eventually, I would like to engage both Scott and Roger in a discussion together, to try to encourage them each to understand the valid educational goals that have led the other to a different approach to teaching. Such a dialogue would likely require that they argue less over the different principles or values that guide their educational choices and instead explain how they try to serve the educational needs and interests of their students. One of these concerns, I would suggest, is helping students to appreciate the relative values of creativity *and* discipline in writing, to avoid falling into simple dichotomies; to formulate their own approaches to writing in light of an understanding of a range of valid approaches and styles. To the extent that each of these fellows wants to preclude students from being exposed to the other's methods or views, they are both in the wrong (though I do not find the situation entirely reciprocal in this respect).

Such a conversation between the two men is a worthwhile goal to work toward. From the details of the story as I have them, Scott and Roger had never actually spoken to one another about their differences before they met in my office—perhaps this is partly why they have demonized one another and why the situation has become so highly charged that they can scarcely manage to conceive of the educational issues from one another's point of view. Both parties have become more and more entrenched in their views as the struggle has gone on. Each believes, I am sure, that he is doing what is best for the students; but it has become impossible, apparently, for either to imagine that the other is motivated by the same commitment. I would see one valid and attainable goal of a dialogue between them to be moving toward that mutual recognition.

Generally speaking, I see conversation as potentially leading toward various kinds of worthwhile outcomes. Sometimes, conversation can lead toward real agreement, consensus, or compromise, as people move from rigid initial positions to a gradual accommodation of one another's views. This may mean one party convincing the other, or both parties changing over time. I do not see this sort of accommodation as very likely in this instance. Alternatively, conversation can lead, even where disagreement persists, to understanding—and through understanding a kind of respect. It is not too much to expect in this instance that even where Scott and Roger do not come to common views, they can come to appreciate the thoughtfulness and integrity that has led each to the view he holds. By seeing that this choice was guided by serious reasons and a sincere concern for students, the other might come to accept it, even respect it, as worthy (even if he continues to disagree with it). Even more modestly, the parties may fail to achieve mutual understanding, but can at least reach a level of tolerance by getting past the clichéd abstraction they have each constructed out of the other's views. Toward this end, I would recommend that Scott and Roger each talk only about *why* he has settled on his own approach and not try to give arguments about why the other's view is inferior. This might shift the focus away from where they differ, and each might glimpse for a moment the human face behind the demon he imagines. This may not yield agreement or even understanding, but it may yield a much-needed measure of tolerance.

I do not think that one has to be sanguine that conversation will *always* be successful at one of these three levels: agreement, understanding, or even simple tolerance. Sometimes further discussion simply heightens the sense of disagreement or reinforces the importance of the issues at stake. Obviously, it is in cases of deep disagreement that our skills of communication are most sorely tested, and we all know that we do not always succeed.

But fostering such conversation is a long-term process, with uncertain prospects of success, given two strong-willed men who bring to this disagreement all their ego, their competitiveness, and their insistence on having things their own way. On this score I am frankly a bit pessimistic, but I see it as my job to try to foster such collegial discussions, and I will do what I can. However, as I have said, I do not think that the immediate issue is about different views on teaching writing, anyway. The present situation has reached a critical point, where students' educational circumstances are being thrown into turmoil and in which students, parents, and administrators are being commissioned into the dispute as partisans on either side. That is a situation I must deal with right away.

This crisis is primarily a result of the ego struggle between these two men. When students are being put in the middle of a dispute between two faculty, or when parents' confidence in the school system is undermined by exaggerated claims about "harm" being done to their children, the time has come to act. Frankly, I hold Scott primarily responsible for this state of affairs, because he is the one (based on the information available to me) who has elevated the dispute to such a level. Roger's criticisms of Scott's approach to teaching, whether justified or not, have been expressed privately, to administrators who have responsibility for the teaching and curricula that go on within their schools. Roger does not, on my reading of things, refuse to allow Scott to teach writing in basically the way that he wants; he is concerned about the preparation of students coming into his own class and would like to see more time spent on skills development and not only on free writing. For Scott, on the other hand, ridding the schools of Roger and people who teach writing as he does seems to be a bit of a crusade.

For these reasons, I believe that before a conversation between them is likely to be at all successful, I will need to speak with Scott and Roger separately. I would try to engage them each in a conversation, away from the distractions of their mutual ill will, in which I can sympathetically hear and respond to their educational commitments and concerns. Part of my interest, frankly, is in trying to model a different way of engaging others in conversation, even when there are disagreements at stake. This would involve, concretely, my *listening* (something neither of them does very well, apparently); my asking for and respecting their own reasons for their educational values and practices; and my crediting the fact that each believes he is doing the best thing for his students. Over time, I would pose some questions about the starkly dichotomous views each has about the freedom/discipline or creativity/structure debate within the language arts. I would try to encourage each to see, in his own way, that creativity and structure are *not* incompatible values in teaching writing and that their caricatures of one another's approaches to teaching are both unfair and unproductive. Perhaps these conversations might be helpful in beginning to change some outlooks or to moderate at least some of the rather dogmatic views that I hear expressed here, and preparing the conditions in which a conversation between them has some chance to proceed successfully.

On Roger's side, I would try to persuade him that it may be easier from a teaching standpoint to take students who already have a love of writing (thanks to Scott) and gradually introduce some of the discipline and skills that allow writers to communicate with a wider audience more effectively. Writing as a form of creative expression does often involve bending, breaking, or ignoring certain rules. Roger says you need to know the rules before you break them; yet there are many examples of great art where that is not true, where untrained practitioners, precisely because of their undisciplined, unconventional styles, break existing molds and explore novel forms and possibilities. Nevertheless, Roger can explain to his students that expressive or creative writing is only one purpose writers might have, and that for many ordinary purposes of writing—such as job applications and business letters—certain conventions are simply necessary for effective communication.

I would try to point out to Roger, though, that it may be easier to develop those skills and discipline when there is a good deal of raw material to work with—and Scott's students certainly are prolific writers. These days, that is a relatively desirable problem for a writing teacher to have to deal with.

On Scott's side, I would try to persuade him that these are not *his* students; that as a teacher he has an opportunity to influence them during the time they are in his charge—to teach, encourage, and inspire them as best he can. But the very same prerogative that allows him the latitude to teach his classes as he chooses, he must extend to others. A bit of structure and discipline *does not* threaten creativity and may support it (for example, poets who by varying rhyme and meter achieve artistic effects through form as well as content). If Scott feels that stimulating the flow of free writing and fostering a pure love of words are his primary goals, well enough; but this does not make those the only goals for teaching writing, nor does it make them incompatible with other goals.

If learning is developmental, there is a time for each thing; enjoying a range of freedom, and a degree of discipline, each have their place in terms of the long-range goal of developing capable and creative writers. It is as true of learning writing as it is of forming moral character, learning how to work and play with others, or any other educational aim.

I would not want to question the integrity or strength of conviction that each of these teachers brings to his teaching. Each seems to be an exceptional teacher, in his own way, and part of that is the fervor and enthusiasm each feels for his way of approaching writing. As I hope is clear from my discussion of the goals of conversation, I would not want to minimize their differences or melt their passions into some soupy compromise of a little of this, a little of that. On the contrary, I would try to impress upon both of these teachers that the dialectic of freedom and discipline needs strong influences on both sides; this is what can maintain a creative tension. Each of them, in a way, *needs* the other in order to have the latitude to teach what he wants. One can focus on spontaneity and creativity, knowing that someone else will take care of the grammar rules; the other can work at developing discipline and structure, because the basic love of writing is already instilled. Neither has the right to expect other teachers to teach to his own expectations, and neither has the right to work actively against the effectiveness of the other simply because he does not personally share the other's values or style of teaching. Finally, and to reiterate the point, it is a *good* thing for students to be exposed to different styles of teaching, different goals, and different representations of course content. It is the student, after all, who needs to interpret and interrelate these ideas in terms of a way of seeing and being in the world that makes sense for him or for her. One might even say that learning to be able to do this is the most fundamental educational aim of all.

On a more concrete and practical level, teachers should extend to one another a certain degree of respect. Schools as communities of teaching and learning cannot be based on strict conformity of methods, values, or expertise. In the face of inevitable diversity and disagreements, a point arrives where simply for the sake of maintaining collegiality and efficacy within the overall effort, teachers must cede to one another a range of autonomy and judgment that they agree to respect for one another. In the staff room, or in other settings, differences deserve to be aired, and the disagreements may be vigorous; maybe they will even result in people changing their minds or changing their teaching practices. But it is more realistic to expect that in many cases the disagreements will remain. I would try to remind Scott and Roger that their dispute is not about negligence, incompetence, or outright misconduct. In this instance, the dispute seems to be mainly about differences in educational priorities, albeit deeply help ones. It is wrong, I would even say irresponsible, for either to try to demonize the efforts of another teacher simply because their approaches—each highly successful and enjoyable to students, in its own way—are based on different pedagogical assumptions. If teachers in schools are not broad-minded enough to encompass this meager degree of diversity, they have little authority in urging upon students the democratic virtues of tolerance and reciprocal respect.

So, in a sentence, the freedom-and-discipline issue I find most interesting in this case isn't the dispute about what these words mean in the context of teaching writing; it is about what they mean in the exercise of one's teaching responsibilities. Scott's freedoms extend broadly, but not to the point of actively undermining the good-intentioned efforts of a colleague. Roger's approach to teaching writing is consistent and rigorous, but it does not extend to trying to "discipline" his colleagues into teaching the way he thinks they should. The creative tension or dialectic between freedom and discipline extends not only to the two aspects of teaching writing, discussed previously, but to two valuable principles in the conduct and organization of human affairs. Both Scott and Roger, I believe, need to appreciate these values and accord one another the respect due to two able and conscientious teacher/colleagues. *That*, for me, is the most salient aspect of this case, both in terms of addressing the short-term problem of the guerrilla war being waged between them and in terms of the long-term problem of creating an atmosphere in which a serious and respectful discussion of their disagreements can possibly take place.

I should explain that I would prefer to keep these discussions "in-house," not because I believe that parents and community members should not have a voice in what is taught in schools, but because this particular way of framing the issue is generating more heat than light. As I have emphasized, the approach that Scott and Roger have taken, extended to its logical limit, can never lead to a better understanding of the subtleties of teaching writing and the actual merits of their different approaches. The form their struggle has taken threatens to be more about who survives in the district or who can undermine the other's reputation and support from colleagues, parents, and students. Such a struggle is about winning, not about good teaching.

Finally, there are a few matters I would like to know more about in this case. I would like to know what the principals or department heads of these schools had tried to do about the dispute before it was elevated to the status of a district problem. I suspect that someone should have seen this problem coming and intervened earlier, before the emotional stakes became so elevated and certainly before it undermined public confidence. I would also be curious to know more about the characteristics of the students in these schools (such as race, class, or ethnic background). If, for example, we were dealing with students from severely disadvantaged circumstances, for whom the attainment of *any* sort of written literacy was a pressing need, I might be more sympathetic to Scott's approach, which sacrifices exact precision for the sake of enthusiasm, confidence, and baseline skills (this does not attenuate the need for developing more finely honed skills and discipline in writing eventually, of course). I would want to know how these two teachers treat other colleagues in the language arts; obviously Scott and Roger are not the only advocates for these opposing views. When they encounter others, do they each treat them similarly? Do they treat all pedagogical disagreements as a life-or-death struggle? Or is this particular dispute actually based on a personality clash between two particularly strong-willed men? I suspect that the vigor each brings to this disagreement suggests something more than a theoretical difference of opinion. And I cannot help but wonder if two female colleagues might have dealt with this sort of conflict differently—might have been less concerned with winning by making the other look bad, more willing to talk things over, and possibly more sensitive to the potential harms being done to the students put in the middle of their emotional battle.

Is It Really Freedom and Discipline?

BY BETTY SICHEL

First Reading and Thoughts

During a first reading I concentrate on the flow of the text, on the situation that at first only seems to concern Roger, Scott, and Andre. But then other shadowy figures emerge from the narrative—principals, parents, and students. I say to the text, "tell me about the particular context, about the school and community." But it does not answer. I wonder about other teachers, about their teaching, their views of methodology and professionalism. As Alfred North Whitehead stressed in his speculative philosophy, what is omitted, what is never experienced, what never surfaces may reveal as much about people and their situations as the characteristics that are explicitly known. Thus, the empty holes, the missing dimensions intrigue and puzzle me.

Wherever there are empty spaces, memory fragments enter, bringing thoughts of movies and literature. Scott seems to epitomize the freedom and imagination of the teacher portrayed in *Dead Poets Society.* Though Roger does not represent a tyrant, certainly not the disciplinarian described in James Joyce's *Portrait of the Artist as a Young Man*, he does represent the "rules" of the discipline, perhaps even primarily as these rules are interpreted on achievement tests.

Another memory trace haunts my reading, again from Whitehead, this time his view of teaching and learning through the rhythmic stages of romance, precision, and generalization. The stage of romance "holds within itself unexplored connexions with possibilities half-disclosed by glimpses and half-concealed by the wealth of material."[1] Systematic, organized structure and precise data are abandoned in favor of the lure of the novel. During the stage of precision, exact formulation replaces the earlier first apprehension. With the stage of generalization, one "return[s] to romanticism with [the] added advantage of classified ideas and relevant technique."[2] General principles acquired at this stage contribute to an understanding of previously dimly perceived relationships.

In their teaching, Scott and Roger each underscores and implements different elements of this "rhythmic" method, but each considerably downplays various elements. Scott moved from romance to generalizations, at times collapsing romance and generalization, as when students wrote and acted in their own plays or read novels or wrote stories. Roger moved from precision to generalization or collapsed generalization into precision, as when students excelled at debating or were assigned "creative" writing.

Throughout the reading, I continually felt that what was missing, what the protagonists and the narrative never mentioned, was more salient than what was included. There was no mention of whole language, of journal writing, of mapping or webbing. No one spoke of the school's structure and governance. Although new initiatives and practices are now emerging in middle-level education, the very grades included in this narrative, there does not seem to be any awareness of these. Initiatives and practices such as teaming, various types of interdisciplinary curriculum cooperative learning, on-site management, adviser-advisee groups, inclusion, action research, conflict negotiation, and the critical role of professional development are not described.

Why be so concerned about these missing pieces? Dilemmas arise out of actual situations. The dilemma that Andre must solve emerged from a context, a situation, from particular educational forms and structures. Within the context of the dilemma, there seems to be minimal, if any, concern with present educational initiatives and innovations. There seems to be acceptance of the independence or autonomy of teachers except when intractable conflict arises between individuals with different interests and methods. The procedure for resolving conflicts between teachers seems limited by a traditional bureaucratic, hierarchical structure. There were few activities, if any, to bring teachers together, to work as teams, to converse about differences or mutual problems, to work together to implement new initiatives. This was my first reading.

Second Reading and Thoughts

As I continued to think about the case, I wondered whether I should confine my search for a resolution to Andre's dilemma to an individual, internal dialogue with good reasons and in the role of Andre presume to know how to resolve this seemingly unresolvable problem. Should I give my stamp of approval to some authoritative decision and thereby reveal confidence in my ability and knowledge? My confidence in espousing real solutions would reveal my belief in being *an* authority and, as the voice of Andre, I would vicariously be *in* authority.

At other moments, when lunching with colleagues and when doing interactive journal writing in a graduate teacher education class, I turned away from the image of the lone thinker, a Solomon judge, who could imprint upon Andre the wisdom of the right judgment that would insure optimum teaching and learning and contribute to a positive educational climate. Because I believe that collaboration and conversation are not just scholarly ideas to write *about* and teach *about* but should be dominant aspects of teaching and learning, decision making, democratic living, and the search for "knowledge" and understanding, how then could I or Andre or I in the garb of Andre make this decision? Was there another way? Yes, there may seem to be some conversation between myself and Nicholas Burbules, but Nick will be a respondent. We may be playing a sophisticated game of give and take, the give and take of an argument, even if that give and take is disguised by a conversational vocabulary. Could there be another way? Could Andre, Scott, and Roger enter into conversation? Could the conversation be expanded to include others, whether my students and colleagues or those of Andre, Scott, and Roger? Could the conversation then be further enlarged to include Nick and his colleagues and students, their perspectives on Andre, Scott, Roger, and their students? And finally, there could be others, those "imagined" readers who would make the text their own.

Thus, the early readings of this seemingly straightforward dilemma are misleading. For I cannot just follow the narrator and accept that the issues involve questions inherent to an academic discipline or the directions given to the reader by the title of the dilemma. Does the dilemma also involve questions about individual style, personality, and values and how these intrude upon issues of teaching as a discipline or language arts as a discipline? Even with this extension of the dilemma's boundaries, something seems awry. Any teaching dilemma has a background, involving taken-for-granted knowledge and assumptions. As hinted, from Andre's thoughts about his first and apparently only interview with Scott and Roger, the dilemma cannot be viewed as an encapsulated situation abstracted from a flow of experiences and from a complex narrative.

As I read the short, suggestive case another time and then again, other questions arise. Should the main consideration be the respective teachers' teaching methodology, how they interpret their teaching responsibilities, their differing beliefs about their discipline, whether their discipline is language arts or teaching, their seemingly opposing views of discipline and freedom? Is an equally serious problem the professional ethics problem of complaining to parents and questioning former students? If these forms of discourse with parents and students are objectionable, should parents and students have some other form of active involvement in the type or quality of education and teaching occurring in each class? Or does someone who is an expert in a field or discipline have ultimate authority regarding what is taught and how it is taught?

Another set of questions emerge about the process that was used to attempt to settle the disagreement between Roger and Scott. Should the issue have been "dumped in Andre Taylor's lap"? This question is asked because two years of escalating "tension" passed before anyone thought of doing something. Could a single meeting resolve the issue? Should Andre have expected that one face-to-face confrontation, entitled "meeting," between Roger and Scott would result in any positive resolution of their ongoing disagreements? Although Andre was given the authority and responsibility to make a decision he should wonder about the efficacy of any directive he might give to the parties. Even if Andre has the right and responsibility to make a decision and order Roger and Scott to modify their teaching styles and to include different content and assignments, would Andre's decision have a salutary effect on teaching and learning? Would an order by Andre infringe on commonly accepted levels of academic freedom for public school teachers? Even if their academic freedom is not at the same level as that for university professors, public school teachers must have adequate freedom to ensure even minimally acceptable or effective teaching. Would a presumptuous decision by Andre so negate this academic freedom that the decision would not merely be an infringement in areas that should be controlled by Roger and Scott, but also have negative collateral consequences for the schools' educational climate and the morale of the teaching staff?

The later rereadings convinced me that my earlier description of Scott as representative of freedom and Roger of discipline would not be accepted by Scott and Roger. When the reader enters into the narrative, the two teachers are argumentative, if not polemic, about what each personifies in his teaching and how each reveres either freedom or discipline. In actuality, however, each teacher believes in freedom and discipline, but they interpret freedom and discipline in radically different ways. For Scott, discipline emerges from freedom; given freedom to explore, imagine, and create, students will acquire discipline and construct necessary rules for skilled writing. On the other hand, for Roger, freedom emerges from discipline; given the necessary discipline by learning and practicing the rules, students will eventually become free, creative, and imaginative. Roger and Scott do not just represent two views of teaching or the opposition of freedom and discipline in relation to the same academic subject, but rather two interpretations of that subject.

Instead of accepting the dichotomy between freedom and discipline as representative of Scott and Roger, instead of accepting that Andre *must* or *should* make a decision about Scott's and Roger's teaching practices and the content of their courses, let's look for a third way, maybe a fourth or fifth way, to interpret and resolve the problems posed in the original case. It may be convenient to engage in "Monday morning quarterbacking," to ask why so many parties waited two years and allowed tension to escalate and positions to become entrenched. Although this procrastination, this "don't fix it unless it's broken" attitude, aggravates the situation and reveals governance shortcomings, we cannot return to the past. We may say what should have been done, we may try to relive our lives, but the historic story is set and interpreted in the insistent present. Andre, Scott, Roger, and their students must go forward into an uncertain future. They must teach and learn, speak and think, at times muddle their way through unknown, uncomfortable lands. They must go on; a decision must be made.

But first, the reader needs to look in still another direction: Can we hear the voices of others, of the students in Scott's and Roger's classes? Are these all the voices of average and above average students? Are these the voices of some dominant group, of students with identical values and beliefs? Do any classes or schools have the nondescript, seemingly homogenous mass of students barely described in this case? Why should the reader worry about students and listen for their voices and thus stray outside the boundaries of the given case? In this circumstance, the assumption is made that teachers and curriculum planners are the ultimate authorities, that they know what is good for students. Thus, the academic discipline does become paramount. If he accepts the primacy of the discipline, the only problem for Andre is to decide which interpretation of discipline is justifiable.

Although Roger and Scott listen to the voices or "dictates" of their discipline, as they interpret that discipline, they do not listen to their students. Students seem to be pawns for their teachers' differing views of the discipline and their teachers' egocentric pronouncements of the superiority of their teaching methods, practices, and curriculum. At this point, Scott chimes in, outraged that he is described as "egocentric." After all, students returned to relate their experiences of Roger's class. Scott did not solicit their criticism. But can this "pied piper" be excused so easily? Did he really converse *with* students? Did Scott ask students to think about the positive aspects of Roger's class? Did Scott remain the "creative," imaginative teacher who sought to transmit his passion for language and critical thinking? Or did Scott retreat into dogma, into the role of the satisfied, knowing authority who dotes on followers?

Returning to the students, we may ask whether there are students from different cultures and ethnic groups. Are there disabled students? Are the teachers actively involved in inclusion projects? Are any students behavior problems? Are all students native English speakers? Are there underachievers or unmotivated students? Comments about above average and average achievement do not express the range of abilities, concrete achievements, or the continuum of talents and interests in the classes. Should all of these student variables affect the decisions made by Scott and Roger? Why did no one—Scott, Roger, or Andre—seem concerned about listening to the students' voices or even mention their individuality and uniqueness?

But in the end, the problem still remains for Andre, "What should I do?" There are different ways to interpret this question. For example, what processes can Andre use to have Scott and Roger resolve their differences? What processes and structures can Andre implement to retain the strengths of Scott and Roger, to further the educational process, to improve teaching and learning for teachers and students? In advocating these interpretations of the final question, this is the recognition that there is no way that Andre can expect that any decision, process, or structure will resolve the problem immediately and for all time. In an argument, as in a fight or war, there may be winners and losers. But who wins and who loses is usually dependent on power, in this case, who Andre sides with. Students do not need winners and losers. Roger and Scott each believe he is supporting the interests of students. They both need to be motivated to join together to create conditions and practices by which all students will be winners and a positive learning community created. If, as described in this narrative, Roger and Scott are creative, competent, and gifted teachers, then they need to reach out to mentor and motivate other teachers.

Andre's Response through My Voice

The question then is what Andre can do to create a different climate and to motivate Roger and Scott to become reflective teachers and, thus, willingly modify their teaching and curriculum when such modifications are desirable. As Andre's alter ego, I suggest three connected paths to reconcile the present dilemma.

Conversation

Andre needs to modify the terms of disagreement from that of a conflict and competition to a conversation in which the respective parties have legitimate, but different opinions and for which there are ground rules that engender basic civility and professional ethics. Unquestionably, to order the two protagonists to begin a conversation would be as futile as commanding them to modify their teaching styles and curriculum. But in his administrative capacity, Andre can design a curriculum activity that will require Scott and Roger to meet and converse on a regular basis.

The Project

Andre decides to bring together four (or six) teachers from different disciplines, two (or three) from the elementary school, the rest from the junior high school. Of course, Scott and Roger would be members of this committee. The teachers would be charged to design a new interdisciplinary curriculum for an experimental, two-year sequence that would span the final year of elementary school and the first year of junior high.

Given the animosity between Scott and Roger, Andre realizes that he must choose the other teachers with care, for example, teachers who will not be intimidated by Scott or Roger, teachers who have good conflict negotiation skills, and so forth. Although the project must be a real one that is deemed important by all parties, the form and structure of the meetings, the process, has greater importance than the final product. To further this process, Andre may also have to appoint a conflict negotiator or group facilitator, perhaps a professional in the school district who possesses appropriate skills.

Collegial Circle

Andre decides to establish a collegial circle for teachers at the elementary and junior high level. He names three people the moderators and facilitators of the circle: Scott, Roger, and a professional skilled at conflict negotiation and group dynamics. The circle is designed as a conversational forum for teachers to discuss various problems and issues, to have a way of communicating with fellow professionals.

Professional Development

Andre examines the forms of professional development that exist in the district and decides that the traditional model for professional development no longer meets the changing needs of teachers. He invites a local college of education to form a school-university partnership to further his goals of professional development and to provide a field setting for the college's prospective teachers. Scott and Roger serve on the planning board with university professors.

A number of activities result from this affiliation: (1) Scott and Roger become mentors to prospective teachers and, thus, are required to articulate their teaching methods and curriculum; (2) at different times, either Scott or Roger team-teach seminars with senior research professors; (3) university faculty members demonstrate some of the recent new methods in language arts or English; (4) university scholars present seminars on recent work on various topics or on the work of contemporary novelists or on the integration of media into curriculum.

As Andre begins each of these three initiatives, he is conscious that the conflict between Scott and Roger will not be resolved overnight. In each of the situations that he designs, Andre clearly enunciates to Scott and Roger in separate meetings that he expects them to be professionals and to maintain professional ethics in dealing with colleagues, other professionals, students, and parents. Andre's aim is not to dictate a solution to the original dilemma, but to create a different educational climate in which issues and disagreements will not escalate into irremediable confrontations.

What of the students? With this solution, students will not remain pawns or passive bystanders, but at various junctures will be brought into the circle of conversation.

Notes

1. Alfred North Whitehead, *The Aims of Education and Other Essays* (New York: Macmillan, 1929), p. 28.
2. Ibid., p. 30.

Further Reflections on "Freedom and Discipline"

Beyond Freedom and Discipline

BY NICHOLAS C. BURBULES

Reading Betty Sichel's discussion of the Roger and Scott dilemma, I am struck first off by some of the similar points we chose to emphasize, as well as some of our differences.

First, I think that Betty and I both wanted to hear more details about the story, especially more about the students, before addressing the values of the two teachers. I think that we both believe that the recurring educational search for One Right Way to teach belies the actual differences among students, their learning styles, and their needs. Too often, competing approaches to education (such as discipline-based versus discovery-based learning) are disputed on the basis of a priori theoretical or even ideological assumptions: ironically, many "progressive" educators are as guilty of engaging in such disputes as traditionalists. The mistake that both make is the hope that a single pedagogy will be successful with every type of student. A stark example of this problem is the perennial debate between phonics and "whole language" approaches to teaching reading. An enormous amount of ink has been spilled as advocates of each position excoriate the views of the other; yet in view of the fact that both methods can legitimately claim benefits for teaching reading to certain types of students, why does the choice need to be either/or? Indeed, isn't trying to make it an either/or issue, seeking an ideal approach to teaching and learning that can be settled once and for all, antithetical both to the need for a pragmatic, experimentalist approach to education and to the diversity of students we actually encounter? Isn't this especially a danger given the many types of students who may not be succeeding in schools under current conditions and who are likely to be disadvantaged under any scheme to impose a single method of teaching and learning upon all? If the history of educational thought should have taught us anything, it is that such questions cannot, and should not, ever be settled "once and for all." The Roger-Scott debate has many of these same elements.

Knowing more about the actual students in these classrooms would help us in deciding whether their needs are actually being put first by *either* of these teachers. Nevertheless, I am also struck by my greater willingness to "dive in" to the moral issues here, as they are presented, without all the contextual information I might desire; for me, wanting to learn more about the students was a topic I raised at the end of my essay, somewhat wishfully. For Betty, it is a basic condition, stated right up front, before being able to cope with the dilemma. Here is an echo, perhaps, of Carol Gilligan's arguments about differences in how men and women deal with moral issues: that men, in general, are more willing to accept limited and artificial parameters to moral examples ("Imagine you are on a desert island . . ."), while women, in general, want to know more about the people involved, their backgrounds and histories, and the context of their relations with one another.

Second, I am struck that Betty and I both proceed from the starting point of seeking to promote moral conversation among the protagonists. Rather than acting, in the role of Andre, to direct or decide the proper actions these teachers should take, we both want to try to find ways for Scott and Roger to explore and understand one another's teaching practices. In the long run, I think we both believe that the resolution of this problem is not in settling this dispute in favor of or against either teacher's views, but in creating a better relation between them, one in which they can respect one another's differences and see in those differences an advantage for the students' educational experience as a whole; for this to happen, they will need to be more tolerant toward these and other disagreements that will inevitably surface between them or between each of them and other teachers. Hence, promoting a better conversation between them is not only a potential avenue of settling their short-term concerns, but of establishing a healthier collegial relation in which further learning opportunities are enabled.

Yet, here too I am struck by some differences in how Betty and I approach the goal of conversation. I am much more concerned with the responsibility of these two men for their intolerant and harshly judgmental responses to one another and want to find ways to foster in them the capacities, attitudes, and values that can make them better communicative partners. Part of this, for me, is trying to engage them each in conversation, trying to get them to appreciate the value of conversation itself. Betty is more concerned with creating broader conditions in which conversations can occur, focusing on the circumstances that might bring out the best or worst in people (her suggestions include working on a joint curriculum project, participating in a collegial circle, working collaboratively together with the university, and so on). Here I would say that both perspectives are important—that is, focusing on the people involved and focusing on the context or circumstances in which they come together—and that the two approaches can be complementary. I will return to this point below.

Third, we both agree that the dichotomy of freedom and discipline is mistaken, that discipline and the formation of skills is a requirement of freedom, and, conversely, that a focus on skill development in education that does not attend to sources of pleasure, purpose, and spontaneity runs the risk of losing students' interest and motivation.

This case is an instance in which the rhetorics of freedom and discipline, and their expression in an oversimplified and exaggerated manner, have become wrapped up with the pride of two strong-willed men who have become very settled in their own approaches to teaching. This gulf of ignorance has led them each to be unnecessarily suspicious of the motives and values of the other.

A general problem of moral conversation is the conflict between the discourses of two or more people, that is, a conflict in which the very terms of discussion are contested such that participants either use the same terms in very different ways (leading to misunderstanding) or use terms that are foreign and meaningless to one another (leading to little understanding at all). In many cases, as with the differences between foreign languages, some explanation or translation across differences is possible; but this can only happen when the parties are motivated to try to understand one another. When differences are characterized as oppositions, or when participants are more concerned with winning a point than with seeking understanding, such explanation or translation is less likely to occur. Now, as I noted in my first essay, such successful explanation or translation would not necessarily lead to agreement—it may in fact heighten or clarify an awareness of differences—but it does humanize these differences and creates the possibility at least of an attitude of respect and tolerance (despite differences) between people. As I have suggested, Scott and Roger would both be better off if they learned this lesson.

There are differences in moral outlook between Betty and myself as well. As noted, I think I am more inclined to hold the individual teachers responsible for their actions and to adopt interventions that are directed toward them specifically. I focus more on the value of personal accountability, Betty more on the ways that communities influence the conduct of their members. Both are true. Here, too, the two perspectives do not need to be strongly dichotomized, though the starting points of our interventions differ to a degree. Our aims, I believe, are much the same: to create an enlarged and more civil conversation among teachers in which a diversity of educational styles and methods can become a strength of schools and not an unnecessary point of dissension. Perhaps this exchange between us provides a kind of model for how such a respectful conversation, despite some real differences, can occur.

Right On, Nick

BY BETTY SICHEL

"Yes, yes, yes," I repeated when reading Nick Burbules's solution to the "Freedom and Discipline" case. Thus, my additional comments here are not a rejoinder, a type of "one-upmanship," or a negative, destructive criticism, but a continuance of our conversation to give greater depth and breadth to Andre's predicaments and even to continue clarifying Andre's dilemma. There are only three areas I want to include in my conversation with Nick: first, the constraints and limitations on actual conversations; second, the constraints on decision making and action in actual schools; and third, the constraints on changing teachers.

Nick appreciates that even if it does not "lead toward real agreement, consensus, or compromise," conversation can lead to understanding and "a kind of respect." Even if the former expansive view does not occur when Scott and Roger attempt conversation, the more minimal outcomes of conversation may possibly occur. Whereas Nick doubts that the expansive outcome can occur, he hopes for the minimal outcomes. I agree with Nick that it would be a utopian dream to expect Scott and Roger to agree or compromise, but I doubt that these two teachers will eventually understand and respect each other. Thus, at least, on a short-term basis, I am more skeptical and pessimistic than Nick.

This pessimism stems from the actual structure and time constraints of schools and teachers' lives. For example, Roger, a dedicated teacher who attends to the small details of student work, probably is teaching five classes (at the very least, four classes) for a total of 100 to 150 students. The correcting of papers, preparing lessons, preparing students for their debates, working with other teachers in his department, and having some sort of family and private life certainly take every minute of his day.

The type of conversation that Nick and I recommend takes considerable time. It is the conversation that both of us understand only too well. For it should be at the heart of university life, where faculty members should continually be involved in conversation with students, colleagues, and others. Such conversation is basic to university teaching and learning and to excellence in scholarship and research. Time is not the issue; the quality of the conversation is. But in schools, especially in crowded, understaffed, underfinanced public schools, such conversations are a luxury, something that is rarely a part of teachers' lives. To expect that Scott and Roger will be able to have this luxury, this conversation over a period of time, is to miscalculate what is possible within the constraints of contemporary schools. In addition, Andre faces a similar predicament in that his time is rationed, the Roger and Scott predicament being only one of many cases that Andre must resolve. Thus, when Andre makes a decision in the "Freedom and Discipline" case, he must consider these constraints. If Andre believes that conversation is the only way, then he must find a way to release Scott and Roger from classes so that such conversation can occur.

Finally, there is the question of whether we expect too much from teachers, whether it is really possible for teachers, such as Scott and Roger, to change, to modify their beliefs and practices, and to understand and sympathize with other ways of teaching and learning. Scott and Roger are examples of the incredible difficulty of changing teachers' beliefs and practices.

Discussion

Right away in the essays by Nicholas Burbules and Betty Sichel we see an activity characteristic of ethical judgment—puzzling out the important aspects and questions in the case. The important things actually may be left out and otherwise obscured in the case as it is described. (What information is needed for judgment here? What do you think about Burbules's and Sichel's apparent differences on that?) And Burbules and Sichel agree that important things are obscured. Freedom and discipline in language arts is not the central problem, they say. Rather, the real problem is the deeper one of bringing Roger and Scott to a recognition of some of their basic ethical responsibilities in teaching and beyond. The important thing for Andre to do is foster a climate for conversation. Scott and Roger need to talk with each other, and perhaps other people. (How about each writer's approach to conversation? Is it better to start small, as Burbules suggests, or to undertake the bigger project Sichel desires? Both?) Maybe they will learn something from each other. At least they might come to understand or tolerate each other. In any event, something needs to be done because students are being hurt.

These points about the limitations of the case are well taken. In this discussion I will follow Burbules's and Sichel's lead and concentrate on their idea of conversation and its benefits. However, I will start with some remarks about freedom and discipline. Clearly, Sichel and Burbules suggest that there may be some benefit if Roger and Scott understood freedom and discipline better. And, beyond this case, freedom and discipline is a recurring theme in this book and in any study of ethics. In a sense, what ethics is all about is trying to figure out how people's freedom should be "disciplined" (if we construe "discipline" loosely) in order that their lives and others' can be worthwhile.

Freedom as an Ethical Value

One aspect of freedom we must consider is its educational value. As Sichel and Burbules point out, it is important for students and teachers, themselves, for teachers to have freedom. Yet this does not require an abandonment of discipline. Good teaching requires both. Roger and Scott need each other.

However, the issue of freedom does not stop with its educational value. The question of individual freedom takes us to the very heart of ethics. We can identify several views on ethical freedom. One is that ethics is above all a matter of individuals creating their own lives in freedom. The existentialist Simone de Beauvoir argues that "human freedom is the ultimate, the unique end to which man should destine himself."[1]The postmodernist Michel Foucault suggests that people's ethical task is to "create one's life by giving style to it through long practice and daily work."[2]The common theme is that individuals must resist the discipline of modern ethical conventions, which are often merely arbitrary and repressive. Yet "discipline" comes from other sources. For de Beauvoir, constraints follow from freedom itself. (We might look at de Beauvoir as an example of Sichel's person who sees discipline emerging from freedom.) To the apparent paradox that to protect people's freedom we must sometimes deny them freedom, she replies, "We have to respect freedom only when it is intended for freedom. . . . A freedom which is interested only in denying freedom must be denied."[3] Foucault does not say any sort of "self-creation" is good. He distances himself from people who are merely "self-absorbed," for instance. One's life should be a work of art, something fine and beautiful, and mere self-absorption does not qualify.

However, these views on freedom are troublesome. De Beauvoir's ethic "recognizes in [the individual] alone the power of laying the foundations of his own existence."[4] Foucault suggests we give up the idea that we are guided by "the truth about desire, life, nature, body, and so on" in trying to give style to our lives.[5] Yet if individuals really are the final authorities for their ethical "foundations," if we really should discard the notion of truth in ethics, then what authority do de Beauvoir and Foucault have to challenge people whose freely chosen ethical foundation is oppression or self-absorption? Giving freedom this sort of status presents the problem of *subjectivism*, the idea that whatever individuals happen to believe is right *is* right. Perhaps "we" can still believe "they" are wrong, but then the only recourse people like Andre would have for dealing with people like Roger and Scott would be sheer power rather than rational persuasion.[6]

Immanuel Kant, whom we encounter in several places in this book, has another view of ethical freedom that has been extremely influential. Kant proposed a "categorical imperative" for ethical agents: "Act only according to that maxim whereby you can at the same time will that it should become a universal law." This notion of ethics also makes individual freedom supremely important. Ethical agents must be free to pass judgment on maxims (principles) in order to test the legitimacy of those principles. It is the idea that if you simply blindly obey what you are told to do you are not acting as a responsible ethical person. Yet, it must be possible to make the judgment a universal law, so in that sense the individual is not the sole authority. An oppressor's proposed maxim that "I should be able to do whatever I want to other people" is not a plausible candidate for a universal law.

As you will see, however, some of our writers argue that even this idea of freedom is excessive. At least some of them take something like a "freedom-emerges-from-discipline" view. For example, Shirley Pendlebury will contend that teachers simply have certain goods and obligations before they have any choice about the matter. Such views need not deny the value of freedom. But freedom has to be earned by first disciplining oneself to the demands of teaching. On the other hand, these views often hold that freedom is overrated. For example, they might say that loyalty and attachment should be valued over freedom. Even if freedom is important, the only freedom worth much is that which is enriched by connections to other persons and things. What these writers and postmodernists might share is antipathy to Kant's emphasis on universal laws, which they agree overlooks or devalues the particulars of individuals' lives. Sichel shows some evidence of this view in her concern to know the "narrative" of the protagonists' lives.

Our understanding of ethical freedom will affect how we respond to a problem like Andre's. Thinking about the issues of freedom we have just raised will help us understand Burbules's and Sichel's recommendation for conversation.

Conversation and Argument

Sichel and Burbules introduce us to a vital question that will occupy us in every chapter of this book: How should we respond to ethical disagreements? They stress a conversational response as opposed to an argumentative one. (Given Sichel's ultimate pessimism about the possibility of conversation, why did she spend so much time developing her (unrealistic) ideal of conversation? Maybe this shows something about the importance of Weber's "ethic of intention." We need to keep a clear vision of the ideal before us even if we cannot or should not pursue it directly. It might help us to fight the conditions that make it unrealistic. Sichel's pessimism prompts us to remember that ethical problems may penetrate beyond particular cases to the broader institutional and social context.) To take one instance, Sichel hints at the importance of the distinction when she wonders about herself and Burbules: "We may be playing a sophisticated game of give and take, the give and take of an argument, even if that give and take is disguised by a conversational vocabulary. Could there be another way? Could Andre, Scott, and Roger enter into conversation?" Why the distinction? What's at stake?

We can begin to answer these questions by thinking about the distinction between arbitration and adjudication mentioned in Chapter 1. Basically, Burbules and Sichel recommend an arbitrator's role for Andre. Rather than seek to determine which views are right or wrong (which is the ultimate aim of argument and adjudication, as I'll be thinking of them), Andre should focus on setting up the conversational conditions in which Scott and Roger can have a better professional relationship.

This tack might be endorsed by existentialists and postmodernists who stress individuals' freedom to determine themselves ethically. They might see value in talking, but it is not Andre's place to say who is right or wrong. However, this would not appear to be Sichel's and Burbules's position. Burbules does consider "it a strength of schools that there is no attempt to impose one best or correct style of teaching." But this reflects doubt about *imposing* any *one* right view, not doubt that there are right and wrong views. (We'll return to this issue below.)

One can emphasize arbitration while still believing adjudication is possible and desirable. Some of our writers' doubts about adjudication simply stem from a consequentialist concern about what would happen if Andre were more directive. He might make matters worse. Of course, a common difficulty with consequentialist judgments is that we cannot anticipate what all the consequences will be. Perhaps parents and other teachers actually would welcome decisive action. Perhaps Roger and Scott would really shape up if Andre were firmly directive. But then there are nonconsequentialist reasons for arbitration, too. For example, some of Burbules's reasoning suggests a nonconsequentialist concern for freedom. There may be grounds for thinking each man is wrong in some ways, but teachers have a right to some amount of professional autonomy, and so tolerance is appropriate. Moreover, if Kant is right about people needing to freely accept ethical maxims, Andre should strive to persuade them rather than simply force them. However, adjudication still could be the ultimate goal. Arbitration might be an initial step necessary to get Roger and Scott to talk to each other, but rather than stop there, Andre should try to persuade them to see the errors and strengths in their own and each others' views. Sichel and Burbules do write about persuasion as an aim of conversation.

However, this puts arbitration at the service of adjudication, and that may not be what Burbules and Sichel have in mind. At another level, emphasis on arbitration can reflect a very fundamental choice against adjudication as the aim of ethical interaction among people. For example, recall that in the Introduction I mentioned how proponents of an ethic of caring might endorse arbitration because it puts human relationships first. Advocates of the caring view, such as Carol Gilligan (whom Burbules mentions), need not deny that adjudication can be a worthwhile aim, but they do deny that it must be the preferred aim. (In Chapter 5 Susan Laird will discuss Gilligan in more detail.) They might endorse tolerance and understanding, not because they are all that can be achieved in the circumstances, but because they are the best aims. (Sometimes, caring is associated with the ethical response characteristic of women. That has been Gilligan's contention, for example. That might be behind Burbules's speculations about how women would have responded in the situation. What do you think about that?)

Alternatively, in Burbules we see evidence of an ethic of virtue that emphasizes character traits over right actions. Burbules's goal is that Roger and Scott develop certain professional and ethical virtues, such as listening and respect for others, and be able to recognize these and other virtues, such as thoughtfulness, enthusiasm, and integrity, in each other. Such virtues are ethically basic. Right actions are important, certainly, but more basic is the inclination to actually think about and do what is right. Also, stressing virtues has the advantage that people who differ on what is right can still agree in admiring these qualities. As Burbules suggests, perhaps each man can admire the other's enthusiasm, even as they think it is misdirected. This mutual admiration can help assuage the conflict that might arise from those differences.[7] (On the other hand, how far can we take this? Should we admire the integrity and enthusiasm of a committed Nazi?)

Still, isn't it important that people strive to be right about ethical matters? Ethically, don't we have to do what we can to help people avoid errors? Even if we are concerned for relationships, aren't we interested in relationships that are really good for people? Concern for getting things right need not be for others' benefit only. Won't people's own lives be better if they don't go through life mistaken about what's good and worthwhile?[8] (We'll discuss this possibility further in Chapter 7.) While a Kantian must respect people's freedom, that does not mean people should have total freedom. Kant's categorical imperative holds people to what they *can* will as a law, not to whatever they *do* will. If a person does not acknowledge a maxim that any normal person can acknowledge, that need not show a problem with the maxim but rather a problem with the person. (Below I'll consider postmodernist objections to "normalcy" as a standard.) We would do them a favor by straightening them out.

This dispute does not show that we have a radical either/or choice between human relationships and ethical truth. (For instance, in the next chapter Noddings will argue that a caring person needs to be competent as a carer. Good caring is not just anything.) As we proceed through the book we will explore ways that they might work together. Yet arbitration is not simply a means to adjudication. It has value independently of its service to adjudication. And the conversation-argument distinction can be one reflection of that.

However, not all the important issues regarding conversation and argument are captured by the arbitration-adjudication distinction. Part of the importance of conversation and argument emerges when we think of them both as means of adjudication. Burbules and Sichel hint at this when they recognize persuasion as a possible (even if unlikely) outcome of conversation. The relevant distinction becomes one between conversational adjudication and argumentative adjudication. When faced with the need to actually change people's minds, should we respond conversationally or argumentatively?

There are several criticisms advocates of conversation offer against argument. One is the powerlessness of argument. Richard Rorty concludes that "a theoretically sophisticated bully and I would always reach an argumentative standoff."[9] Rorty does not say we shouldn't fight bullies, but we should do it by trying to make vivid to them the consequences of their cruelty, redescribe to them what they are doing in such a way that they will be repelled by what they do. (Might Scott be repelled by Sichel's redescription of himself as a "pied piper," a "knowing authority who dotes on followers"?) It's those sorts of images that move people, not arguments and claims to truth. Rorty admits that the notion of truth may have some useful purpose, yet "whatever else truth must be, it is something we are more likely to get as a result of free and open encounters than anything else. . . . [I]f we take care of political and cultural freedom, truth and rationality will take care of themselves."[10]

Clearly, freedom is extremely important for Rorty. But his point is not just about freedom. Part of his point is that we may not be able to argue, even if we wanted to. Rorty claims that if argument is to happen people must share a sufficient background of beliefs. If Roger and Scott are to fruitfully argue with each other about the merits of their teaching, they have to share, or come to share, some beliefs about what good teaching involves, otherwise they'll just talk past each other. This view of argument is not necessarily controversial. What is at issue is the extent of sharing required. Rorty contends that, by and large, we do not have the resources needed for argument, or at least not to the extent many people have tended to think. (Burbules's point about how "the very terms of discussion" may be contested reflects this issue.) This does not mean we should not try to reach consensus, but, where background beliefs are not sufficiently shared, consensus must happen through conversation rather than argument.

However, as a final point against argument, we might attack the very aim of consensus. William Connolly, who draws upon Foucault a great deal, says consensus "inflicts wounds on life" by suppressing differences.[11] This "normalization," as Connolly calls it, may be inevitable and desirable to some extent, but we also must "establish more space for otherness to be."[12] Seeking conversation rather than argument may be one way to give space to the "otherness" Roger and Scott embody. (In light of that, Connolly might warn against conversation aimed at persuasion.)

How might we respond to these claims? Regarding the first, it's true that argument can be ineffective. But what does that show? Martha Nussbaum agrees that philosophical argument has limited usefulness. Like Rorty, she stresses how vivid images, particularly those drawn from novels, are important for cultivating the imagination, sensitivity, and perception needed in ethics. (Note how Sichel drew images from a film and a novel.) But Nussbaum does not claim novels are sufficient. In her own writing she weaves together strands from literature and strands of philosophical argument. As argument alone cannot produce the vivid images, images alone can distort reality rather than expose it.[13] For example, *Dead Poets Society* clearly is intended to vividly show the tragedy of excessive discipline. Is this a true account of freedom and discipline or is it a distortion? Even if it is not exactly false, does it capture the whole truth? Is it enough just to oppose it with a different image, such as the tragedy of excessive freedom in Sophocles's *Oedipus the King*?[14] Or shall we also argue about it?

It is unclear that truth and rationality will take care of themselves if only freedom is secured. Sometimes truth needs to be helped along. Although we should not make the decision lightly, there may be times when we have to fight for what is right. Likely, the people we fight won't be convinced by our arguments for why our cause is right. But if we are to fight them it seems insufficient to tell them we have only a "good story" to back us up. Sure, we might be kidding ourselves when we believe we have the truth. But that doesn't show our aim should be less than the truth. (We will return to the issue of truth in Chapter 7.)

But what about Rorty's claim about the possibility of argument? Rorty is right that we should not simply assume people always do or can share background beliefs. But neither should we overestimate the differences and the difficulty of achieving common ground. How much common ground really is needed? Richard Bernstein argues that Rorty exaggerates what is needed:

> *He [Rorty] writes as if it is appropriate to speak of argument only when there is enough common agreement so that we can all agree on what counts as a better argument. Argument is appropriate when the rules of argumentation are commonly accepted. But it is never clear why we should restrict argument in this narrow way. . . . [T]here is rarely (if ever) complete common agreement about the "rules" for clearly distinguishing better and worse arguments. If there were algorithms for deciding among competing arguments then there would be no need for argument!*[15]

So what sort of agreement is needed, then? Charles Taylor provides a hint with his idea of "common meanings." He says that common meanings

> *can subsist with a high degree of cleavage; this is what happens when a common meaning comes to be lived and understood differently by different*

> *groups in a society. It remains a common meaning, because there is the reference point which is the common purpose, aspiration, celebration.*[16]

People who disagree about the value of the freedom lived out in *Dead Poets Society* might still see freedom as a "common purpose, aspiration, celebration." There is enough common ground that people can see themselves as all on the same field of play. They can recognize each other as concerned for the same aspirations. This sort of idea seems to be at work in Burbules's advice that the discussion shift from the specific "guiding values" Roger and Scott have to a common aspiration of meeting student needs. How far might this get us? Perhaps not far. As Sichel points out, even though Scott and Roger believe in both freedom and discipline, they interpret these in quite different ways. Neither of our writers is overconfident about the possibility of progress, and with good reason. Yet, Scott and Roger do have access to more common ground than they realize. Despite their differences they do share concern for students' interests (even if they have lost track of that) and some idea that freedom and discipline are both needed. In regard to the example of Burbules and Sichel themselves, whatever their differences, there is considerable overlap in the sorts of questions they deem important to confront in the case. Even this much sharing is important.

But now how about the problem of "normalizing" one or both of these teachers? Connolly and Foucault have a point that social institutions, such as schools, have become extremely concerned with "normalization." Does the ever-growing population of therapists who treat an ever-growing list of maladies reflect heightened sensitivity to real human needs or just our intolerance for differences and frailties in ourselves and other human beings? On the other hand, how tolerant must we be of different views, particularly when it comes to teachers, who have responsibility for other human beings? Do the sorts of "discipline" suggested for Scott and Roger "inflict wounds" on them? Are all restrictions on their freedom unreasonable? Connolly is right that we must be careful about consensus, but the need to be careful about it does not mean that seeking consensus through argument is an illegitimate aim.[17]

If Taylor is right, searching for legitimate common meanings through argument can still permit "cleavages," deep differences of views. It leaves space for differences. Or better, it actively seeks to create spaces for differences. This may not be obvious. When Burbules and Sichel emphasize conversation they contrast it with such things as being a "Solomon judge" and seeking the "One Right Way" to teach. But argument and adjudication do not have to mean those things (and I'm not proposing Sichel and Burbules disagree). Following Bernstein we can contrast an "adversarial" or "confrontational" style of argumentation with a dialogical style.[18] Adjudication can be a cooperative dialogical effort. Argument need not be a competition. There need not be winners and losers, because the aim is to understand the issues and what should be done, not defeat opponents. Good argument strives to see others' views in their strongest forms, because the idea is to arrive at good answers, not just defend one's own. (Is there evidence of that sort of argument in Sichel's and Burbules's writing?) If other persons cannot present their views strongly or at all, one attempts to do so oneself; hence the urge to create space for differences. Good argument thrives on the clash of strong views, the dialectic that Burbules describes. But the aim is not just to present views (although that may be enough at times). The aim is to work toward better views. This does not happen unless people are willing to challenge others and accept challenges themselves. So this is more than conversation. Yet, to be clear, neither does this exclude conversation. Good dialogue is likely a blend of conversation and argument. Bernstein refers to participants in his dialogical encounter as "conversational partners," and perhaps the dialogue our writers recommend can be understood the same way. The point is that there is a need for both.

Conclusion

This chapter has involved us in issues of freedom and human interaction (among others). We have seen that finding the proper relationship between freedom and discipline can be difficult. But at least we have reason to believe that it *is* a matter of relationship, rather than choosing for the one or the other. Also, we have seen the importance of dialogue in sorting through these and other ethical questions. Dialogue is itself an issue. There are some fundamentally different ways to understand it. As with the freedom and discipline issue, the conversation-argument issue is complex. It presents some fundamental issues of how we think about human beings, what is important, and the possibility and desirability of ethical truth. At this point, perhaps we can at least agree that there are issues here that merit further study. The next chapters aim to encourage that study, as well as introduce other issues for your scrutiny. Each chapter attempts to contribute something to the dialogue we have begun here.

Whatever the particular issues in each chapter, a constant theme is that any treatment of ethical disagreement requires dialogue. All of our writers share a basic view that these issues should be confronted through dialogue with other human beings and are not just a matter of subjective opinion and exercise of power. There are people who would challenge this view, and certainly we need to be careful about the limitations of rational dialogue, as we have tried to be in this chapter. But as Burbules says in regard to his exchange with Sichel, we have here models of respectful dialogue that is carried on even in the face of some pretty basic disagreements. You will need to think about the worth of these models, for they certainly do imply particular ideas about ethics. One thing they imply is that if we look at the ethics of teaching this way it puts a big burden on educators and schools. For if Sichel is right about what one finds in schools, the conditions for good dialogue often are lacking. So, educators and schools face a double challenge; not only must they try to act ethically, they must also strive to establish the broader contextual conditions that are needed for the full ethical project to be pursued.

So, what's next in our exploration? In this chapter we have thought about Roger's, Scott's, and Andre's freedom largely in regard to their responsibilities to others. But many other questions have yet to be addressed. What about concern for oneself? What about the teachers' family and private lives that Sichel mentions? What about teachers' particular ideas about what is good? In this chapter we have not emphasized what Scott and Roger might be thinking. As Sichel asks, should we expect them to give up sincerely held beliefs? What forms of resistance, if any, should be open to them? Is it true that they should have kept things "in-house"? Burbules mentioned integrity and compromise. Does compromise require that they sacrifice their ethical integrity? How much, if at all, should they compromise their views? Burbules advises against a "soupy" compromise, advice with which we might agree. But what are legitimate forms of compromise then? These are some of the questions we will confront in the next chapter.

Notes

1. Simone de Beauvoir, *The Ethics of Ambiguity*, trans. Bernard Frechtman (New York: Philosophical Library, 1948), p. 49.

2. Michel Foucault, "On the Genealogy of Ethics: An Overview of Work in Progress," in *The Foucault Reader*, ed. Paul Rabinow (New York: Pantheon, 1984), p. 351.

3. de Beauvoir, pp. 90–91.

4. Ibid., p. 156.

5. Foucault, p. 350.

6. For sympathetic critiques of existentialism and postmodernism see (respectively) Richard J. Bernstein's *Praxis and Action* (Philadelphia: University of Pennsylvania Press, 1971) and his *The New Constellation: The Ethical-Political Horizons of Modernity/Postmodernity* (Cambridge: MIT Press, 1991).

7. See Michael Slote, *From Morality to Virtue* (New York: Oxford University Press, 1992).

8. For an argument of this sort, see Joseph Raz, *The Morality of Freedom* (Oxford: Clarendon Press, 1986).

9. Richard Rorty, "Truth and Freedom: A Reply to Thomas McCarthy," *Critical Inquiry* 16 (1990); reprinted in Gene Outka and John P. Reeder, eds., *Prospects for a Common Morality* (Princeton: Princeton University Press, 1993), p. 282.

10. Ibid., pp. 279–80.

11. William Connolly, *Politics and Ambiguity* (Madison: University of Wisconsin Press, 1987), p. 10.

12. Ibid., p. 11.

13. For a particularly clear statement see Nussbaum's paper "Sophistry about Conventions" in her *Love's Knowledge* (New York: Oxford University Press, 1990), pp. 220–29.

14. See John Kekes's analysis in his *Moral Tradition and Individuality* (Princeton: Princeton University Press, 1989), pp. 12–33.

15. Bernstein, *The New Constellation*, p. 281.

16. Charles Taylor, "Interpretation and the Sciences of Man," *Review of Metaphysics* 25 (1971): 30–31.

17. See Thomas McCarthy, "Postscript: Politics and Ambiguity," in his *Ideals and Illusions: On Reconstruction and Deconstruction in Contemporary Critical Theory* (Cambridge: MIT Press, 1991), pp. 76–82.

18. Bernstein, *New Constellation*, pp. 337–38.

3

Self and Others

CASE

The Sweetwater Board of Education is instituting a program of achievement testing for students in its schools. At the end of the fifth, eighth, and twelfth grades, students will be given comprehensive achievement tests in the areas of reading, writing, math, and science. Students who do not pass all these tests will not be allowed to graduate or move on to the next grade level.

This policy was adopted after a series of public meetings on the proposal. Ultimately, a majority of the community supported the proposed policy. There were dissenters, however. Lucy Williams was one of these. Lucy has been teaching freshman and sophomore math at one of the town's two high schools for 23 years; it was her first and has been her only teaching position. At the public meetings she firmly and clearly stated her opposition to the proposed policy.

It was not that Lucy opposed the idea that students need to achieve in school. She had seen too many students just passed along even though they were not learning what they should. She knew that some students came to her as freshmen without knowing all the math they should. She also knew that with patience and hard work she had been able to help many of these students achieve satisfactorily. Some even excelled. Nothing would have been gained by holding these students back, by making them repeat the same experiences that had been unsuccessful before.

Lucy realized that not all teachers had her sort of commitment. But to the depth of her soul she felt that the proposed testing was not the answer. The answer was to improve instruction. And more than merely ignoring that issue, the proposed policy threatened to actually exacerbate the problem. Lucy suspected that the emphasis on passing tests would lead to the experiences of students in math and other courses being narrowed. For the sake of guaranteeing that students could give a show of knowing the "basics," the "extras" that made math alive and meaningful for students would be sacrificed. People responded to Lucy's fear by saying that that problem could be taken care of by constructing good tests, ones that really required thought and knowledge and not just memorization. But this did not satisfy Lucy. For one thing, she wasn't sure that people were committed to creating good tests. Nor was it clear to her that the sorts of things she stressed—such as developing a good attitude about math—could be "tested." The pressure of the tests might actually work against students' development of that attitude. Even if good tests were constructed, this wouldn't alleviate the problem of the tests determining the curriculum. It should be the needs and interests of students that are the driving force, Lucy believed.

But what angered Lucy most was that the community seemed only to be interested in passing the buck. Voters had turned down several bond issues in the past few years, and the schools were hurting. It seemed to Lucy that the community was demanding results without making the commitment of resources that was needed to help students learn. Even if tests were a good tool, what would be their point if students weren't given an adequate opportunity to learn?

Lucy tried to be open to points made by supporters of the policy. But there was no getting around the fact that these were unconvincing to her and that she was now being asked to be part of a program that clashed with her deepest beliefs about good teaching, gained over many years of study and experience. Lucy shared her anger and sadness with her principal, Carole Carter. Carole was receptive. Carole herself had spoken out against the proposed policy, and Carole told Lucy of her own unhappiness about the final decision. However, Carole also expressed her belief that the best course now was to make the best of the bad situation. The policy was in place. As professionals they had an obligation to obey the community's wishes. But they shouldn't despair. Over the next several years, as the consequences of the policy started to emerge or the economic and political winds changed, people might begin to change their minds about the policy. Besides, Carole pointed out, to follow the letter of the policy need not require adherence to its spirit. There was much they could still do to provide students with good experiences even within the demands of the new policy. But they had to realize that overt resistance to the policy would not be tolerated. Although Lucy and herself were respected, tenured faculty members, the school board could dismiss them on the grounds of insubordination.

Lucy could see the sense in Carole's points. But to give even the appearance of cooperation with this policy was abhorrent to Lucy. She thought of her obligation to serve students' welfare. She thought of her obligation to her teacher colleagues. Many of them were looking to her, a respected senior colleague, to see what she would do. If she would make a stand against the policy, perhaps they would join her. Even if they did not now, perhaps her actions would be an example for them that personal sacrifice may be preferable to subservience. How could she live with herself if she did not act? Her commitment to her own image of herself as a teacher seemed to demand that she continue to resist, to force a showdown, even at the risk of censure and dismissal.

On the other hand, Carole's comments prompted Lucy to think about other things important to her. Lucy had one child in college and another about to enter. Lucy and her husband had prided themselves on the fact that their children would not have to work their way through college. If Lucy lost her job that might well change. Besides, could she really leave teaching? That was so much of who she was. She relished the contact with students and her fellow faculty. Could she do them more good if she kept her job?

Moreover, as an African American woman and educator, she felt a particular bond with Carole. Carole was the first African American, and first woman, to be an administrator in their school district. It would reflect badly on Carole if there was dissension at her school. It might give people an excuse to conclude that Carole was incapable of handling her faculty. And besides, Lucy wondered, where's the virtue in sacrificing yourself for a losing battle? Rather than being noble, maybe that would just be stupid.

Lucy's conception of her self is very important to her. Ethically, what sort of guidance can and should this conception afford her? Should she do more to turn her attention toward the interests and wishes of others? It seems that doing so might go some distance in serving her own self-interests. Yet how far should she go? As she says, she still has to live with her self. What ought she do?

Reflections on "Self and Others"

Lucy's Dilemma

BY NEL NODDINGS

There are two major aspects to Lucy's problem: first, she must consider the options for action; second, she must reflect on the meaning of each of these possibilities. What would a given choice mean to her own sense of self? What might it mean to others for whom she feels a sense of responsibility?

Let's begin with the first. It seems clear that her options are fairly well outlined as follows:

1. She can leave Sweetwater,
   a. giving a frankly honest reason for doing so or
   b. giving a reason that will not prejudice her references or suggest to another district that she is a troublemaker.
2. She can remain in Sweetwater,
   a. actively opposing the testing policy,
   b. passively opposing the policy, or
   c. working to make the best of a policy she deplores.

Outlining the possibilities is just the beginning of Lucy's work. Now she must consider the ethical, practical, and personal implications of each choice. Suppose she seriously considers leaving Sweetwater. The practical difficulties could be decisive here. She has been in her school for 23 years. It may not be easy for her to get another position. Few districts are eager to hire teachers at the top of the salary scale, and personal factors may make it impossible for her to move very far. Thus, on practical grounds alone, option 1 may be out for Lucy.

But suppose she can secure a position in a nearby school. Should she resign in protest or just quietly leave, giving personal reasons for her decision? Life is so complicated that, indeed, personal reasons may emerge during the time that Lucy wrestles with the ethical problems. She may, thus, be justified in giving personal reasons for her departure. However, most of us would find such a decision at least questionable ethically. In the Kantian tradition, for example, lying is absolutely forbidden, and Lucy—whether or not she adheres to this tradition—may well reject that choice.[1]

Although it isn't our purpose here to analyze theoretical positions, it is important to be familiar with some basic theories. The Kantian tradition has grown out of the work of Immanuel Kant (1724–1804), whose work attempted to ground ethics in practical logic and rationality. Previous ethics had depended heavily on authority (often religious) or tradition. In contrast, Kant insisted that every normal adult human being has the logical capacity to decide for himself or herself what is right. This does *not* mean that whatever an individual thinks is right; it is not a relativist doctrine. Indeed, Kant thought that every person using reason properly would have to make the same decision in a given situation. His categorical imperative—so act that you can logically will that your choice should become law—forms the foundation of an absolute ethic of duty. Kant argued that one can logically derive absolute rules from the overarching categorical imperative. Killing and lying, for example, are absolutely forbidden. Following Kant, Lucy could not lie about her decision.[2]

It seems to many of us, however, that in this case a decision to tell the truth (or not) is a relatively unimportant ethical question. From the perspective of an ethic of caring, the major issues for Lucy are how to care for her students and how to preserve herself as a faithful and competent carer.[3] Given how deeply she feels about the well-being of her students, Lucy will probably decide against leaving Sweetwater, but a decision to leave could be compatible with caring. Lucy might decide that with the objectionable testing policy in place, she simply cannot care for her students as she always has in the past. Perhaps, knowing herself well, Lucy can accurately predict that she will just "not be herself" under the new program. If she is right in that assessment, she would do better to leave and preserve her capacity to care for other students. Practically, she might want to secure a new position before stating her reasons for leaving. But, ethically, we cannot say whether she *should* say publicly why she is leaving. If she thinks it will further the welfare of her students to make such a statement, she should do it. However, if she thinks that her statements would make things harder for her students and colleagues, she should not do it.

Now let's analyze Lucy's deliberations as she considers remaining in Sweetwater. Should she remain and actively oppose the policy? What would active opposition involve? Clearly, she cannot, by herself, prevent implementation of the policy. Other teachers, or even outsiders, can be assigned to create or select the tests, and her students will be tested regardless of Lucy's opposition. She could refuse to prepare students for the test and go on teaching in her usual way, but this might hurt her students. She could try to muster enough support among her colleagues to launch a strike against the district, but, given that a majority of teachers and parents approve the policy, it seems unlikely that she would succeed in such a radical effort. Further, regardless of the probability of success or failure, Lucy has to consider whether extreme measures are ethically justifiable.

Although Lucy (and many other responsible educators today) feels strongly that the testing policy described in this case is educationally wrong and potentially harmful, many well-intentioned educators advocate such testing programs. Reasonable people differ on the issue, and debate is lively at every level of educational policy making.[4] The testing policy is not clearly unethical or immoral. Therefore, Lucy has to consider personal action that is appropriate to the problem.

This is a very important point. One can imagine situations in which teachers could be ethically obligated to resist the implementation of official policies. From the perspective of any and all legitimate ethical theories, teachers should have resisted the exclusion of Jewish students from public schools in Nazi Germany. Similarly, it would be hard to find a philosophically defensible ethic that would have justified teachers in the U.S. in excluding black children from white schools in the 1960s. Today, if California's notorious Proposition 187 is allowed to stand, teachers may have to resist the law's demand that they report students suspected of being illegal immigrants. In cases such as these—where the moral nature of the problem is so obvious—teachers may indeed be obligated to engage in civil disobedience.

As she mulls over the choices before her, Lucy may be troubled by the examples above. Some readers, too, may question my inclusion of Proposition 187 with cases as repugnant as the exclusion of Jewish and black students. However, one must note that the cases of Jewish and black students are historically finished cases. There is no philosophical defense currently recognized for the positions taken against admitting Jewish or black students. But at the time of these events, there were influential people who made ostensibly legitimate arguments for the positions we now find so morally offensive. This lack of agreement among people in a position to speak is what makes ethical decision making so hard and, ultimately, soul-searing. One could argue, and clearly a majority of California's citizens believe, that illegal immigrants have no right to ordinary health and educational services. By definition, as *illegals*, they have broken the laws that protect legal citizens. How could I possibly argue, then, that teachers might have an ethical obligation to resist the demands of Proposition 187? I would have to argue the innocence of children and their need for education, the likely harm done to children and families of legal immigrants who would surely be called into suspicion, the dissension induced among teachers and staff, the fear that would keep many parents from enrolling their children in school or seeking medical help, and the horror of living in a society in which people who should respond as carers respond instead as agents of an oppressive state.

What Lucy faces does not seem to trigger such moral urgency. But I say this tentatively. Perhaps, for Lucy, this problem does have great moral significance. Perhaps she sees the potential harm to minority students as enormously compelling. If she does, then, according to many traditional ethicists, her first task is to develop an argument that will justify her position.

A feminist ethic of care does not put such great emphasis on philosophical justification. It constantly poses the questions: How can I best care for those I encounter? How can I preserve myself as a carer? From this perspective, the primary issue about active resistance is its possible effects on Lucy's students and colleagues. As Lucy reflects, she may reject active resistance, even if she still thinks the policy is potentially very harmful.

Perhaps she should consider a form of passive resistance. Passive resistance is often thought to be synonymous with nonviolence. The methods of Mohandas Gandhi and Martin Luther King, Jr., are sometimes referred to as "passive," but most of these methods are both active and nonviolent. Sit-ins, occupations, and confrontations that invite the opposition to use violence but reject violence themselves are all highly active and public modes of resistance.

Genuinely passive methods of resistance involve nonperformance. Often, lying and manipulation are required. Workers in Nazi-occupied countries, for example, often obstructed projects by feigning stupidity, clumsiness, or illness. Such tactics can be enormously effective. But are they applicable to Lucy's situation?

In my own earlier career as a high school mathematics teacher, I sometimes used passive tactics. School rules required teachers to record and report all tardiness to class. I believed that this practice did nothing to develop self-responsibility in our students, that it was rude and disrespectful to students (after all, we don't treat adult students this way), and that it was a waste of valuable teaching time. Instead I asked my students to come on time as a general rule. If they were late, they were to take seats nearest the door and wait for a break in my lecture to consult a friend on what might have been missed. When occasional queries or warnings came from the front office about the lack of tardy reports, I always shrugged them off, saying, "Oh, yeah, I keep forgetting that," or, "I don't have many tardies." The latter was true; in a way the former was, too, but the forgetting was deliberate.

Another rule I regularly disregarded was one that blocked students without valid excuses for absence from making up missed work. They were to receive zeros for each such missed class. I thought this was ridiculous and counterproductive, and I argued against the rule at faculty meetings. However, when the rule was passed, I quietly ignored it. With some humor, I firmly reminded occasional offenders that the responsibility of students is to learn and that they could not escape that responsibility by being absent. The work (and full credit for it) awaited them on their return.

In both cases above, my resistance was passive. I didn't announce my moves publicly, nor did I discuss them in private conversations. I just quietly ignored the rules and did what I thought best for my students. When opportunities arose in faculty meetings, I expressed my opposition to the rules but did not confess my disobedience. This made it possible for the administration to ignore my noncompliance.

In Lucy's case, however, there is nothing comparable to be done. She cannot ignore the tests because they are neither voluntary nor in any way dependent on her compliance. Therefore, passive resistance seems inapplicable.

There are interesting theoretical matters to discuss here even though the tactics are inappropriate for Lucy's case. Was my behavior in the two cases described above ethical? Many would argue that it was not—that one must either obey legally constituted rules or disobey them in the grand tradition of civil disobedience. In the latter, objectors disobey a rule they think is unethical but accept the legal consequences of their disobedience. It is, to be sure, a grand and admirable tradition.[5] Quietly ignoring a rule has rarely been credited as moral behavior. Exceptions include rescue and obstruction tactics in time of great danger—activities such as the rescue of Jews during the Holocaust, assistance to escaped slaves in our pre–Civil War period, and worker bumbling in occupied territories. Activities of this kind, at their moral best, signify a rejection of the very source of authority. They arise in a different tradition. In contrast, civil disobedience disavows only a particular law or practice while pledging allegiance to the basic structure of governance. My practice fits neither of these traditions, but I would still defend it as an appropriate choice for a caring teacher. You might want to press the case by asking what I would have done if the administration had challenged me, if many students had taken advantage of my trust, or if other teachers had complained.

Let's return to Lucy's case. Active resistance (at least as I've described it) might hurt her students; passive resistance seems to be inapplicable. That leaves option 2(c): working to make the best of a policy she deplores. This choice can combine features of active resistance and vigorous cooperation; that is, Lucy can still speak out against the policy while she cooperates to make it work for her students.

Both active opposition and vigorous cooperation require competence. In my own work on caring, I have emphasized that "caring implies competence."[6] When we care, we try hard to do well what is really needed. That means that we exercise the competence we have with great care and that we continually strive for greater competence.

Lucy should study the issues in considerable depth. Part of her active opposition must involve the study of arguments on all sides and the careful articulation of her own position. People will be more likely to listen to her if she can present facts, logical arguments, and moving stories of student experiences to support her position.

Vigorous cooperation also demands competence. Lucy might work to achieve the best test possible. If this course of action seems "too cooperative"—and I think it might to me—then she has to turn her attention to helping her students do well with whatever test is established. Many of us who have never been involved in creating standardized tests, for example, have nonetheless studied them carefully so that we can help our students do well on them. We are highly practical people who accept the fact, but not the spirit, of such testing. We would not cheat, and we would not advise Lucy to cheat. (Why not?) But we would hone our own skills to perfection and teach our students every legitimate trick of test taking in addition to the content prescribed by the test.

To do this—to teach the content prescribed by the test—may violate Lucy's professional judgment on curriculum. She may have to work hard to include both the test material and the content she judges to be educationally valuable. But in most cases, I believe it can be done. The teacher works harder and under more difficult conditions, but if the students believe she is on their side, they too will work harder, and together they will make the best of a bad situation.

Notes

1. For an introduction to Kantian ethics for teachers, see Kenneth A. Strike and Jonas Soltis, *The Ethics of Teaching*, 2d ed. (New York: Teachers College Press, 1992); Strike and P. Lance Ternasky, eds., *Ethics for Professionals in Education* (New York: Teachers College Press, 1993); Nel Noddings, *Philosophy of Education* (Boulder, CO: Westview Press, 1995).
2. For a comprehensive and fascinating discussion of lying, see Sissela Bok, *Lying* (New York: Vintage Books, 1979).
3. See Nel Noddings, *Caring: A Feminine Approach to Ethics and Moral Education* (Berkeley: University of California Press, 1984); Carol Gilligan, *In a Different Voice* (Cambridge: Harvard University Press, 1982).
4. See the discussion in the Summer 1994 issue of *The Educational Forum* 58, no. 4.
5. The classic work is Henry David Thoreau, "Civil Disobedience," 1849. This work influenced both Gandhi and King. Their works, too, should be read.
6. See Nel Noddings, *The Challenge to Care in Schools* (New York: Teachers College Press, 1992).

Her *Self* in Compromise: Carving a New Path of Integrity

BY DILAFRUZ WILLIAMS

Lucy Williams and I have more than our last names in common. She has been teaching mathematics in high school for 23 years; I taught mathematics at a secondary school for six years. She is an African American woman; I am South Asian. She is a mother of two children; I am a mother of one child. Lucy faces an ethical predicament in her profession related to a board of education policy on comprehensive achievement tests as determinants for graduating and promoting students. Cooperating with the implementation of this policy brings into question her very sense of *self*; similar quandaries have been and currently are an indispensable component of my professional life as an educator.

Why do I feel that it is necessary to provide some of this personal information regarding our similarities? Of course, while I have alluded to just a few resemblances between Lucy and me, features that Lucy and I do not have in common can also be located in the above description. Plus, there is probably much more that is dissimilar than similar in our backgrounds and experiences. Yet, I offer this brief introduction because I must admit at the outset that while I have tried to look at Lucy's case as specifically applicable to Lucy, I found *my* story to be quite related to this case. The particularities of mathematics teaching, motherhood, and nonwhite membership are those commonalities between us that primarily began to define how I was addressing and judging the case. I was constantly being challenged to reconsider how I was viewing the ethical predicaments in light of who *I* am. In other words, the kind of predicament Lucy is facing by virtue of who she is, and by virtue of her profession, is not new to me. I can closely identify with her and with her predicament. Hence, in responding to the question "What should Lucy do?" while I deliberate by looking at her specific circumstances, my own voice of membership and experience unfolds.

To me the case study clearly indicates that Lucy genuinely cares about her students and about good pedagogy. However, her sense of *self* is at stake as she is caught in a web of ethical difficulties resulting from the implementation of the achievement test policy. She is a strong opponent of such tests. Nonetheless, she must implement the board of education's policy or protest it. For Lucy, neither option is without its problems.

As I explore Lucy's problems, I assess the risks of her noncompliance and her reluctance about compliance. In carefully considering her loyalties to certain people and constituencies, and the ways she defines who she is, I find that Lucy's ethical problems are not adequately resolved unless she complies with the new policy. This may appear to be a poor solution, requiring Lucy to compromise her self in a way she wants to avoid. She *will* have to compromise, although she can do this by carving out a new path of integrity for herself. That is, *how* she compromises will determine to a large degree whether she really can preserve her integrity and self-identity.

I present my ethical deliberation about Lucy's case in two parts. First, I outline the ethical predicaments that Lucy encounters at various fronts. In doing so I present the voices and choices she must confront and the relevant moral claims that demand Lucy's attention. That is, the initial phase of assessing her dilemma is to take up the matter of inclusion: Who and what should count in her deliberation and why? I explore the likely implications of compliance and noncompliance in light of these claims and how Lucy defines her *self*. In the process, I find myself suggesting that Lucy can resolve her ethical dilemma by compromising the position she's taken on the various issues. In the second part I tease out the compromise that Lucy would need to make and argue that this path would leave her with an integrity that is so crucial to her own sense of *self.*

Confronting Voices and Choices: Matters of Inclusion in Ethical Deliberation

In this part, I explore the relevant elements of the case as they arise from Lucy's professional and personal commitments. I wonder, for instance, who and what does Lucy care about? What are her institutional obligations and loyalties? Is she committed to these? What about her obligations and loyalties to the community? Her vulnerabilities? Her own convictions regarding these things? In what ways do these mesh with her more personal commitments, her obligations to her own children, for instance? For which constituencies do her commitments hold strongly? What are the claims that each one of these makes upon her? How is she to determine what and who counts, as she deliberates on all these claims?

I pursue these questions as "voices and choices" that Lucy encounters in her ethical deliberations; she faces matters of inclusion, since *others* play a significant role in how she defines her *self.* On examining her case, I find myself using voices such as *caring*, *commitment*, *obligation*, *loyalty*, and *honor* that involve her relationships and hence her concerns.

Caring about Students and Good Pedagogy

I find that Lucy cares deeply about students and about her own practice of teaching. She does not seem capable of separating her sense of self from who she is as a teacher. I find it important that Lucy participated in the public deliberations and firmly and clearly declared her opposition to achievement tests. This *public* participation, declaration, and voicing of her convictions presents a critical dimension to how I address her dilemma. Had Lucy been passive and had she not made her position known prior to the board's decision, other things being the same, I would have probably found her reluctance to comply with the policy puzzling. Since she had the courage to let her opposition to testing be known, I feel more convinced about her integrity related to her convictions.

A new policy that contradicts Lucy's professional beliefs about good educational practice has to be implemented. These professional beliefs, it seems to me, are an integral part of how Lucy views who she is. Lucy feels that when such tests are forced on educators and students, teaching gets aligned with testing, and passing the test rather than developing a positive attitude toward learning becomes the goal. Furthermore, holding back those students who do not pass these tests, Lucy believes, is not going to accomplish much—repeating a grade and being made to go through the same failed experiences seldom do. She finds the new policy to be detrimental—neither students nor teaching practice would gain from policies of promotion and graduation based on achievement tests.

Consequently, what if Lucy does not comply with the policy? How would that affect her ability to fulfill her obligations to students and to teaching? It is clear that her difficulty centers around the fact that it is not a simple matter not to follow the new policy. The measure was passed by a majority of community voters, despite the opposition Lucy and others voiced. This alerts me to the strong likelihood of community and board displeasure were she not to comply with the policy. Noncompliance might result in her dismissal. I'm sure this would be a serious loss to students. Given the information in the case, this loss, it seems to me, would be difficult for Lucy herself to handle. So much of how she defines who she is is embedded in this role of hers as a teacher. Also, I feel that Lucy would probably rather be a teacher who can at least give something to her students than not be there to give anything at all to them. I feel that the possibility of dismissal and its impact on her students would weigh her down since she cares so deeply about her students.

On the other hand, knowing her commitments to students and to good pedagogy, I ask how Lucy can comply with the testing policy when it is at great odds with her convictions concerning who she is as a teacher. Her sense of *self* is so deeply woven with her convictions about good teaching that compliance would clash with what she considers critical to who she is. This fact is likely to play a vital role in Lucy's decision to comply or not comply. Yet neither compliance nor noncompliance seems like a promising prospect.

Loyalties to Principal and Colleagues

Lucy cannot ignore how her actions would impact what her colleagues might do regarding implementation of the testing policy. Being a senior and respected colleague, other teachers are looking up to her for leadership in this matter. On the one hand, protest and noncompliance would likely be supported by those who, like her, opposed the policy. If these teachers joined her in protest now, would there be a powerful enough force for the board to reconsider the measure, bringing it back to the public's attention and vote? More than likely, no, since public hearings were already held on this matter. On the other hand, some otherwise supportive teachers might be skeptical about what protesting would accomplish. Moreover, I have a feeling that seniority and tenure would greatly determine who among the teachers would take the risks involved with noncompliance.

Therefore, what is at stake here? What if there simply isn't a critical mass of teacher colleagues who would support a protest? Noncompliance with the testing policy might leave Lucy facing dismissal without having any impact on the policy. And, what if teachers who supported her were to be dismissed? It seems to me that for Lucy the uncertainties of affecting many more lives than her own would be problematic. Furthermore, it would seem that the very teachers who would join the protest would be the ones who cared about their students more than the tests. Hence, it appears that students would lose, if noncompliance results in dismissal of caring, courageous, and committed teachers. If, on the other hand, such dismissals would cause public furor against the policy, then noncompliance would be worthy of pursuit. However, again, from the case study it doesn't appear that such a public outcry is likely to occur. More than likely, Lucy and other teachers would be seen as violating the verdict of the community—hence, there would be little sympathy for them from the community and the board.

In addition, since the principal of the school, Carole, happens to be the first African American and the first woman to be an administrator in the school district, if there were protests and noncompliance, this could have negative repercussions for how Carole's leadership is viewed by the school district, the board, the community, the teachers, and students. However, I find myself torn over the issue of Lucy's loyalty toward Carole based on the fact that Carole, too, is a woman and an African American. I wonder whether such memberships are relevant for the decision Lucy needs to make. In cases such as this, do we have obligations to others by virtue of our gender and ethnicity/race? I don't think so. I ask myself, if Lucy were a white man, would he have to consider the fact that Carole was the first woman and the first African American to be principal in the school district? I feel that this fact could not simply be ignored as irrelevant in ethical deliberation. What counts is not so much loyalty by virtue of the *same* status (gender, ethnicity/race) as obligation because of the *kind* of status someone has due to prior injustices and inequities. How Carole is affected by compliance or noncompliance matters simply because of her minority status. It still is possible that Lucy's loyalty to Carole is more pronounced because they are both African American women. In any event, Lucy cannot discount the consequences her protests might have for Carole. Carole's credibility as a leader might come into question, thus jeopardizing future hiring of people from underrepresented groups for administrative positions.

I feel that Lucy's loyalty to Carole and her colleagues is going to count in her deliberations. Also interwoven is, once again, how her protest might affect students. Noncompliance poses a great risk in that significant others in her professional life would be affected to a degree that it would be difficult for Lucy to live with such an action.

Obligations of Motherhood

Because Lucy and her husband have prided themselves on the fact that they could free their children from having to work when in college, Lucy faces a dilemma on this front. If she does not comply with the policy and is dismissed, her two children (one already in college and the other ready to enter college) would definitely face the economic burden she wanted to avoid. Would they forgive her for their economic hardships? Possibly. They are old enough, I believe, to place no moral demands of financial support upon her. Perhaps her children might feel a sense of pride if their mother took a stand on her convictions. Such pride could conceivably compensate for any remorse or resentment they might feel over economic sufferings. While Lucy herself might feel the pain, I think she might be able to justify noncompliance to herself. Her obligations as a mother are not necessarily violated by the consequences of protest against the policy, even if dismissal results. I do not find the choice of noncompliance to be especially risky insofar as her obligations of motherhood are concerned. If, on the other hand, Lucy were a single parent and the sole supporter of two small children, my judgment on this issue would alter significantly.

The Voice of Honor

This voice is much more challenging than I thought at first. In the case study, Lucy doesn't seem to consider that she ought to honor the verdict of the community. That puzzles me. No doubt, she is frustrated and angry that the community has not passed bond issues in the past and has merely "passed the buck," expecting results from schools without providing resources. She is justified in her feelings. However, honoring the voice of the community does count, I believe. This has to do with trust in the process of democracy and upholding that trust.

But doesn't the honor element put Lucy in a double bind? If she participates in implementing the policy, Lucy could be considered a hypocrite by those voters who opposed the policy. In contrast, those who voted in favor of the policy could consider her noncompliance to be dishonorable. In either instance her honor is at stake. I think, however, that the claims of the majority need to be upheld by the dissenters, including Lucy. Therefore, while the majority's vote does not appear to count in how Lucy views who she is, I find myself considering honoring this vote to be critical.

Where does Lucy's confrontation with the voices above lead her, then? Should she comply with the new policy? Compliance appears to fundamentally contradict what Lucy considers to be good educational practice. It also clashes with her deep commitments to students. Yet equally demanding of her moral attention are the consequences of noncompliance. Her obligations, loyalties, caring, commitments, and sense of honor leave Lucy in a quandary about her choices. Can she find a way out of her dilemma? What should she do?

To Comply or Not? Creating a New Path of Integrity

If reversal of the testing policy is Lucy's aim, her most immediate option is noncompliance. At one front (that is, in standing by her beliefs) she would maintain her credibility and honor, and her sense of *self* would be served. However, she must face the possible outcomes of this choice and gauge the ways in which they *threaten* her sense of self.

1. The policy would most likely stay unchanged, despite her protest, hence she would not accomplish what she set out to do through her noncompliance.
2. The students would be losers if she and other teachers like her were dismissed by the board.
3. The African American principal Carole's credibility as a leader would come under scrutiny, more so if other teachers joined the protest; future hiring of administrators from underrepresented groups would be jeopardized.
4. Lucy's children would go through economic hardships if she were dismissed.
5. Not upholding the community's majority ruling would be dishonorable.

Given these possible outcomes, it seems to me that noncompliance would ultimately *weaken* Lucy's sense of self. Most likely, she would be dismissed and so would not remain a teacher and take care of the very things she opposes. Given Lucy's commitment to students and to teaching; given the importance to her of significant others such as the principal, students, her teacher colleagues, and her children; and given the need to honor the vote of the community, noncompliance does not appear to be a viable choice for Lucy.

So, I feel Lucy would need to comply with the new policy. But, as has been discussed, she feels that compliance threatens her commitment to students and good pedagogy, and inevitably her sense of self. This commitment, I believe, demands the most significant moral attention as she considers this choice of compliance. If what she cares for—students and good pedagogy—are impacted by the new testing policy, surely compliance would affect her integrity. Hence, what is required here is to figure out whether there is any way Lucy could strike a compromise with the policy so that she could still maintain or nourish her integrity.

I believe that compromising here need not lead to a loss of Lucy's sense of self. By operating within the educational system, Lucy has already obligated herself to the system, thereby not having total control over how education is conducted. For instance, she probably has no jurisdiction over why, in the first place, all students are required to study mathematics, or when in the course of their schooling they are required to study certain matters in mathematics. Testing, I believe, is a problem symptomatic of a much broader issue of why students must be regimented in the educational system to learn certain subjects at certain times, in a certain sequence. As long as Lucy has already accommodated her *self* to these institutional demands, I feel that she could still comply with the policy and figure out how to maintain her integrity within this compromised position. *How* she carves her path is the challenging task at hand now, so I explore some possibilities for compliance below:

(a) Lucy might wholeheartedly comply with the policy because she is swayed to believe in the merit of achievement tests. If Lucy changes her position because she believes it is the right thing for students and for good practice, then she would not lose her sense of integrity. However, given Lucy's strong opposition to the proposed use of achievement tests and given the fact that she is considering risking her job by protesting, I do not believe she would be capable of suddenly changing her mind about the merits of testing. Perhaps, if implementation succeeds in students achieving higher test scores and without higher rates of retention of students, she might reconsider her strong opposition to the tests. But, that is not an immediate possibility and not a morally attractive path.

(b) Lucy could follow the letter of the policy but not its spirit. This was Carole's advice. When I first saw this advice I felt uneasy. I wondered what exactly it meant for a teacher in Lucy's position. Would teachers simply "appear" to implement the policy but not "really" do so? How could this even be possible? Achievement tests are tangible and the community would demand accountability, I'm confident. Or, would "not following the spirit" of the policy mean that if achievement tests were administered, ways would be figured out to promote or graduate those who failed? I do not see how anyone could "work around" this policy. This would be tantamount to noncompliance and so would not be a viable option, for the reasons discussed above.

(c) However, there are other ways that Lucy might comply with the letter of the policy yet not discredit her own teaching. Lucy would not have to align her own teaching to testing. Compliance with the letter of the policy does not require that she do so. What she might consider doing is to prepare her students on how to take the tests so that they could do well. This would not greatly affect her own teaching, nor would it harm her students. Good pedagogy, so crucial to her sense of self, would still be possible. She could still emphasize the "extras" that make math meaningful, for instance. However, merely pursuing this path would not take care of how students in classes other than her own might be impacted, leaving Lucy in a moral quandary as to the effect of the policy on students who could not even make it to high school because of poor test scores. This requires that she consider yet another path.

(d) Lucy could comply with the letter of the policy, not discredit her own teaching, and become involved in developing better tests and in assisting other teachers (especially at the lower grade levels) with staff development on good pedagogical practices. This kind of extension of herself would probably be morally appealing to Lucy. Her ethical predicament, I believe, is not so much how she herself can continue to be the good teacher that she is, but how she can prevent or mitigate the harmful effects of the policy as implemented by *other* teachers. To attend to this, Lucy needs to get involved outside her own classroom and school. If students' attitudes toward mathematics could be changed when they are young, they would have greater chances of not only passing the tests, but also of learning more as they progressed through the educational system.

In conclusion, in pursuing these latter two paths I feel Lucy would comply with the testing policy while simultaneously maintaining her honor, credibility, and obligations to students and good practice. But in pursuing the last path, Lucy would carve for her *self* a stronger path of integrity.

Further Reflections on "Self and Others"

Thinking with Dilafruz Williams about "Self and Others"

BY NEL NODDINGS

Professor Williams and I agree on many of the issues and also on what is likely the best decision for Lucy to make. Williams calls this decision a compromise; I've called it "working to make the best of a policy she deplores," and I've suggested that such work demands vigor and competence. There are two points on which we may have more than superficial disagreement, and I'll discuss these in a bit.

First, I would like to draw readers' attention to a slight difference in the language we have used. Professor Williams uses "noncompliance" to cover what I have referred to as active and passive resistance. I rejected the term "noncompliance" because, in this particular case, there seems to be no action that could correspond with it. No matter what Lucy does, the tests will be given, and her students will have to submit to them. Although the choice of language does not signal a substantial difference in our analyses, it is worth pointing out. I prefer to use "noncompliance" in cases where one can engage in clear acts of noncompliance—cases such as my not recording "tardies" and allowing students to make up work even if their absences were officially unexcused.

Second, I want to say that I like very much Professor Williams's careful consideration of each group and each individual for whom Lucy must care. This is a nice way to draw attention to the kind of ethical thinking actually used by those embracing a "care approach." From the care perspective, we ask what our actions will mean for each party involved and how we can best respond as carers.

Let's turn now to the areas of possible disagreement. Professor Williams suggests that Lucy should be concerned about supporting the principal, Carole, because she is the first woman and the first African American to be principal in her school district. Indeed, Williams says, "How Carole is affected by compliance or noncompliance matters simply because of her minority status." I'm not sure I agree with this, even though I recognize that women leaders are more likely than men to be accused of not being able "to handle things." But the issue is more complicated. Lucy is strongly opposed to the policy. Should she cooperate just because the principal is an African American woman? Should this fact figure importantly in her deliberations? I don't think so.

It would be useful here to separate Lucy's general support of Carole from her support of this policy. Clearly, Lucy can support Carole in many other ways and even speak out strongly on matters she thinks Carole has handled well. To support Carole *on this issue* because of her minority status seems a mistake. This is a point worthy of considerable discussion at this time because our nation seems to be caught up in a tremendous debate about "identity politics." How far might Lucy go in supporting someone on the basis of racial or gender identity alone? If, by "take into account," Professor Williams means that Lucy should consider the effect her opposition may have on Carole, I agree entirely. As I indicated above, Lucy might well increase her efforts to show general support for Carole. But she should not support the policy simply to show solidarity.

A second point on which Professor Williams and I may disagree involves the "voice of honor." Williams suggests that it would be dishonorable not to uphold the community's majority ruling. I'm not convinced of this. It would be dishonorable for Lucy not to abide by the terms of her contract with the district or to engage in frankly insubordinate actions. But I see nothing dishonorable in continuing to oppose a policy even if it has been passed by an overwhelming majority. Indeed it may be dishonorable *not* to continue one's opposition.

Again, we see that it is important to judge the moral status of the policy in question. If it is judged clearly immoral, Lucy has to oppose it. If it is morally questionable or just educationally wrong-headed, I believe she has an obligation to continue raising questions while she cooperates "to make the best of a policy she deplores." It is true that, in a democracy, a majority vote must count for something. We should not engage in civil disobedience lightly. But there is also a long democratic tradition that treasures the loyal opposition. Lucy can claim an honorable place in that tradition.

Finally, Professor Williams's approach to Lucy's dilemma raised further questions for me about the concept of integrity. Readers might want to consider Jeffrey Blustein's account and contrast it with one found in the work of Mary Catherine Bateson.[1] Blustein's account follows that of Bernard Williams in concentrating on the unity of the individual as the center of integrity. Bateson, in contrast, seems to hold a dynamic and relational view of integrity. As people care for one another and reach out to respond, they consider actions well outside their former definition of integrity. They interweave these new behaviors with established ways of being, thus composing a richer life and, perhaps, a new integrity. Both views are worthy of study and discussion.

Using integrity as a focus, we can see that Lucy might oppose the testing policy vigorously as a "matter of integrity." This might be her initial stand. But as she considers the possible effects of her opposition on those for whom she cares, she might modify her stand and develop a newer and richer sense of integrity. Some critics would surely scoff at such an approach to integrity. Surely, they might claim, any compromise with what one considers wrong represents a loss of integrity. How are those people defining integrity? Answering this question should lead to lively discussion.

Under what circumstances might we all agree that Lucy had lost her integrity? If she used the policy as an excuse for lazy and slipshod teaching ("What's the use? My judgment isn't respected anyway."), she would surely have lost her integrity. She would have failed in her commitments to students, colleagues, and community. Further, she would have betrayed her own ideal for herself as a teacher. That such things actually happen to teachers, that they give up and "just collect a paycheck" is a sad fact of professional life.

Can you think of other ways in which Lucy might lose her integrity? Suppose she not only cooperated with the testing policy but insisted that she had been for it all along? Suppose she supplied her students with advance copies of the test or parts of it? Suppose she subtly encouraged them to find their own ways to cheat?

Perhaps the most important part of this discussion centers on the relative emphasis we should put on integrity as an individual property and integrity as a relational property. Although we have not discussed the issue explicitly, I believe Professor Williams and I may be in substantial agreement on the balance between individual and relational integrity. Both of us want Lucy to maintain her ideal of herself as a teacher. Both of us want her to define herself as a person who cares—someone who responds to the needs of those who address her and who honors her commitment to them. Can you anticipate issues on which we might disagree?

Notes

1. See Jeffrey Blustein, *Care and Commitment* (Oxford: Oxford University Press, 1991); Mary Catherine Bateson, *Composing a Life* (New York: Plume, 1990); and Bateson, *Peripheral Visions* (New York: HarperCollins, 1994).

Thinking with Nel Noddings about "Self and Others"

BY DILAFRUZ WILLIAMS

Although Nel Noddings and I have approached Lucy's dilemma from different perspectives and considerations, central to both of our deliberations is the fact that Lucy cares deeply about her students and good teaching. Keeping this at the heart of our discussion, we have considered what Lucy's options might be, assessing the ramifications of her leaving or staying at Sweetwater. Interestingly, both of us have argued that if Lucy stays at Sweetwater, tests need not define how she teaches, and implementation of the board's policy need not hinder her teaching. Since our paths of ethical deliberation differ, however, I will focus here on matters that require further clarification and discussion. Noddings's essay has triggered some critical questions in light of what I have already covered in my essay: (1) Who are the significant *others*, besides students, that should count in Lucy's ethical deliberations and why? (2) What predicaments does Lucy confront when she addresses the voice of the majority of the community? and (3) How might we address the question of morale that arises when Lucy compromises?

Significant Others

In the case study, the *self*, for Lucy, is implicated in her relationships with *others*—her colleagues, her principal friend Carole, her children, and her students. I will take up the matter of her relationship with the community in the next section, since the issues are different and more complex. While at the heart of the matter is how her action would impact her students, all of the above constituents demand her moral attention as she considers her choices. I find missing in Noddings's essay the dilemmas posed by these relationships and wonder why she has not addressed them when considering Lucy's options. I feel that our ethical judgment is incomplete unless we confront the impact of Lucy's choices on *all* these fronts; hence I wish to take up this matter here to provide further clarity.

In my deliberations, while I included leaving Sweetwater as a consequence of being dismissed by the board for noncompliance, I did not consider leaving quietly to be an option for Lucy as Noddings did. I believe, though, that whether leaving voluntarily or being dismissed because of noncompliance, Lucy's ethical deliberations would still need to include how her choice of action would affect significant others besides students. Let's take Noddings's discussion of the option to leave Sweetwater, which is prompted by two considerations—a practical one and one driven by the ethic of care. On practical grounds, she is right that this is not a likely option for Lucy. Noddings does support Lucy's leaving, though, if Lucy decides to do so, on grounds that "a decision to leave would be compatible with caring." Lucy's ability to perform as a teacher counts strongly and hence her decision to leave could be viewed as a strong case for caring, as Noddings has argued. However, I believe that equally demanding of Lucy's deliberations *in the realm of caring* would be the following: How would the risk of leaving Sweetwater affect her children? If she left, what would be the consequences on her teacher colleagues and the principal of the school? The first matter, which relates to her obligations of motherhood, would be taken care of if she found a job. Or, she could justify to her self her actions by claiming that her children were old enough not to demand financial support from her. Based on such a justification, Lucy might decide to leave Sweetwater. Her ethical predicament would not be resolved, though. Since Lucy is a senior and respected colleague, other teachers are looking to her for guidance; therefore, leaving Sweetwater quietly is not without its moral dilemmas. If Lucy leaves quietly after finding a job elsewhere (an option that Noddings proposes), her colleagues might feel betrayed. What would such an action convey to others when a "respected" leader quits without any prior warning and explanation? I believe this would have broad and long-term implications for the morale of her colleagues, a matter that Noddings would need to assess. If, on the other hand, Lucy protests in noncompliance, other teachers may or may not join her—but at least they will have acted on the basis of knowledge of the risks their senior colleague is willing to take on the issue. Along similar lines, as I argued in my essay, I feel that Lucy's loyalties to the African American principal, Carole, would count in her ethical deliberations, not permitting her to leave quietly. She would need to consider how her action would affect the future hiring of minorities in administrative positions, if Carole's leadership comes into question.

Thus, when Lucy considers the option of leaving Sweetwater voluntarily, as Noddings has proposed, she would still need to confront how her choice would affect the significant others identified above, by virtue of caring for them. In all likelihood, because she has been a teacher in the same school for over two decades, the moral dilemmas posed by her loyalties to her colleagues and the principal would prevent her from leaving Sweetwater quietly.

Dealing with the Voice of the Community Majority

As I stated in my essay, I found the issue of the majority verdict of the community to be a challenge when I was considering how Lucy should respond to it. Noddings's examples of Proposition 187, the Holocaust, and her own experiences of passive resistance to certain school policies have provoked several issues that warrant further discussion.

For me, a significant moral question raised by Noddings is In a democracy, should an individual ignore institutional rules and policies when these clash with his or her personal moral code? Let's begin with the example of Proposition 187. Although the ramifications of its implementation are more serious than those of the Sweetwater board's testing policy, I would like to clarify the position that I have taken in my essay, in light of Noddings's essay. No doubt, many teachers and other educators are disturbed by Proposition 187. However, I believe that instead of an individual teacher taking the matter into his or her own hands and refusing to implement the measure, it would be more appropriate and effective if, through collective action, the public is roused (as is happening at present) about the detrimental effects of such a proposition on innocent children. Through such collective undertakings, enough support can be garnered to legally repeal propositions such as 187.

My argument for cautioning against individuals resisting the verdict of the community that has been reached through a democratic process has to do with my trust in the democratic process for repealing such propositions. It also has to do with the likely harmful consequences of ignoring majority votes. Let me give an example to clarify my reluctance. In recent months, a measure in Oregon—Proposition 13, also known as the Anti-Gays Measure—was defeated by a close margin. How would we feel if those teachers who supported Proposition 13 were not to uphold the verdict of the community and were to begin to act individually to discriminate against gays and lesbians? I am convinced that there are possibilities for revoking measures and policies through proper democratic channels such as nonviolent resistance; there are also possibilities for educating the public about the harmful consequences of these measures and policies. By virtue of working in educational institutions and other organizations, we are bound by their codes, codes to which we often should accommodate our personal moral codes. When the tussle between institutional and personal moral codes is too strong, we should either work with others to collectively change the institutional codes, or we should leave.

So what does all this have to do with Lucy's predicament? I want to point out that I made a case that Lucy should honor the verdict of the community even though she was against the testing policy. If she is repulsed by the policy so strongly that she simply cannot operate as a teacher any more (which, by the way, is not suggested by the case study), then of course her only option would be noncompliance with the policy; but then she should leave Sweetwater. Even if she stayed, however, she could actively resist the policy, persuade the community by making a strong case against tests, and seek community support to repeal the board's policy. However, it did not seem to me from the case that this would have positive results—at least not immediately.

Addressing the Question of Morale

Often, when we have no choice but to compromise our position on issues, we are left with the issue of our personal morale. In other words, when we are caught in a bind that requires us to cede our personal beliefs to institutional obligations, we might feel like pawns fighting a losing battle. How are we to overcome the detrimental effect of the low morale likely to result? I proposed a path that I thought would help Lucy with nurturing her sense of self, thereby going beyond "making the best of a bad situation," as Noddings has suggested. In my assessment of the case, I felt that as an African American woman who had been a mathematics teacher in the same school for 23 years, Lucy would most likely have much to offer other teachers. Hence I proposed that since Lucy would need to compromise her position on testing by implementing the board's policy, she could maintain her sense of self by getting involved in designing good tests and also by extending herself beyond the parameters of the high school, to lower grade levels, thus having a greater impact on the formation of students' attitudes toward mathematics. I felt that it would be in Lucy's best interest to work toward implementation of the policy while simultaneously keeping up her morale. It is of equal importance that this course of action would also be in the best interest of her students.

Ethical dilemmas sometimes require that we compromise our position. This is not to suggest that we do so all the time—if we did, it seems to me we would not be left with the integrity so crucial to how we identify our selves. However, when we do, we need to skillfully carve a path that helps us grow with each ethical judgment.

Discussion

Teachers are not alone in their schools and classrooms. (Although they may sometimes feel like they are, or wish that they were!) They have responsibilities to others, and other people have all sorts of ideas about what those responsibilities are. So much is obvious. What may not be so obvious, but is no less important for a teacher to think about, is "How about the things that are important to *me*? What place does the unique self that *I* am have in all this?" Nel Noddings and Dilafruz Williams explore three fundamental dimensions of these questions, which I will focus upon in this discussion. First, there is the issue of *self-interest*. For instance, is it all right for teachers to look out for their own well-being, or must others' interests always come first? Second, there is the question of *ethical point of view*. When it comes to judgments about what is ethically correct, what place should a teacher's personal point of view have? Common sense suggests that there needs to be some mutual give-and-take among people's views, but how far should a teacher go in this? Williams's and Noddings's thoughts about *integrity* and *compromise* help to address this question, and this issue is the third dimension that I will examine in this discussion.

The Interests of Self and of Others

Both Noddings and Williams give Lucy's self-interest a prominent place in their discussions, but what sort of place should her self-interest have? There is a long and strong philosophical tradition that ethics requires people to give equal consideration to the interests of all relevant persons. We need not leave our personal interests out of the picture, but we must understand that they do not count any more than anyone else's. Kurt Baier represents this view when he says that the very purpose of ethics is to put impartial restraints on pursuit of self-interest.[1] In Baier's terms, Lucy must look at things from "the point of view of anyone," not the particular person she is.[2] Therefore, for instance, granting that Lucy has a personal interest in preserving her chances of getting another job, she is thinking ethically only insofar as she bases her decision on how it impacts the overall balance of good. Her personal interest in protecting her job opportunities is just one of the interests she must consider. To the extent that she gives priority to her own interests she is acting *prudentially*, not ethically. (Prudence is often contrasted with ethics. Arthur Brown will raise the issue of prudence in Chapter 4.)

Some philosophers question this "impartial" view on self-interest. Bernard Williams puts the point this way: "There can come a point at which it is quite unreasonable for a man to give up, in the name of the impartial good ordering of the world of moral agents, something [called "ground projects"] which is a condition of his having any interest in being around in that world at all."[3] True, from the point of view of the impartial universe, we all are equally important, and so we have to grant to all people the same sorts of value, freedom, and so on that we would wish for ourselves. Still, from *our* point of view, our own projects, our own loved ones, may have special significance. There are times when people can or should be partial toward their own interests just because they are their own. There is a legitimate and important "self-other asymmetry" that should be recognized.[4]

Our writers appear to take something like this "asymmetric" view. (Is that a proper view for teachers? For instance, even if "asymmetry" holds for people in general, might teachers as teachers have special obligations to be impartial, or even altruistic, giving priority to others' interests?) The ethical task then is to judge when and how it is ethically reasonable or unreasonable for Lucy to give up or limit or modify her "ground projects" in light of others' interests. Much of the essays can be read as an attempt to show where Lucy should draw the line, and this issue is the focus of much of the disagreement between Williams and Noddings.

Of course, nothing says one's ground projects have to conflict with others' interests. As Williams and Noddings show, Lucy's concern for her self as a carer is not simply self-interested but serves others, too. Even the "impartial" view can support that sort of self-concern. But other things may be trickier. How about Lucy's concern for her own children compared with her responsibilities to students? Or how about Noddings's proposal that Lucy might be less than completely honest in order to enhance her chances of getting another job? From the "impartial" point of view this might be a paradigm example of putting prudence—or even selfishness or cowardice—before ethics.

I suggested one possible response to this in the Introduction: Even if being disingenuous is unethical, maybe that's still acceptable. Could this be a time when ethics isn't especially important? Noddings might be saying this when she distinguishes "ethical, practical, and personal implications" and says that certain actions might be eliminated "on practical grounds alone." (What do you think about those ideas? Williams, too, gives a good deal of weight to "practicalities." Properly? Should Lucy do more to act *in spite of* the "practicalities," to act in a supererogatory way?)

On the other hand, Noddings's and Williams's challenge is not just that self-interest may come before ethics but that we may need to rethink ethics itself. Thus, when Noddings proposes that whether or not to lie is a relatively unimportant ethical question she challenges us to shift our whole understanding of ethics and the place of the self in it, similar to the way Weber asks us to shift our understanding of ethics. What are we to make of that challenge? This gets us into the issue of ethical point of view.

The Self and Ethical Point of View

To begin to understand the full significance of Williams's and Noddings's challenge we need to understand Noddings's conception of an *ethic of care* and how that compares with an *ethic of duty*. An ethic of care focuses on the particular, concrete relationships Lucy has to other people. Hence the need to ignore school rules that preclude or hinder a caring relationship between a teacher and her students. Hence the reason for Lucy to lie and save her job prospects, if that is needed to preserve her ability to care, which is the important thing. In all this, Lucy must approach her situation from the point of view of *Lucy*, since only she as a unique individual has the particular relationships and capacities for care that she does. Hence Williams's concerns about how Lucy's various options would clash with "who she is." (If their view is correct, how can Noddings and Williams make recommendations for Lucy? Williams begins her first essay by describing her similarities—but also her differences—with Lucy. Must people be similar in order to give ethical advice to each other?)

This view puts Williams and Noddings in tension with what can be called an *ethic of duty*. (Below I'll suggest that Williams gives this ethic a larger place than Noddings does.) Noddings herself points to this tension in her remarks on Kant, who is perhaps the paradigmatic representative of the ethic of duty. If an ethic of caring emphasizes *particularity*, we can say an ethic of duty emphasizes *universality*. Far from advising Lucy to act and think as a unique self, a Kantian would stress that Lucy must act and think as any rational being would in her situation. (Thus this view stresses a sort of impartiality.) From this point of view, principles, duties, and rights are Lucy's ethical guides. These sorts of things have a law-like quality; they are binding on all relevant persons. In that sense, "who she is" is largely irrelevant for Lucy's ethical judgment, at least in so far as we are trying to determine her ethical duties. (For Kant, "who she is" may have some place in ethical judgment outside the question of duties. Here is where the ethics-morality distinction comes up.)

To think more about what is at stake here, let's look at two ways Noddings draws the contrast between these two ethics. One regards justifying ethical beliefs and actions. The other concerns the role of principles, duties, and rights.

Noddings raises the issue of justification when she suggests in her first essay that whatever her (Noddings's) reservations about the urgency of Lucy's problem, it still may be urgent *for Lucy*. Furthermore, Noddings says, Lucy is not required to give a philosophical justification for her sense of urgency. She need not try to show that she is right. But shouldn't Lucy be concerned for the truth? Don't we need to know whether the problem really is urgent or not, not just that Lucy *thinks* it is?

What is Noddings getting at? Neither Noddings nor Williams advocates the subjectivism I mentioned in the preceding chapter, the position that ethics is all a matter of personal opinion. (Noddings acknowledges the "soul-searing" difficulty of ethical judgment but clearly believes that certain actions and policies can be identified as right or wrong on the basis of caring.) Neither says that Lucy should do whatever she feels like. What Noddings might be saying in this passage is that, even when all evidence and arguments are in, different people might arrive at different justifiable judgments. But that sort of view is not unique to an ethic of caring. Noddings is saying something more here. It is not just that justification is inconclusive; it is, in an important way, beside the point.

What's most important, Noddings says, is to care. Giving priority to philosophical justification can distract from that. Less vital than being right is the disposition to care about people, or, more accurately perhaps, less vital than justifying the impulse to care is being right about *how* to care. (In this we can see elements of an ethic of virtue. We can also see a consequentialist strand as shown by Noddings's and Williams's concern for the consequences of Lucy's actions. Both these general features conflict with an ethic of duty's nonconsequentialist concern for principles.) After all, it is caring that motivates attention to ethical issues in the first place and leads people to be careful about what they do to and for other people.

A Kantian could give several responses. For one thing, calling upon people to justify their actions can be a way of showing respect for them, because it acknowledges that they have a perspective within which their action makes sense to them and that we are interested in understanding that perspective.[5] People have an obligation to respond to such requests for justification. Furthermore, caring may be a good thing, but is it always the right thing? Of course Lucy should care for her children. But aren't there limits to what she can do for them? Isn't her first ethical responsibility to know what is right? And regarding the impulse to care, it's true that Lucy should do the right thing for her children because she cares for them, not just because she believes it is her duty. Still, even if her immediate motive should be care, a background sense of duty and justification can be a valuable motivation when caring flags; and, again, it provides necessary limits to what caring can justify.[6]

I won't pursue this exchange any further. But before leaving it to you to think more about it, I'll reiterate my claim that Williams and Noddings do not say that caring justifies anything and everything. The issue is what needs justification and when.

A further issue is what sorts of things justify Lucy's actions. Should they be principles, duties, and rights? Noddings's remarks on Proposition 187 and the argument that illegal aliens have no right to public services are informative. In support of illegal aliens, we could deny that they lack rights to services. Appeal to rights is something an ethic of duty would tend to emphasize. But that is not Noddings's tack. Her view may be that rights is "a relatively unimportant ethical question." (Even if she would not say this, some philosophers do.) At least, she does not appeal to rights. She appeals to "innocence," "harm," "dissension," "fear," "horror." The appeal is to feelings and experiences of concrete individuals—enactors and victims of the policy. It is those feelings and attachments that provide the basic ethical guidance needed, not talk of principles, duties, and rights. (Noddings writes of the need for "logical arguments" as well as "moving stories." Is she endorsing the sort of conversation described by Burbules and Sichel? Something else?)

Part of Noddings's concern about principles is that they are unresponsive to the particulars of people's situations. (Another part of her concern, suggested when she refers to a *feminist* ethic of care, is that an ethic of duty does not adequately incorporate the perspectives and experiences of women.) Thus, she expresses doubts about Kantian ethics, claiming it absolutely prohibits lying. (So far as "absolutes" are a concern, does Noddings treat caring as an absolute?) But an ethic of duty need not be absolutist. In fact, in his *Lectures on Ethics* Kant himself says that lying may be permissible. A white lie is permissible if one is forced to make a statement when convinced improper use would be made of the truth.[7] The universalist claim is that *anyone* faced with that situation could acknowledge the permissibility of lying. Even so, Kant says, a lie is always evil, even if justified. In this sense, Noddings may be correct that Kant claims the principle against lying is "absolute." But in that sense, maybe the principle *should* be absolute. Even if ethics permits, or even requires, that we lie under certain conditions, shouldn't we always see that as an ethical violation and feel regret about having to lie?

We can see these tensions between duty and care in at least some of Dilafruz Williams's disagreements with Noddings. In Williams's essays we see a greater role given to an ethic of duty. While Williams does give caring a central place, she appears to think of it more as one "voice" among several, in contrast to Noddings, who makes caring fundamental. For example, consider Williams's objections to Noddings's idea of ignoring a rule. Williams contends that "[b]y virtue of working in educational institutions and other organizations, we are bound by their codes, codes to which we often should accommodate our personal moral codes." We might think of being "bound by codes" as based on a duty to keep promises. In taking a job in a school there is some promise to abide by its rules. Later, one might find they are bad rules; an ethic of duty by no means advocates slavish obedience to school rules. One can try to change them or leave the school. Yet, Williams says, ignoring them is another matter. Her call to speak out about one's objections echoes a Kantian's concern for rational agency, which implies public discussion of disputed ethical issues.

Noddings does not say that the voice of duty is irrelevant. She does not deny that Lucy should "abide by the terms of her contract." Nor does she deny all place to school rules and traditional civil disobedience. But, again, their worth depends on their contribution to caring. If that contribution is not there, they are dispensable. Williams, by contrast, would appear to give more weight to at least some principles or duties in and of themselves, which is characteristic of a nonconsequentialist ethic of duty.

These views embody importantly different emphases, but the issue as I see it is not between an emphasis on people and an emphasis on duty. The issue is *how* we should be concerned for people. Should we emphasize our more personal, particular connections with people, as an ethic of caring tends to stress (I say "tends" because Noddings is not against all universals. For her, caring is a universal capacity and need), or the more general and perhaps universal things we share with a wider range of people, which I interpret to be the concern of Kantian ethics? The point of impartiality need not be to detach ourselves from our selves but rather to put us in touch with certain aspects of our selves, namely the parts that we share with anyone. We should not just be concerned for how Lucy Williams the unique individual should live but also for how Lucy Williams the human being should live; not just the Lucy who has to pay her bills, but the Lucy who has dignity as a human being and connection to others as human beings. And there may be a whole range of questions in between: How should Lucy Williams the teacher live? How should Lucy the African American woman live? How should Lucy the citizen of a democracy live? My suggestion is that the questions "Who is Lucy?" and "What is her ethical relationship to other people?" have both particularistic and universalistic answers as well as answers in between. We shouldn't lose sight of any of them.[8]

That's easy to say, of course. Our relationships may produce conflicts. Williams and Noddings confront such conflict in several places. It appears in their dispute over the significance of Carole's status as an African American woman. (What do you think about that dispute? Should Carole's status as a woman and African American have greater weight than Noddings allows?) It shows up in Williams's question about how far Lucy's circle of concern should extend. (Does Lucy really have a responsibility to all the people Williams suggests?) It is also involved in the dispute about honoring majority wishes.

These are important differences. Yet we should not overlook possibilities for common ground. For example, Williams's concern for majority wishes is not just a concern for an abstract notion of democracy but for persons whose bond with us is through a common citizenship, even if we do not have a more direct connection to them. At the same time democracy is certainly about protecting the powerless against tyranny by the majority, which may be Noddings's concern. There is plenty of room for disagreement here, but it is worth noting that this disagreement occurs between people who share a commitment to democracy. The source of the difficulty is within democracy itself, not just in the views of individuals.

When faced with these sorts of disputes, we often look for some one view that is superior or more basic that can settle the dispute for us. It may be important to pursue that project. (What do you think about that by now?) But however we think about that, we should be careful not to assume that an ethic of care and an ethic of duty is an either/or choice. While Williams and Noddings may disagree about the relative importance of these two ethics, they do grant some place to both. When faced with such conflicts, we may need to take a "both/and" attitude. That may make things more complicated and difficult, but we risk stultifying our ethical understanding if we do otherwise.[9]

Integrity and Compromise

Whatever their disagreements on these issues, Williams and Noddings are in basic agreement that Lucy can and should be open to modifying her views on things. (And they also agree a good deal on what sorts of modifications are appropriate. At least in this case, their differing views on an ethic of care and an ethic of duty do not lead to widely different conclusions.) She can modify her views while still properly preserving her self. This is an important claim, for it offers the possibility of doing justice to both self and others when these conflict. But as Williams and Noddings show, "integrity" and "compromise" are tricky ideas.

Let's start with "integrity."[10] In her response to Williams, Noddings makes a distinction between integrity as an "individual property" and integrity as a "relational property." This distinction captures a tension between preserving a unified self on the one hand, and, on the other, being open to change for the sake of preserving or achieving integrity in relationships with other people. As the essays show, trying to determine when one goes too far one way or the other can be difficult. But it seems pretty clear that we *do* want some sort of balance between them. Some people can be so wrapped in preserving their image of themselves that they fail to take proper account of their connections to other persons. This is not acting with integrity but rather being self-indulgent. At the other extreme, we want to avoid being "chameleons" who change to fit every situation and thus have no unified self.

Personal transformation need not threaten integrity if we look at the complexity of a person's commitments and the whole pattern of that person's life and not just an isolated incident. This explains why Noddings's and Williams's claims about Lucy's preserving of her integrity are plausible. For instance, Lucy's opposition to testing may be a relatively peripheral commitment. More basic to who she is are commitments to caring and being a good teacher. This explains why Noddings's example of Lucy's giving in to slipshod teaching is a clearer example of sacrificing integrity. (How about Noddings's question about other ways Lucy could lose her integrity? Can you think of examples?)

Maybe it is possible for Lucy to back off from her stand on some of the issues she is concerned about without sacrificing her integrity. But wouldn't that still be unfortunate? She would still have to compromise, would she not? As Noddings notes, some people might say any sort of compromise is a betrayal of integrity. But compromise isn't always bad or "soupy" or integrity sacrificing. We must be clear about what is a compromise and what isn't. If, as Noddings and Williams suggest, Lucy's opposition to the tests is in some sense a mistake, or at least questionable, Lucy could go along with the testing without compromising her sense of self. She would not have to sacrifice a commitment against the testing because she comes to see the commitment is mistaken; she is *changing* her commitment rather than *compromising* it. Similarly, Williams's suggestion that Lucy "carve a new path of integrity" need not imply compromise (even though Williams suggests it does). Lucy could honestly say that her original stance was mistaken, or, if not mistaken, at least inferior in that it is less rich, sensitive, realistic, and so on, than the new image she has fashioned. Both Williams and Noddings describe how Lucy has an opportunity for growth.

Real compromise involves sacrifice, but even genuine compromise can still preserve integrity in the ways suggested above. Compromise can be a way of preserving relationships with people. It can show loyalty to democratic dialogue as a means to settle disagreements. Even if we conclude that what Noddings and Williams recommend for Lucy really is compromise, Lucy can still preserve her integrity and her morale in a legitimate and significant way. (*Do* they recommend compromise? Is there a difference between compromise and "making the best of a bad situation"? In "Freedom and Discipline," how could Roger, Scott, and Andre compromise yet preserve their integrity? Should they compromise?)

Before we leave the issue of compromise, we should note that the essays focus on compromise as a possibility for Lucy. But compromise could have been an objective for the whole political process in this case and not just for Lucy. Given that there was dissent over the testing policy, and particularly dissent voiced by some of the educators who would implement the policy, "splitting the difference" could be a viable aim—democracy does not justify the tyranny of the majority. The board's "all or nothing" stance may be unjustified. For example, why not phase in testing, say at just one grade level at first, and/or in just one or two subject areas? Perhaps parties could agree that after a specified amount of time, say a couple years, the policy would be reviewed and a new vote taken. In these examples, each side would give up something. Perhaps if something like this had happened, there would be less doubt about the need for Lucy to honor the process. Indeed, perhaps the whole agonizing dilemma Lucy faced could/should have been avoided. It is worth remembering that ethical action is not just about dealing with problems reactively, but also about preventing problems. (Would argument have been a good approach to the testing issue? Conversation?)

Conclusion

So, what place does a teacher's unique self have in the ethical world of education? Our discussion suggests that it should have a big place, although I think it's safe to say that its proper place may not be clear always, particularly since there are some fundamentally different ways to think about the ethical importance of the self. In my discussion I've tried to keep the issues alive, to show that there is much to ponder here. But let's also remember that in spite of the complexity it is possible to arrive at plausible judgments that do justice to both self and others. Despite their disagreements, Williams and Noddings arrive at conclusions that are quite similar. At the very least, they agree that teachers should be concerned for their selves, ready to stand up for their principles, but they should also critically reflect on themselves and adapt and even compromise as situations warrant. Some of their agreements are even more substantial than that. (Let's not overlook their disagreements, however. We need strong differing positions to keep the dialectic going.) I think this agreement holds promise for the possibility of dialogue and a "fusion of horizons."

In the next chapter we will continue to think about teachers' freedom and their interactions with other people. It focuses on teachers' responsibilities to others, although concern for individual freedom and integrity is central, too. It continues the discussion by asking to which people teachers are responsible. Do teachers have special ethical obligations to their students, say, or must they cast their net of concern more broadly? And what is the basis of this concern? For example, we'll return to an issue similar to the one with which Noddings and Williams grappled: Do teachers have some special obligation to honor the wishes of their local community? We will look at these questions from different perspectives than those represented in this chapter. This variety should add some helpful insights.

Notes

1. Kurt Baier, *The Moral Point of View* (Ithaca, NY: Cornell University Press, 1958), p. 309.

2. Ibid., p. 310.

3. Bernard Williams, "Persons, Character and Morality," in Amelie Oksenberg Rorty, ed., *The Identities of Persons* (Berkeley: University of California Press, 1976), p. 210.

4. See Michael Slote, *From Morality to Virtue* (New York: Oxford University Press, 1992).

5. Charles Larmore, *Patterns of Moral Complexity* (Cambridge: Cambridge University Press, 1987), p. 64.

6. Jeffrey Blustein presents this sort of view on caring and duty in his *Care and Commitment* (New York: Oxford University Press, 1991).

7. Immanuel Kant, *Lectures on Ethics* translated by Louis Infield (Indianapolis: Hackett, 1980), p. 228.

8. Martha Nussbaum tries to integrate the universal and the particular. While she is a strong advocate of the need to understand people's particular circumstances when making ethical judgments, she also says that the starting point of ethical inquiry is the question "How should a human being live?" See her *Love's Knowledge* (New York: Oxford University Press, 1990), p. 25.

9. See Eve Browning Cole and Susan Coultrap-McQuin, eds., *Explorations in Feminist Ethics* (Bloomington: Indiana University Press, 1992) for discussions of the relationship between the ethics of care and the ethics of duty. Some of the essays show how both ethics are needed. See Rita Manning, "Just Caring" (pp. 45–54) and Robin S. Dillon, "Care and Respect" (pp. 69–81).

10. Many of the points made in this section are drawn from Blustein, *Care and Commitment*; and Martin Benjamin, *Splitting the Difference* (Lawrence: University Press of Kansas, 1990).

4

Communities Near and Far

CASE

All beginning teachers expect that their first year will be difficult at times, but Stan Stankowski was not prepared for the mess he was in now. The year had begun promisingly enough. Stan had gotten the job he wanted—social studies teacher at Coolidge High School, the inner-city school at which he had done his student teaching. Stan knew the job would not be easy; his student teaching experience had shown him that. But he had some success, and he relished the challenge. The Coolidge teachers, parents, and students who had gotten to know him during his student teaching had enthusiastically supported his application. With the advantage of this support and his own experience, Stan felt that he had a "leg up" on things and so had faced the beginning of the school year with great confidence and enthusiasm. However, by now, the last week of October, things were beginning to unravel. Among parents and other teachers there was considerable unhappiness about what Stan was doing with his students.

During college Stan had gotten heavily involved in volunteer work for an international relief agency. He had even made a commitment to act as coordinator of fund-raising activities for his part of the state. He was proud that the activities he oversaw had collected a sizable amount of money for famine relief in Africa. The agency had requested that Stan continue on as district coordinator after college, and Stan had agreed.

This commitment required considerable time. It hadn't interfered with his responsibilities as a student teacher, but he had greater teaching responsibilities now. Stan found that he couldn't devote quite so much time to his teaching as he would otherwise desire. Of course, he didn't believe that this hurt the students any. In fact, he felt that the students would benefit from his example of involvement, and he even included them in his charity activities. In class they discussed issues of poverty and global economy and politics. His experience with the relief agency had given him some insights into these issues. He got the students involved more than just intellectually. As a class assignment the students planned a fund-raising activity, composed flyers and advertisements, solicited the needed permits, and so on. Stan and the students planned to drive out to several large shopping malls in the suburbs every Saturday during November and solicit donations for Stan's relief agency. Afterward, each student would write a paper about the whole experience.

This project had seemed to be going well. At least, the students were engaged and excited. However, complaints from parents and other teachers began to come in. Parents were upset about several things. Would the students be academically prepared for college entrance tests? For many students, if they were to go to college they would need a good deal of financial aid. High test scores could only help their chances of getting some. They were concerned that the students were not getting the social studies curriculum that would prepare them for the tests and for college. Also, the parents felt that Stan was not devoting enough time to his students. Several parents noted instances when their children had approached Stan for help after school only to be told by him that he was unavailable due to his charity commitments. Charity may be nice, but we have to worry about *our* kids, parents said. Besides, if Mr. Stankowski wanted to get students engaged in charity work, there was plenty to be done closer to home in the inner-city neighborhoods where these kids lived. The feeling was that Stan was spending too much time worrying about distant people and not enough about those to whom he had his first obligation—the local community and its children. Some parents who had supported Stan's application for his teaching job felt that he was betraying them.

Several teachers shared the parents' concerns about academics. Others were more willing to think that there was a connection between Stan's project and the social studies curriculum. But all the teachers agreed that Stan was being too much of a "lone wolf." The social studies team had been working hard to reconceptualize the social studies curriculum. The principal and superintendent had been pressing the social studies team to do this, and they were watching the process closely. Stan had been only an occasional attendee at the meetings because of the demands of his work with the relief agency. His curricular ideas may be good, his colleagues said, but he should be thinking how his sort of project could fit in with the entire social studies curriculum. He should be thinking more about his obligations to the other students in the school and to his faculty colleagues.

Stan did not take these complaints lightly, but he did not believe that he was shorting his students. Perhaps he didn't give students all the attention that they and their parents wanted, but what he gave them certainly was adequate. Anyway, he felt, what counts is quality, not quantity. Perhaps his students weren't getting as much "book learning" as other students, but he was giving them something more lasting and worthwhile—practice in real social and political action. He knew there were social and political problems closer to home; but wasn't he fostering the sort of caring and disposition to act that might prompt students to tackle those problems?

He contacted the relief agency to see if he could be released from his commitment to them. They told him they would try to find someone else if that's what he wanted. He also thought about scaling back his class's fund-raising, maybe to just one Saturday. Ultimately he decided against making any changes, as he feared that backing off from his activities would give students the wrong message. He wanted students to see service to others as something that should be a real commitment. It couldn't always be convenient and without sacrifice.

Concerning his colleagues, Stan knew he was not pulling his weight so far as the curriculum reconceptualization. He went to meetings when he could manage it. But he wasn't sure what he could accomplish if he went more often. It was unclear how much real change would occur. More than likely, any attempt by other teachers to repeat his project in their classes would result in merely half-hearted efforts; one couldn't expect all the teachers to have the sort of commitment he had. Stan had the sense that this didn't let him off the hook completely. Even if the meetings weren't all that productive, maybe loyalty to colleagues demanded that he participate nonetheless. But he had loyalty to many communities, Stan thought, including the community of distant human beings who were suffering.

Meetings with parents and colleagues have not resolved the dispute, and things are coming to a head as the time for the trips to the suburbs approaches. Several parents are saying now that they won't allow their children to go with their classmates on the trips. They are demanding that Stan set aside more time for meeting with students before or after school. Stan's principal and superintendent are pushing for action on the new social studies curriculum. Should Stan rethink his whole understanding of his ethical commitments? What should he do now?

Reflections on "Communities Near and Far"

Principles, Politics, and Prudence

BY ARTHUR BROWN

Like diamonds, teachers can be forever. Most teachers have little discernible effect on our character, on our personalities, on our understanding of ourselves, or on who we want to be. Not so for the good ones or the bad ones. The good ones change our lives for the better; the bad ones leave scars. You can depend on having bad ones. But good ones are rare and, like anything rare, should be prized, nurtured if necessary, but, insofar as possible, left alone. Stan looks like a good one, a diamond—in the rough.

When I use the word "good" in reference to teachers, I am not referring to how much subject matter we learned from them. I remember very little of the subject matter taught by any teacher. I am referring to who they were—their personalities, their passions, their insights, the way they went about their business. Advocates of "knowledge-based education" may not be pleased with what Alfred North Whitehead had to say in this connection, but it surely must ring true for most of us: "Education is what's left over after everything else has been forgotten."

I am reminded of two of my own good teachers. There was Mr. Nash, my high school Latin teacher. At the time I learned a lot of Latin; however that is practically all gone now. What I learned that persists is caring—caring about words, about grammar, about precision. Even now, as I ponder whether to use the nominative or the accusative case, his ghost looms above me. I dare not make a mistake. But Mr. Nash, good grammarian though he was, did not or was not able to help me learn about the deeper human issues to be found in Ovid or Virgil or Julius Caesar.

It was several years later, at the University of Massachusetts, when I met Professor Ray Torrey, that I discovered someone who could help me understand "what it all means." Suffering as I was the despair of growing up, I latched onto Torrey. Although my philosophic views are now different from Torrey's, he is responsible in large part for my *real* education, however modest it is. And I am not alone in my admiration. Listen to what other former students have said about him. Dr. Oswald Tippo, former chair of Yale's botany department and later chancellor of the University of Massachusetts: "He taught his students botany, but he did more than that—he sought to awaken their sluggish minds in the hope that this would awaken their even more sluggish spirits."

The poet Robert Francis, describing Torrey's lecturing style:

> *He* was *talking about cells a moment ago, but at this moment he is talking about classical music or the Dark Ages or the Fourth Dimension. Like a magician he can draw almost anything out of the tall hat of botany and do it so quickly you do not see the move. His avowed aim is not to teach botany merely, but to relate that science and all science to the whole of education, to philosophy, to history, to religion, and particularly to what a young man or woman is thinking of today.*

Torrey, I should note, was not one of the more gregarious professors on campus. Indeed, he was regarded by many as an eccentric, a loner. I doubt that he was collaborating with anyone except his assistants not only because of who he was but also because collaboration at the university level or in the schools was not exactly in vogue at that time.

It is only in recent years that the idea of extensive collaboration among teachers and between teachers and other stakeholders in the educational enterprise has acquired a degree of popularity. I myself have been for many years an ardent supporter of the concepts of collaboration and shared authority and have attempted to implement those conceptions in political activities both in my home community and in my university. Not, I should add, without causing considerable consternation on the part of my superiors and certain government officials, and not, I might also add, without some personal costs.

I have argued for participation both as a philosophical ideal and as a practical desirability. I have maintained that genuine participation in decision making by the various constituent groups in social organizations is a human right, that it is consistent with political and social democracy, and that, fortuitously, in the long run it promises greater efficiency than do pyramidal, hierarchical social structures. And in this connection I am fond of citing an especially lyrical passage in John Dewey's *Freedom and Culture*:

> *[Democracy] can be won only by extending the application of democratic methods of consultation, persuasion, negotiation, communication, cooperative intelligence, in the task of making our own politics, industry, education, our culture generally, a servant and an evolving manifestation of democratic ideas.*[1]

Yet . . . I hesitate. There is something about the role of the individual teacher that is substantively, if not uniquely, different from the roles of people in most organizations and institutions. This is especially the case in a democracy—and for two reasons.

The first reason is to ensure the generation of ideas. Ideas are generated by individuals. A group may discuss an idea, accept or reject it, may elaborate on it or modify it, but a group does not generate an idea. Hence, teachers (and others, too, but teachers especially) must feel free and be free to express their ideas and act on them, to be, as Bertrand Russell put it, "directed by an inner creative impulse, not dominated and festered by authority."

Consider Stan in this regard. He has been accused by his colleagues of being "too much of a lone wolf." "His curricular ideas may be good," his colleagues said, "but he should be thinking how his sort of project might fit in with the entire social studies curriculum." Yet teaching is a highly personal activity. *One* person teaches. That is the case even for team teaching. Moreover, there are important social benefits which accrue to the exercise of personal intellectual freedom, as pointed out some years ago by Nobel Prize winner Dr. Ernest Chain when he expressed concern about the reduced flow of new ideas in medicine:

> *[T]he need . . . is for more attention to far-out investigators in biology and to make more room for the scientist whose work does not lend itself to rational, planned team effort.*
>
> *It is our job . . . to recognize [these scientists] and to give them the opportunities to develop their talents, which is not an easy task, for they are bound to be lone wolves, awkward individualists, non-conformists, and they will not fit very well into any established organization.*[2]

A second reason for giving teachers freedom is to provide protection for them in their role of expressing unconventional or politically unpopular views, views that do not correspond with those in authority or with those of the general public. Freedom of speech is, of course, a First Amendment right, but too often it is considered a right to be exercised only in a public forum, not in the workplace, including the academic workplace. Indeed, as anyone experienced in workplace politics knows, exercising that right is a risky business.

We come then to a major ethical problem that confronts all of us: How to live by one's principles in a world that doesn't necessarily share them. In Stan's case, how can he harmonize his professional rights and responsibilities as a teacher and citizen with the demands imposed by the social setting in which he works and lives? In addressing that question, I shall allude to three interrelated issues: principles, politics, and prudence.

Principles

Teachers enjoy the privileges of academic freedom and professional autonomy. This is to ensure that the integrity of teachers is protected and ultimately to protect the democratic character of society. In contrast to a closed society in which teachers are expected to echo the party line, to indoctrinate or proselytize, in a *truly* democratic society teachers are charged with educating their students in such a manner that they will be inclined to question social policies or conventional wisdom, to search for the truth, to acquire the habit and disposition to *inquire* into matters rather than simply *acquire* information, to arrive at judgments using their own intellectual powers, and to become sensitive to the problems of humankind. In a democratic society, *all* teachers are responsible for helping students acquire the habits, attitudes, and dispositions necessary for democratic living in the process of studying their respective disciplines.

However, it would not be appropriate for a physics teacher engaged in teaching physics to undertake the kind of project Stan took on with his students. If the physics teacher were to do that as an *integral* part of teaching physics, he or she would be violating a public trust and, in my judgment, would not be justified in appealing to the principle of professional autonomy or in asking for the protection of tenure—however worthy the project. This is, of course, not to say that if there is a clear and present danger to society or to a fundamental principle of justice, the physics teacher *as a citizen* would not be justified in speaking out or in taking action or in mobilizing people and resources. But he or she would do so as a citizen, not as a physics teacher.

On the other hand, it would *not* be a violation of a public trust if a physics teacher were to discuss the ethical problems associated with producing hazardous waste during the manufacture of nuclear weapons or to take a strong stand on the issue in class. Nor would it be a violation of a public trust if a biology teacher were to discuss in class ethical dilemmas associated with the human genome project or even speak out against the project. In each case, the issues are an integral part of the subject matter. I would also contend, though, that in each case the teacher must take great care in taking a stand and should do so only if all sides are given a fair hearing and only if the topic does not receive undue attention. It is one thing to incorporate, as did Professor Torrey, ideas or facts from related fields. It is another to expound on or to become excessively, if not obsessively, partisan about *social and political matters*. When teachers of physics or biology do so, in my view they are not only violating a public trust, but also by abusing that trust are endangering the principles of professional autonomy and academic freedom.

Turning to Stan, his famine relief project is without question appropriate to the discipline of social studies, for we can assume that by being engaged in raising money and in other aspects of the project, such as applying for permits to solicit funds, students are acquiring a greater understanding of the discipline. Moreover, in acquiring that understanding, it is conceivable that Stan's students are also acquiring those qualities, described earlier, which constitute the goals of an education for democratic living.

However, notwithstanding his right and even obligation *as a social studies teacher* to have his students participate in a project of this kind, the question arises: Should Stan continue to pursue the course of action on which he has embarked in the face of objections, which may be legitimate, raised by parents and colleagues? That question leads to a consideration of the matter of politics.

Politics

The deontological position that moral principles are primary has much to commend it. But one cannot live by principles alone. The *consequences* of acting on principles must be considered. Otherwise serious damage may be done. Thus, I have claimed that the principles of academic freedom and professional autonomy are essential for the generation of ideas and for the protection of professional integrity and ultimately a democratic society. But schools exist in a sociopolitical arena in which parents, students, colleagues, administrators, and the public at large are all stakeholders and, as such, have a legitimate claim to the opportunity to participate in the construction of educational goals and practices. Furthermore, the participation of all stakeholders in the educational enterprise is necessary for the attainment of optimal educational results. How can we harmonize the conflicting values entailed?

We need to recognize that the teacher's role is in part a political one. And politics has been aptly described as the art of the possible. I am not suggesting that the teacher should not fight for principles or should accept the role of functionary. (I myself have "gone to the mat" on a few occasions.) I am suggesting, however, that a teacher must accept the political nature of his or her position and that performing the political role effectively can strengthen public support for the principles of professional autonomy and academic freedom. Teachers can no longer remain "above" politics while politicians, especially in state houses and governors' mansions, are taking greater control of the educational system, including mandating educational content and methodology. The view prevails that education is too important to leave to educators.

The overriding concern of the American public regarding the school is its instrumental value. The idea of the intrinsic value of education and the principles of academic freedom and professional autonomy are becoming antiquated, as is the idea of the school as a means for promoting American democracy's highest ideals and educating for democratic life. Until teachers face up to the fact that the educational system is an extension of our political and social system and recognize that in order to ensure its integrity they must become politically involved, teachers will be forever subject to the vagaries of those in power and those who control the media. To use current terminology, they will become deskilled and deprofessionalized. Except for certain unions, and they are always suspected of self-interest, there is not a professional organization of educators which, to my knowledge, is engaged in the kinds of political activity that are needed.

All that is a sort of macro view. But what about Stan? What can he do as an individual to become politically involved such that he can be a more effective teacher and protect his personal integrity and that of his colleagues? First, he must become more conscious of the fact that as a teacher he lives in a political world. Therefore, Stan must redouble his effort to educate those with whom his professional life is intertwined and who, as I have said, have a legitimate stake in the education of students: his colleagues, his administrators, and the parents of his students. He must continue to make the case to skeptics that involving his students in the project of raising money for starving Africans is an integral part of his course, that it has pedagogical value, social value, and value as a means for sensitizing his students to the plight of others, particularly at a time when caring for the "stranger" is an attribute losing, I am afraid, its appeal in a world torn by ethnocentrism. Stan may not prevail, but at least he will have tried. And even failure may gain him some respect, which might some day redound to his benefit and to that of his colleagues and his profession as well. The question for Stan, then, is how to go about being political. For some suggestions along those lines, I turn to the matter of prudence.

Prudence

If discretion is the better part of valor, prudence is the better part of politics. You can't beat City Hall with a frontal attack and little fire power. Politics requires the building of alliances, it requires lobbying, and it requires earning respect. And, as important as anything else, academic politics, at least, requires knowledge and the ability to make a case. All this doesn't happen overnight.

Stan seems to be energetic, certainly concerned. His idealism, of which there is not enough these days, is to be admired. As I said earlier, I think he is a diamond in the rough. If he survives, his brilliance may some day shine through. But Stan is politically inexperienced. However meritorious his project and however good he is as a teacher, he and his project will fail unless he goes slowly and unless he is willing to engage in the political process. That willingness is essential in making a difference in any organization, but especially in schools. (Educational politics, according to some, is the most vicious of all.)

Since old people relish giving advice, I shall make a few suggestions as to what Stan might do to increase his chances of successfully pursuing his project and, also, I might add, to save his job. Above all, Stan should demonstrate more respect for the parents of his students and for his colleagues. I am not suggesting that he kowtow, become submissive, and not stand up for the principles in which he believes. But parents and colleagues do have a stake in the school and in its educational program. Stan must engage them in the political process, the process, as Dewey said, of "consultation, persuasion, negotiation, communication, cooperative intelligence."

Consider the parents. Many are concerned that their children will not do well on standardized tests because they are spending so much time on Stan's project. Not only do they believe that their children's chances for admission to college are being weakened, but also their chances for financial aid. Understandable and legitimate concerns. Now Stan could categorically reject the parents' objections and claim the right to pursue his project as he sees fit. But this would be rash and not appropriate to the situation. Or, although at this stage in his academic career it would probably be difficult for him to do so, Stan could argue, as many of us have over the years, that test scores have little to do with genuine education, that they do not really matter in the long run, that undue emphasis on teaching for the test undermines genuine education, that test scores, and grades for that matter, predict little or nothing about students' competence on the job or teachers' competence in the classroom, and that, therefore, parents should not be so concerned. Parents live in the real world, however; they know that, regardless of the merit of the policy, colleges do take test scores seriously and that admissions and financial aid are, in fact, to a greater or lesser degree dependent on them.

What should Stan do? For one thing, he might inform parents that research exists that shows that academic achievement and test scores have, in fact, *been raised* as a result of students having the sort of course and experience he's proposing. In this way, Stan may be able to reconcile his primary interests and principles with those of the parents without necessarily coming to agreement on certain antecedents, such as the value of tests.

Consider Stan's relationship with his colleagues. Just because his prior attempts have not been eminently successful, Stan should not assume that his colleagues are uneducable and that his presence at social studies team meetings will make no difference at all. Even if his colleagues prove to be obdurate, Stan cannot escape the charge given to the team to reconceptualize the social studies curriculum; this is one of his professional responsibilities. Furthermore, whatever eventuates from that reconceptualization will affect his professional life and, if only for that reason, he should participate fully in the discussions. Of equal importance is that by demonstrating his respect for his colleagues, by attending meetings, by seeking out colleagues for private conversations, by voicing his views and listening to theirs, Stan is far more likely to enjoy political success.

There are other matters about which Stan could be prudent. As a first-year teacher, he is in a precarious position; therefore, he should cool it. Stan is perceived as spending an inordinate amount of time on the project to the neglect of his other duties, including refusing to set aside more time for meeting with students—an action that is inexcusable and that he himself questions. And his worry about setting a bad example regarding commitment if he were to reduce the time spent on the project is simply misguided. There are obviously many commitments to be fulfilled in life, and students would be better off knowing that sooner rather than later.

Postscript

However laudable his ideals, Stan, I am afraid, is guilty of self-righteousness, a not uncommon human frailty. On one hand, we do not have enough people like Stan, people of principle; on the other hand, the world is often torn apart by people of principle. On one hand, principles provide the basis for a just and humane society; on the other, they tend to blind us to the consequences of our actions. Ideally, of course, principles should inform our action and, conversely, the consequences of our action should inform our principles. But that ideal is difficult to realize. Frequently the only recourse to settling conflicts among contending parties who cannot agree on certain antecedents is negotiation. In which case, ethics becomes politics.

Being political does not necessarily mean we should suffer every kind of fool or make deals with every kind of charlatan or put up with every kind of oppressor. Nor does it mean necessarily turning the other cheek. What it does mean is that insofar as possible, we should be sensitive to the needs, interests, and values of others whose views are different in an effort to arrive at a mutually acceptable accommodation. No easy task! But what's the alternative? Good luck, Stan.

Notes

1. John Dewey, *Freedom and Culture* (New York: Capricorn, 1963, reprint of 1939 ed.), p. 175.
2. Ernest Chain, *Detroit Free Press,* January 7, 1967.

Living the Life of a Teacher: Reflections on Stan's Dilemma

BY SHIRLEY PENDLEBURY

Arrogant and deluded about his own motives and capabilities—these were some of my first, harsh thoughts about Stan Stankowski on a quick reading of the case. A deeper reading jolted me into putting such snap judgments on hold.

"What should Stan do now?" we are asked. This question marks the case as one calling for practical reasoning; the intransigence of Stan's dilemma marks it as a hard case, as opposed to a routine or soft case. In hard cases of practical reasoning, principles and precedents may serve as guidelines for ethical choice, but they provide no rules for morally appropriate action, no straightforward solutions, no unambiguous signs about what direction to follow under problematic circumstances. Stan finds himself in exactly this situation.

Stan seems to be a principled man. He appeals to principles both in trying to understand his quandary and in defending the choices he has made so far. Against the claim of loyalty to his colleagues, he appeals to his loyalty to many other communities "including the community of distant human beings who were suffering." In defense of his decision to engage students in a fund-raising drive, he appeals to the principle of sacrifice for the sake of service: he wants students "to see service to others as something that should be a real commitment," something that "couldn't always be convenient and without sacrifice."

Yet the very principles he values are constitutive of his predicament, for they point simultaneously in more than one direction. The principles of loyalty and commitment bind him not only to his students and fellow teachers but also to his fund-raising activities. The principle of sacrifice in the name of service says nothing about the nature, direction or extent of appropriate sacrifice; it is silent on the question of whether it is better for Stan to sacrifice his teaching career for the sake of serving a famished community in a distant land or to sacrifice his fund-raising position (and the deep sense of personal fulfillment it brings) for the sake of service to his students and professional community.

If these and other pertinent principles cannot be decisive in resolving Stan's dilemma, what should he do? Just leap in one direction or the other and live with the consequences? But this would be out of character. As far as we can tell, Stan isn't the kind of person who simply forsakes one set of obligations for another. So, the question persists, What should he do?

Hard cases of practical reasoning require an astute and rich situational appreciation.[1] Stan's primary task, in my view, is to discern all the salient particulars of his situation, for it is these that will help him see how best to act. This is no easy task. Salient particulars do not always leap to the eye ready-labeled for identification. What counts as salient will depend in no small measure on how Stan sees himself and on what kind of life he regards as a good life for him. It will depend, too, on his standing commitments and on the principles he values. At the same time, in coming to an appreciation of his situation he may also come to change his mind about who he is and what he conceives as a good life for him. Hard cases of practical reasoning confront us not only with who we are at the time of confrontation but also with who we might become as a consequence of our actions. This is partly what makes them hard; they involve conflicts of personal identity as well as conflicts of value and choice.

Although there is no recipe, there are many ways of coming to a fuller and richer appreciation of a problematic situation. All call upon imagination and emotion at least as much as they call upon reason.

As an outsider reading Stan's story, I take two approaches to picking out some of the salient particulars in his situation. I begin by reading Stan's case in the light of the given title, "Communities Near and Far." Then I propose some alternative titles and attend to the different details and different sets of principles illuminated by each. "Communities Near and Far" illuminates those aspects of the situation that present Stan's predicament as involving a conflict between responsibilities to a local community and responsibilities to a different one. Each of the alternative titles I propose arises from my sense that this is too narrow a view of the issues at stake.

Of course, it would be impossible for me to discern anything like a complete range of the salient particulars. For one thing, I am not Stan. Although I may face (and indeed have faced) very similar dilemmas, his situation is not mine. We have different life histories and perhaps different temperaments, we have different sets of personal and professional relations, and we work in different contexts. For another, Stan's story (as it is told in this book) omits many details that may be salient to his predicament. We know nothing about his family and friends, nothing about his obligations and interests outside of teaching and fund-raising. We don't even know very much about his relations to fellow fund-raisers.

Communities Near and Far

On the surface, Stan's approach to resolving his conflict is sensible and sensitive: he tries to integrate his various responsibilities in a single, principled, moral vision. For him charity neither begins nor ends at home. He brings his charitable concerns into his classroom teaching, and he takes his class into the domain of charitable work. Telling himself that students will benefit from his example of involvement, he uses his volunteer work as a basis for class discussions of poverty and global politics, as well as for an out-of-school project. In these various ways, Stan might be seen as bringing members of his local community (his students) into moral touch with a remote community, thus extending the scope and range of students' moral concerns.

Whatever his own view of the case, Stan has not taken proper account of the salient particulars unless he also attends to the views of salient other people. Within the school community, salient others include students, parents, and fellow teachers. Beyond the school community, salient others include members of the fund-raising organization and members of the distant African community served by the organization. I shall focus on salient others in the school community.

We know very little of what the students think, apart from Stan's observation that they are "engaged and excited." Two sets of questions are pertinent here. One relates to the accuracy of the observation, the other to its significance for Stan's curriculum decisions. Is it true that all or most of the students are engaged and excited, or has Stan deceived himself about their response to the project? What would he have done had they not been engaged and excited? Would he have taken this as a strong enough reason to change his approach to social studies teaching?

These questions all but disappear from view if we read Stan's predicament only in the light of the title "Communities Near and Far." I revisit them later under an alternative title.

"Communities Near and Far" does illuminate a prominent facet of the parents' concerns. For them, charity begins (and perhaps ends) at home. They believe Stan is spending "too much time worrying about distant people and not enough about those to whom he had his first obligation—the local community and its children." Yet the dispute is not simply about whether his primary obligation is to a local or a distant community. It is also a dispute about what is involved in fulfilling the responsibilities of a teacher or, more specifically, a dispute about the nature and aims of education and the importance of time and care in the profession of teaching. Stan is sensitive to these facets of the dispute. He defends himself against parents' complaints by appealing to his perception of what is educationally worthwhile, namely, "practice in real social and political action" and "fostering the sort of care and disposition" necessary for moral action. Embedded in his appeal is a challenge to parents' myopic conception of secondary education as little more than preparation for college entrance tests.

What of Stan's fellow teachers? Like the parents, their concerns are partly captured by the title "Communities Near and Far," but with an important difference in what they regard as the relevant local community for Stan's commitment. Teachers believe that Stan owes allegiance, time, and care to his professional community, especially to that section of the community made up of fellow social studies teachers and students at the school, including those not in his class. Teachers are unanimous in their unease about how thin a commitment Stan has to his immediate professional community. Implicit in their concern is a thick conception of what it means to take on the role and accompanying responsibilities of a teacher. For them, good curricular ideas may be worthy of praise but they are insufficient for the fulfillment of a teacher's responsibilities. Part of what it means to be a teacher is to be a member of a community of the practice of teaching and thus to bring one's good ideas to bear on the curriculum as a whole for the good of all the relevant students and all the relevant faculty. At best Stan is a restricted professional; his colleagues expect him to be an extended professional.

Precisely because it throws such strong light on some of the salient particulars of Stan's situation, the title "Communities Near and Far" casts a shadow over others. Three retellings—"Lone Wolf"; "Beginnings, Middles, and Ends"; and "Living the Life of a Teacher"—will help to bring these other particulars to light.

Lone Wolf

The teachers see Stan as a lone wolf. Should this worry him? *Roget's Thesaurus* includes "lone wolf" in two separate lists of synonyms, one for an odd person (for example: "outsider," "alien," "pariah," "lone wolf"), the other for a selfish person (for example: "self-seeker," "individualist," "loner," "lone wolf"). To accuse Stan of being a lone wolf is to say either that he has no community (Stan as Pariah) or that he cares too little about "his" community, perhaps is too disdainful of it, to invest his energy in its projects (Stan as Individualist).

Like Frankie in Carson McCullers's *A Member of the Wedding*, Stan as Pariah would not be a member of anything. There would be no "we" of which the "he" of

Stan is a part. Certainly he is not a member of the remote African community served by his fund-raising activities. And, while he is contractually a member of the teaching profession, there do seem to be good reasons for denying him the status of a fully fledged and active member of the professional community. But this doesn't make him a pariah. He is an active member of something (if not a community) and that is the local fund-raising branch of an international relief agency. In any case, a pariah is an outcast. Stan has not been cast out either by the remote community he serves or by his local professional community. Indeed, he could not be cast out by the remote community since spatial and cultural distance make him ineligible for membership in it. To be eligible he would have to live and work among the people for a time, sharing their way of life and coming to understand the ravages of famine from lived experience.

Lone wolf though he may be, Stan is no pariah. At least not yet. If his fund-raising activities continue to absorb his attention and time, he may find himself cast out from collegial respect and recognition, as well as from other more tangible goods like promotion and pay increases. If he had been working at a black township school in South Africa prior to the demise of apartheid, he might have found himself hounded out of the school by students who saw his fund-raising involvements as neglectful of his teaching duties and as a betrayal of their educational aspirations. In apartheid South Africa a profoundly unjust political system, extensive unemployment, and exceptionally high drop out and failure rates in African schools, coupled with the growth of grassroots democratic movements, all contributed to student militarism and deep suspicion of any teachers whose attention was seen to be diverted by concerns outside of local struggles for education and justice.

If Lone Wolf Stan is not a pariah, is he an individualist? A few of his responses to the concerns of fellow teachers hint at the arrogance typical of many strong individualists. Although he acknowledges he isn't pulling his weight in the school's curriculum reconceptualization project, his skepticism about the possibility of real change suggests a dismissive attitude to the project and his colleagues. "More than likely," he thinks, "any attempt by other teachers to repeat his project in their classes would result in merely half-hearted efforts; one couldn't expect all the teachers to have the sort of commitment he had." Whatever the truth of this view, the tone of the thought is at once disdainful and self-congratulatory.

Insofar as he has chosen to act independently of his teaching colleagues, Stan is a loner. Independence is not a fault. We surely want teachers who can think for themselves, and independent teachers can help a community of practice to thrive by breaking new ground. The trouble is Stan appears to have neither interests nor projects in common with his teaching colleagues; he engages as little as possible in their cooperative endeavor to bring about a commonly desired end (the reconstruction of the curriculum) and so whittles away the enabling conditions for mutual care and respect between himself and fellow practitioners. Yet the very things missing from his collegial relations at school may well be present in his volunteer work. If so, we may want to ask Stan whether his heart is in teaching and to ask how far he is willing and able to live the life of a teacher (with its attendant calls for sacrifice and commitment).

Beginnings, Middles, and Ends

As is so often the case in critical moments of a moral life, Stan finds himself at the intersection of several runs of life narrative, each at a different stage of completion. His story of qualifying as a teacher and securing a position has come to a happy end. He has been appointed to the position he wanted, with enthusiastic support from parents and teachers, and with all the challenge that appears to be temperamentally necessary for him to thrive. (We are told that "he relished the challenge" of teaching in an inner city school.)

Where one story ends, another begins. Qualifying as a teacher is not the end of becoming a teacher. Becoming a teacher, in the full sense, involves living the life of a teacher. In the few months of his employment Stan has entered the territory of teaching without taking on all the demands and habits of the life. He certainly isn't an interloper or a blundering explorer. His qualifications give him legitimate entry and, together with his previous experience as a student teacher, provide a rough map of the territory and a set of tools for traversing and making his place in it. Yet many of his thoughts and actions suggest the confidence of an authority, or someone who knows it all and has little to learn from insiders. It is as if Stan took on the job at Coolidge High without recognizing that to be a beginner teacher *is* to start afresh, with fresh challenges to meet, fresh impediments to overcome, fresh relationships to nurture.

Cutting across these two stories of teaching (one story ended, the other barely begun) is a third: the story of Stan the Fund-raiser. In this established, continuing story—a story somewhere in the middle of its trajectory—Stan is emerging as a hero. Things depend upon him, and he has proved his dependability. As district fund-raising coordinator he has acquired responsibility, recognition, and the authority of his office. He has also become more knowledgeable through the insights the work has given him into global politics and economics.

This is a story of someone who tackles each project with pride, energy, and considerable personal satisfaction. The results of his efforts are tangible—a sizable amount of money for famine relief. Because the story is an established one, so too are Stan's commitments and his sources of personal fulfillment—pride in his accomplishments to date, the challenge of raising even more money and of choosing the best ways to do so, a deep sense of service to people in real and desperate need. All these are reasons why he may find it difficult to relinquish his involvement in volunteer work, especially since he has yet to establish his sources of fulfillment in teaching, and these he may find more fragile, more difficult to sustain than those in fund-raising.

Passion for his volunteer work and pride in it have bonded Stan's identity as a fund-raiser. These emotions propel much of his activity in thought and deed; they direct his attention and color his vision, heightening his awareness of the many things that might connect with this work. But what colors vision may also cloud it; what propels a hero to action may also be his self-defeating flaw. Stan's pride in his fund-raising achievements may have led him to exaggerate his own importance in the work of the volunteer agency. Pride, coupled with arrogance, sometimes encourages us to believe that we are indispensable, and though passion for a project may be contagious, it may also blind us to others' indifference to the project. Perhaps, affected by his energy and enthusiasm (and by his novel approach to teaching), Stan's students are indeed engaged and excited by the fund-raising project he has set them. On the other hand, carried aloft by his own passionate interests, he may simply not have noticed the indifference of some students.

As we have seen, the beginning of Stan's story as a teacher is none too promising. After only a couple months, things have begun unraveling. Beginnings are risky times to put the trust and goodwill of one's colleagues and clients to the test. In doing so Stan puts his own future as a teacher at risk. But beginnings are also openings, times of possibility when a great many things could happen, constrained only by context and character. This is why the question "What should Stan do now?" is so critical.

Living the Life of a Teacher

Interpreting William James' account of the moral life, Ruth Anna Putnam writes:

> *Moral life consists of normal stretches punctuated by critical moments. . . . During the critical moments we choose new ideals or reaffirm or modify old ones guided by nothing but ourselves. Our character limits our choices and will be modified by the choices we make. The right act is the act that fits into a certain life, fits the character one is and wants to become.*[2]

I would add that the right act doesn't have to fit with a life lived now, for that would preclude the possibility of shaping a different sort of life. Stan's dilemma, although he may not see it this way, is partly a dilemma about the kind of life he wants to live.

Think about different ways of living a life. There's deep immersion in a single practice or pursuit, a consuming passion for one thing. There's the drive for balance, for integrating several interests and activities into a full and rich life. There's the life in which what one lives for must be kept in the margins precisely because it cannot earn a living. There's the chaotic, fragmented life of darting from one thing to another, buffeted about by the winds of circumstance, and accomplishing nothing.

Stan's initial response to his predicament was a move toward balance and integration. One of the reasons for the failure of the move, I believe, is that Stan is not yet sufficiently immersed in teaching to understand its demands on him. He has several of the qualities that distinguish real teachers from pretenders: an imaginative approach to his subject, pleasure in his students' engagement, a holistic understanding of education, a sense of how to ensure that the class fund-raising project is an educational enterprise and not simply an exploitation of student labor. Yet his identity as a teacher is precarious.

Whatever his other commitments, Stan has not committed himself to living the life of a teacher. The evidence suggests that he is not willing to do so, at least not now. Does this matter? I think it does matter, deeply, and this because I regard teaching as a practice in the sense that Alasdair MacIntyre uses the term. According to MacIntyre's tortuous but useful definition, a practice is

> *any coherent and complex form of socially established cooperative human activity through which goods internal to that form of activity are realized in the course of trying to achieve those standards of excellence which are appropriate to, and partly definitive of, that form of activity, with the result that human powers to achieve excellence, and human conceptions of the ends and goods involved, are systematically extended.*[3]

On MacIntyre's account, a fully fledged practitioner becomes one through the sustained pursuit of two kinds of goods that are definitive of the practice. The first is excellence in the products of a practice; the second is excellence in the lives of practitioners. The two kinds of goods are interdependent. Living one's life as a teacher means devoting time, effort, and attention to keeping alive the knowledge, skills, and interests necessary for excellence in products. (Examples of the definitive products of the practice of teaching are students' learning, a whole range of classroom processes including the teacher's performance, curricula, and curriculum texts.) Living the life of a teacher also means sacrificing on occasion one's personal interests for those of the practice.

Teaching is a practice in and of time—a practice of patience as well as pace, a practice that requires time for teachers and students alike to immerse themselves in activities that will extend their knowledge and understanding, a practice that requires time to become familiar with and appreciate different ways of doing things, and a practice that requires time for talking and thinking about the goods of the practice with colleagues and clients.

Stan hasn't yet done his time in teaching and already he seems to be nudging it into the margins of his life. Perhaps he will decide to leave teaching at a point when his contractual and moral obligations, as well as his financial means, allow him to do so. In the meantime, given the pressures on him from parents and teachers alike, he would be wise to push his fund-raising concerns and activities into the margins. Perhaps, in time, he will find a way of doing both without compromising either, although this, too, will extract its toll.

Notes

1. Shirley Pendlebury, "Practical Arguments and Situational Appreciation in Teaching," *Educational Theory* 40 (1990): 171–79; and David Wiggins, "Deliberation and Practical Reason," in Amelie Rorty, ed., *Essays on Aristotle's Ethics* (Berkeley: University of California Press, 1980), pp. 221–40.

2. Ruth Anna Putnam, "The Moral Life of a Pragmatist," in Owen Flanagan and Amelie Rorty, eds., *Identity, Character, and Morality: Essays in Moral Psychology* (Cambridge: MIT Press, 1993), p. 87.

3. Alasdair MacIntyre, *After Virtue: A Study in Moral Theory* (London: Duckworth, 1981), p. 175.

Further Reflections on "Communities Near and Far"

An Addendum to "Principles, Politics, and Prudence"

BY ARTHUR BROWN

I find that Dr. Pendlebury and I are in wide agreement on philosophical matters as well as on our advice to Stan.[1] Consider, for example, the similarities on two central issues:

1. Life presents us with many obligations (as Stan has discovered), and we are forced to make a selection from among them such that some cannot be fulfilled, at least to the extent desired.

   Pendlebury: In hard cases of practical reasoning, principles and precedents may serve as guidelines for ethical choice, but provide no rules for morally appropriate action, no straightforward solutions, no unambiguous signs about what direction to follow under problematic circumstances. Stan finds himself in exactly this situation.

   Brown: We come then to a major ethical problem that confronts us all: How to live by one's principles in a world that doesn't necessarily share them. In Stan's case, how can he harmonize his professional rights and responsibilities as a teacher and citizen with the demands imposed by the social setting in which he works and lives?
2. A single-minded commitment to a particular principle may be commendable, but it also may be destructive.

   Pendlebury: But what colors vision may also cloud it: what propels a hero to action may also be his self-defeating flaw.

   Brown: On one hand, we do not have enough people like Stan, people of principle. On the other hand, the world is often torn apart by people of principle. On one hand, principles provide the basis for a just and humane society. On the other, they tend to blind us to the consequences of our action.

Since there is nothing of a substantial nature in Dr. Pendlebury's elegantly written essay with which I would take issue, what I should like to do in this section is elaborate on a few ideas that she or I or both of us touched on in our first essays.

First is the idea that contingencies exist in almost all human situations and, hence, one must take into consideration the values, needs, and so forth, of others in resolving problems. (This may be belaboring the obvious but, too often, sad to say, actions suggest otherwise.)

Conflicts, as we all know, are pervasive. We have conflicts within the family, between employees and employers, between students and teachers, between students and students, between teachers and administrators, among members of Congress, among ethnic groups within a nation, and, of course, between nations. In recent years many educators have become increasingly concerned about such matters, particularly about the level and intensity of conflicts within the school. As a consequence, programs in "conflict resolution" are being instituted. Unfortunately, for many people the "resolution" of a conflict—the cessation of open hostilities, the settling of a strike, the avoidance of a divorce—is what is all important. I am afraid, however, that much more is at issue. The *means* by which the conflict is resolved and the sense on the part of all parties that the conflict has been resolved *justly* are of special significance. If these matters are not given sufficient consideration, the resolution may well be short lived.

Witness the seeds of the Second World War planted in the treaty arrived at in Versailles. Witness the impact on morale of the interminable bickering between teachers and school boards and between faculty and administration in many school systems and universities at contract time. And witness the damage done to employer-employee relationships as business and industry downsize to raise profits and please stockholders. It is not simply that lives have been shattered; so have traditional values. Organizational loyalty, for example, has suffered irreparable harm, and that does not bode well for either individual businesses or society at large.[2]

I say all of this to emphasize the point that in order to arrive at lasting accommodations, we frequently must rise above our principles, above our personal values, above our assumptions about what constitutes ownership or distributive justice or what we claim to be our individual rights or the rights of business. In a word, we may have to make sacrifices in light of the values, interests, and sensitivities of others—even if it is only a matter of enlightened self-interest.

This is politics, but a different kind of politics. It is not a politics of seeking advantage, of winning or losing, of settling for the moment. It is a politics that merges with ethics, a politics that recognizes the other as being possibly *defensibly* different, a politics guided not only by principles but also the envisioned consequences of our actions. It is only through such a merging of ethics and politics that a lasting accommodation can emerge from the negotiations between Arab countries and Israel, between ethnic groups in Bosnia, between labor and management, and between Stan and his colleagues and the parents of his students. It is in light of such considerations that I have made my specific recommendations to Stan.

That I have emphasized the necessity for a political-ethical stance that takes into account the values of others does not obviate the necessity for engaging in the act of persuasion. It is for this reason that I recommended that Stan not give up trying to persuade parents and colleagues of the merits of what he was trying to do with his students. But there is a larger political problem here, one that I touched on earlier and about which I should like to say more now. I said:

> *Until teachers face up to the fact that the educational system is an extension of our political and social system and recognize that in order to ensure its integrity they must become politically involved, teachers will be forever subject to the vagaries of those in power and those who control the media. To use current terminology, they will become deskilled and deprofessionalized.*

Hence Stan and the rest of us academics have a special responsibility to try to educate the public with respect to those two important values I have emphasized throughout my remarks—academic freedom and professional autonomy—and with respect to how essential they are to a democratic society and to quality education. Deprofessionalizing teachers with, say, narrowly conceived assessment and accountability systems focusing on grades and tests and controlled by those outside the profession corrupts the educational process and will, in the long run, prove to be a disservice to both students and the public.[3] (As Alfred North Whitehead, the eminent mathematician and philosopher whom I find so quotable, observed almost 70 years ago in his "The Aims of Education," the uniform external examination may test for slackness, but it kills the best part of culture.)

Teachers are not the only group threatened with deprofessionalization. Scientists engaged in basic research, who have long enjoyed a large measure of autonomy, are being increasingly challenged to justify their work and are experiencing the same kinds of pressures as educators to come up with immediate or near-term payoffs to the neglect of basic research. In response to such pressures, Alan Schriesheim, Director and CEO of the Argonne National Laboratory, has declared that scientists must "strive to blend scientific potential with political reality" and that science can no longer remain "above" society and politics. Scientists, Schriesheim maintains, "have a clear obligation to increase scientific literacy in American society in order to foster greater understanding of what they do," and he cautions scientists that the extent to which they "avoid the political process is precisely the extent to which others will decide their future."[4]

Teachers and scientists can, if they wish, close the door and work at their desks or benches. They may, as many do, isolate themselves. But if they continue to do so, they will not only lose control of their lives as professionals, and, hence, become functionaries, they will deprive society of the benefits that attend academic freedom and professional autonomy. They will deprive themselves, in addition, of the opportunity to grow as professionals and as persons.

A final word about that. As they struggle to survive in their work situation, it is no doubt difficult for young people to take on political responsibilities. But the fact is that engagement in the political process is essential not merely for social and professional reasons. Political engagement educates us and helps us grow. It is easy to become disenchanted, as Stan has become, about dealing with parents and colleagues. Admittedly, the political process is emotionally draining and time consuming. (Oscar Wilde once declared that socialism would not work because it takes too many evenings.) But people don't grow without struggle.[5] In the Garden of Eden, only fruits and vegetables grow.

And so I leave you, Stan, with this thought: Stay the course. But act in such a way that your several constituencies will respect you for not only what you believe in but also for your respecting what they believe in as well.

Notes

1. The fact that Shirley Pendlebury and I reacted to the situation described in "Communities Near and Far" in much the same way belies, to some extent at least, current thinking about the subjective nature of reality and the discourse about how gender, culture, age,

personal experience, and other such variables affect our thinking and direct our judgments. Some who call themselves deconstructionists, or postmodernists, or critical theorists might find this of interest.

2. We should not ignore, too, the potential long-range economic damage that may attend layoffs. Increased unemployment and underemployment promise to decrease purchasing power, which eventually affects profits and the nation's economic welfare. For a succinct and insightful analysis of this predicament, see Bob Herbert, "Firing Their Customers," *New York Times*, December 29, 1995, p. A-11.

3. The low correlation between grades and professional competence has long been recognized and amply documented, but the public and politicians persist in identifying quality in education with grades and test scores. Roland Pace has interestingly put it: "School grades predict school grades and not much else—not compassion, not good work habits, not vocational success, not social success, not happiness." (Cited in John Goodlad, *What Schools Are For*, 2d ed. (Bloomington, IN: Phi Delta Kappa Foundation, 1994), p. 61.

4. Alan Schriesheim, "U.S. Science Confronts a New Uncertainty Principle," *The Scientist*, December 12, 1994, p. 12.

5. Shirley Pendlebury puts it this way: "Hard cases of practical reasoning confront us not with who we are at the time of confrontation, but also with who we might become as a consequence of our actions."

Teaching and Trust

BY SHIRLEY PENDLEBURY

My dialogical partner Arthur Brown construes Stan's case as one that calls upon Stan to "harmonize his professional rights and responsibilities as a teacher and citizen with the demands imposed by the social setting in which he lives and works." Professor Brown's conception of rights and responsibilities is nested within his conception of democracy and democratic education. Academic freedom and professional autonomy, in his view, are not simply privileges; they are the sine qua non of democratic education and ought therefore to be safeguarded. Stan's decision to use fund-raising activities as the focus of a social studies project is defensible, Brown suggests, in so far as it involves the appropriate exercise of academic freedom and professional autonomy. In principle, then, Stan is on morally safe ground, if not on the moral high ground. However, schools are located not in the rarefied domain of principles but in the messier domain of politics, where parents, students, and teacher colleagues, as well as administrators and the public at large, are stakeholders who may have competing purposes and values. Together, stakeholders in education set constraints on teachers' exercise of professional autonomy. Challenging these constraints and winning both space and trust for unusual approaches to teaching are largely political tasks whose accomplishment depends upon prudent action. So far Stan has been anything but prudent. Captivated by his fund-raising project, he has neglected to negotiate and build alliances with colleagues and parents.

Professor Brown's analysis yields a neat guiding maxim for Stan: Act prudently, with due regard both for principles and for political constraints and possibilities. A wise maxim, and one that prods me to extend my own analysis of Stan's case. I shall do so via a discussion of trust, taking as my starting point Annette Baier's characterization of trust as "letting other persons . . . take care of something the truster cares about, where such 'caring for' involves some exercise of discretionary powers."[1] In two prominent areas of his life Stan holds positions of trust, each of which places in his care something that others care about. A comparison of the two positions of trust offers some important insights into Stan's case.

As a fund-raiser for famine relief, Stan is entrusted with the accurate accounting and delivery of funds to his organization, which, in turn, is entrusted with the safe delivery of funds or food to needy communities in Africa. Presumably once he has submitted funds and supporting financial records to the organization, Stan has fulfilled the formal requirements of his position of trust. But donors may hope for more, wanting assurance that donated money reaches its intended destination. In his capacity as a regional fund-raiser, Stan may not be in a position to give such assurances, but if he accepts donations given in good faith to a worthy cause, he is under some moral pressure to find out what happens to the money once it leaves his hands. In other words, while he may have little discretionary power over the distribution and channeling of funds, if he is to serve as a strong link in a chain of trust he—at the very least—has to be familiar with the organization's distribution procedures and to be alert to signs of misappropriation. Ignorance does not establish innocence.

As a teacher Stan is entrusted with the education of students in his class. The trust endowed in Stan as Teacher involves considerably more discretionary scope than does the trust endowed in Stan as Fund-raiser. And so it should. Professional autonomy requires a wide range of discretionary powers, including discretion about how and what to teach within a broadly specified set of curriculum guidelines. Without these discretionary powers, the definitive goods of teaching remain unattainable, and the office of teaching becomes ossified. Currently the range of Stan's discretionary power is curtailed by the pressures from his school principal, fellow teachers, and students' parents, all of whom are stakeholders in education or, as I called them in my opening essay, salient others in Stan's moral predicament. Stan's discretionary power is also curtailed by virtue of his being a first-year teacher who has yet to prove his worth. We might interpret Professor Brown's advice to Stan as a call to negotiate for an extension of discretionary power in the interests of professional autonomy and responsibility. If Stan is successful in following this advice, he will have won the trust of parents and colleagues alike.

While I agree with Professor Brown that it would be prudent for Stan to win the trust of colleagues and parents, and I agree that this is a political task, I think it is crucial to distinguish between trust won and trust earned. Sweet-talking politicians may mislead us into believing they are trustworthy guardians of the values or assets we entrust to them. Likewise, articulate and politically astute teachers may be adept at presenting merely personal pursuits as educationally sound practices. Entrusting others with discretionary powers involves a special sort of vulnerability on the part of the truster and that is "vulnerability to not yet noticed harm, or to disguised ill will."[2] From a stakeholder's point of view, trust busting or trust suspending may be wise until trust is seen to be earned. Stan is a new teacher who has not yet shown himself to be worthy of parents' wholehearted trust. His unconventional approach to teaching social studies has given them reason, so they believe, to doubt whether he is taking care of what they care deeply about—the education of their offspring. His obvious impatience with the concerns of parents and colleagues hardly helps matters, hinting as it does at an inclination toward what Michael Walzer has called the insolence of office—the arrogant belief that because of specialist knowledge or official status, one is not answerable to one's clients or colleagues.[3]

How might Stan go about winning and earning the trust of his colleagues, his students, and their parents? There is no easy answer, for trust is a double-edged sword whose goods depend upon the risks of harm. The discretionary element that introduces the special dangers of trust is also "essential to that which makes trust at its best possible."[4] In teaching, as in other professions, too limited a range of discretionary power results in the ossification of office.

From one point of view, Stan's involvement of his students in a fund-raising project can be seen as an educationally proper use of his discretionary powers as a social studies teacher. From another, it can be seen as a disguised abuse of discretionary power. Professor Brown takes the first point of view: Stan's famine relief project is not a violation of public trust because it "is without question appropriate to the discipline of social studies." "Without question" is too strong, I think. Academic disciplines and school subjects are part of a contested terrain. It is debatable whether social studies is more about what makes societies tick or about acquiring the values of tolerance and concern for others; whether it is more about learning to use evidence appropriately or about becoming a democratic citizen. Professor Brown argues that a physics teacher who undertook a project like Stan's would be violating a public trust. If a teacher of physics or biology speaks out against clear and present danger or against injustice, he or she does so as a citizen, not as a teacher. So Professor Brown's argument goes. In his view, one speaks or acts properly as a teacher in so far as what one says or does is integral to the subject, and while questions of social justice are not integral to physics they are integral to social studies. Perhaps so. In my view, however, this does not justify Stan's fund-raising project. Fund-raising per se is not an integral part of social studies. Little, if anything, in the act of collecting money contributes in any obvious way to "a greater understanding of the discipline." The distinction between teacher and citizen is blurred in Stan's case. His work in famine relief could be classed as an undertaking in his capacity as a citizen of the world; similarly, involving his students in the project might be classed as an initiation into world citizenship. Whether such initiation is an appropriate undertaking for a high school social studies teacher is a debatable point and hardly one to be tested by a novice teacher who has not yet won or earned the trust of clients and colleagues.

So we come full circle to a question posed and as yet unanswered: How might Stan go about winning and earning the trust and accompanying discretionary powers that are necessary for him to flourish as a teacher? I cannot fault Professor Brown's guidelines for winning trust. In some respects they are also guidelines for earning trust. I think that some additional guidelines might be drawn from a reflection on the relationships between time, teaching, and trust.

We earn and sustain trust through doing our time as novice practitioners, through concentrating time on developing our capacities within a practice, through enduring setbacks and disappointments, and through investing time in refining and advancing the practice once we have become fully fledged practitioners. The time of teaching is both contemplative and energetic time; it is both solitary and collegial. As long as Stan's time and energy is directed away from the practice of teaching, he is unlikely to win the wholehearted trust of parents and colleagues, and—in my view—he certainly will not have earned it.

Notes

1. Annette Baier, *Moral Prejudices* (Cambridge: Harvard University Press, 1995), p. 105.
2. Ibid., p. 104.
3. Michael Walzer, *Spheres of Justice* (New York: Basic Books, 1987).
4. Baier, p. 106.

Discussion

Arthur Brown and Shirley Pendlebury address an "ethical interests" issue similar to the one in "Self and Others": Which community's interests should Stan serve, and what are their interests? Pendlebury and Brown agree that if Stan is to remain a teacher, he needs to "marginalize" his concern for the "far" community of African famine victims to some extent and give more attention to the "near" communities of students, parents, and school colleagues. A major reason for this is that Stan is mistaken (at least in some ways) in his understanding of his students' educational interests. (This is a place where Brown and Pendlebury appear to disagree. Brown, more than Pendlebury, thinks that the fund-raising project is consistent with the students' interests to be served by their social studies education. What do you think about that?)

However, Pendlebury is quite explicit in her doubts about the wisdom of framing the relevant issue as "communities near and far." Her point is well taken. As we've seen before, the "lenses" used for looking at a situation will affect what is picked out as "salient particulars." (What do Pendlebury's alternative lenses prompt us to see that we might not otherwise? What other lenses could be used? How about a "caring" lens? A "virtue" lens? A "duty" lens?) She and Brown both go beyond the "communities near and far" issue. As Pendlebury notes, the issues are about the very nature and aims of education. (But then, all of our chapters are about that.) Yet the chapter title does capture an idea that runs through their essays: *community.*

Like the contributors in "Self and Others," Brown and Pendlebury take the issue of community to the level of "ethical point of view." This is particularly clear in Pendlebury's appeal to the "practice of teaching." It is also present, though in an importantly different way, in the Deweyan conception of democratic community Brown presents. The common theme is that community provides in some fundamental way a (the?) basic ethical orientation for Stan. But this gets us into the final issue I will consider, and it is another one familiar from previous chapters: What are the ethics of living and working in a community that does not share your principles? Brown says Stan must be political and prudent. But is that ethical? Sometimes, being "political" and "prudent" is contrasted with being ethical. Pendlebury's care about distinguishing between winning trust and earning trust may reflect this sort of concern. Once again, we confront questions about the nature and proper domain of ethics.

Community as Ethical Point of View

In recent years, a number of philosophers have argued for a *communitarian* view of ethics. For communitarians, community provides the basic ethical point of view for people. Pendlebury's emphasis on the practice of teaching suggests a communitarian perspective (although she objects to some aspects of communitarianism, as will be explained below). She says: "Becoming a teacher, in the full sense, involves living the life of a teacher. In the few months of his employment Stan has entered the territory of teaching without taking on all the demands and habits of the life." Community—here the community of teaching—provides Stan's ethical point of view in that there is a "life of a teacher" to be "taken on." Alasdair MacIntyre, to whom Pendlebury refers, expresses the idea this way:

> *[W]e all approach our own circumstances as bearers of a particular* social *identity. I am someone's son or daughter, someone else's cousin or uncle; I am a citizen of this or that city, a member of this or that guild or profession; I belong to this clan, that tribe, this nation. Hence what is good for me has to be the good for one who inhabits these roles. As such I* inherit *from the past of my family, my city, my tribe, my nation, a variety of debts, inheritances, rightful expectations and obligations.*[1]

Charles Taylor explains the point in terms of a community providing a "horizon of significance, whereby some things are worthwhile and others less so, and still others not at all, quite anterior to choice. . . . [*I*]*ndependent of my will* there is something noble, courageous, and hence significant in giving shape to my own life."[2] What is good for Stan, insofar as he wishes to be a teacher, is what is good for someone who inhabits the role of teacher. Stan inherits the debts, expectations, obligations, and other significant things that go along with teaching. These things are there for him independent of his will. This does not mean there is no room for freedom or change. (This might be described as a "freedom-emerges-through-discipline" view such as we considered in Chapter 2.) They provide a "horizon," not a detailed landscape. There still is room for innovation and debate about what the practice of teaching requires.[3] Still, to take a legitimate part in that debate Stan needs to immerse himself in the practice. From the communitarian view, Stan's mistake is that he has done too much to try to *create* his own conception of good social studies teaching rather than try to *discover* what it is to be a good teacher. In this sense it is the community of teaching that is ethically authoritative.

Stan's freedom is a concern here. Communitarianism typically is contrasted with *liberalism*.[4] Individuals' freedom and ethical authority is a focus of their debate. As the self-described liberal (and strong critic of communitarianism) Will Kymlicka explains, "Liberals . . . insist that we have an ability to detach ourselves from any particular communal practice. No particular cultural practice has authority that is beyond individual judgement and possible rejection."[5] Kant is often described as a liberal because of the sort of freedom embodied in his categorical imperative. According to liberals, individual will and choice do have a place; community is not authoritative.

Now, as we've already seen, we need to be careful about what we mean by the authority of individual judgment. Regard for individual judgment can go to the subjectivist extreme that it would be impossible for individuals to make mistakes; they create ethical duties in the sense that their duties are whatever they happen to think they are. Or it could go to the egoist extreme that licenses disregard for what other people think or desire. Liberalism, however, by no means implies those things. Kant certainly does not, and John Dewey, who can be described as a liberal, advocated a normative notion of (democratic) community that fosters many and varied shared interests among people with the purpose of using those to guide social action and seeks free interaction among groups for the purpose of adjusting social habits.[6] While it is not clear how we should classify Brown's ethical point of view, to the extent he shares Dewey's views (as he suggests he does) he can be described as a liberal. And clearly Brown has a great deal of regard for community.

So, there need be no disagreement between communitarians and liberals that community is important. But there is an issue of *why* community is important. And part of this involves what's meant by "community." Michael Sandel criticizes liberals for having only "instrumental" or "sentimental" conceptions of community.[7] In the "instrumental" conception, community is looked on only as an instrument useful for permitting harmonious pursuit of individual aims. Communitarians see this conception reflected in our (excessive) concern for rights, obligations, and contracts. These sorts of things help guarantee that we do not interfere with each other as we associate for our mutual benefit, but community is not valued in itself. Community may actually be seen as a threat of some sort. According to some communitarians, we would be better off if we did away with rights talk and safeguarded the interests of individuals through strong feelings of communal regard for each other.

Stan might not be looking at his communities only instrumentally. But then he may only have a "sentimental" sense of community. Here community attachments are still understood as a matter of choice by a self somehow held independent of these attachments. Stan could still be accused of seeing himself as too independent of his local communities. At the same time, he may be accused (similar to the way Pendlebury criticizes him) of seeing himself too easily "choosing" to be part of the African community. He may have some sentimental attachment, but that is not enough to qualify him as part of the community. This is not to say Stan should have no concern for famine victims. But he cannot be part of their community. Claiming membership in the community, rather than being a noble attempt, may be a form of imperialism because it downplays the real differences between Stan and them.

Sandel argues for a "constitutive" conception of community. This "describes not just what [people] *have* as fellow citizens but also what they *are*, not a relationship they choose (as in a voluntary association) but an attachment they discover, not merely an attribute but a constituent of their identity."[8]

Why do communitarians think this strong sense of community is so important? We can identify at least two reasons that are commonly given and that we see at work in Pendlebury's essays. One is that the goods inherited from concrete communities provide the sort of guidance that is necessary for good ethical judgment. This theme is particularly strong in MacIntyre. For instance, in the quote above MacIntyre says that teachers have obligations. But talking about obligations in the abstract is not much help. We need to talk about the obligations *of a teacher*. MacIntyre also emphasizes virtue. Virtues are even more substantive than obligations. Note, for instance, how Taylor referred to what was noble and courageous. (How about some of the virtues Burbules identified?) The claim is that we know more about an action if we're told it is noble than if we're simply told that it is good or right. Virtues still might not be substantive enough if taken out of context. Teachers may need to be noble and courageous, but so do people in other vocations. Again, Stan's task is not just satisfying abstract duties or virtues but satisfying them *as a teacher* ought.

However, community is not important only so that Stan can do well by others. The second way communitarians see community as important is for Stan's own well being. In a significant sense, Stan himself would be nobody without the communities he is part of. He inherits more than debts. He inherits who he is. His identity is a *social* identity. Sandel stresses how without this understanding of ourselves and our relationship to others we have an impoverished conception of self; life lacks meaning.[9] That is part of why it is important that Stan not be an outcast, a pariah.

This role for community is part of the broader communitarian emphasis on "narrative," which Pendlebury (and some of our writers) stresses. If Stan is to lead a good life, he has to take account of who he is and where he is, which includes his roles and communities but also many other aspects of his situation and experience. Again, this does not mean he can make teaching into just anything he wants. Regard for the narrative of his life might show that teaching is not for him. (The essays do not explore that possibility to any great extent. Given what you know about Stan, would leaving teaching be a good idea? If so, how should he leave? How might his situation compare to Lucy's in "Self and Others"?)

Liberals could agree with some amount of this. Yet liberals stress the need for critical distance from roles and communities. (So could Noddings, as we have seen, although to the extent that she would base this on care rather than freedom she would not take a liberal tack.) Are all the roles and expectations we inherit good ones? For example, we might think about what "the role of women" has been in the past and ask if that's something we should perpetuate. In a personal communication Shirley Pendlebury cautions how communitarian arguments were used to justify apartheid in South Africa. Now, communitarians could join in the criticism. They could attack apartheid for being anti-democratic, say. Yet liberals would not endorse democracy just because it is a community value but because (among other things) it provides for individual liberty. So, for liberals, the communitarian challenge still is not sufficient.

Regarding the guidance point, "thick" values may be needed for guidance. ("Democracy" might be an idea that at least approximates the needed thickness.) Nonetheless, we cannot dispense with "abstractions"—such as rights—that are ethically primary even if insufficient for ethical guidance. Stan may need to stick to the obligations of teaching, but we need to know that the obligations are ethically correct; the teaching community is not the final authority on that. Similarly, in regard to Stan's self, it may be that his communities provide essential resources for development of his self. But the ultimate aim is to develop *his* self, and so he must retain the ability to adjust or reject the conceptions of self provided by his communities. (We will return to the issue of liberalism and identity in Chapter 6.) And, as Brown suggests, cannot this sort of individual freedom actually serve the democratic community?

How might this debate affect our conclusions about the case? How about the "near and far" issue? We might think that there isn't much effect, given the extent to which Pendlebury and Brown appear to agree on that issue. Yet, if we take the communitarian view to heart, we must be especially concerned for the particular communities to which we belong. Pendlebury questions whether Stan really should consider himself a member of the distant community. She says that community membership requires a tighter bond of experiences and sharing than now exists between Stan and famine victims. This is a significant issue, for community membership in Pendlebury's strong sense implies particular ethical priorities. Typically, we think that we owe more to our fellow community members than to outsiders. Certainly, this can be taken to an ethnocentric extreme in which the well-being of distant others or other strangers is ignored. On the other hand, however, we simply may not be able to genuinely share much with people who are culturally and experientially "distant," and to claim otherwise may distort their experiences to fit our own. (Recall Rorty's point.) Of course, some people take this to the unreasonable extreme of saying members of different communities cannot possibly understand each other to any appreciable degree.[10] So we get into the "identity politics" Noddings warned against. Again, Pendlebury does not say that Stan cannot have legitimate sympathy or empathy for African famine victims. However, if he does decide to give them priority he must leave teaching; part of his dilemma is deciding the kind of life he wants. The bottom line is that Stan must conform to the demands of whatever practice he enters.

For liberals, in contrast, the demands of the practice are not the bottom line. They would be prepared to give at least relatively more weight to far communities. R. S. Peters presents this point when he says, "there is one sort of kinship that must be appropriate for a rational being, whatever he feels about his loyalty to family, state, class, or club, and that is his kinship with other rational beings as persons."[11] Liberals might agree with communitarians that this kinship is not community in the communitarian sense, yet dispute the significance of that. This sort of kinship does not mean the interests of the far community must take priority. It could be that from the point of view of any rational person it is permissible or even required to be partial to those people with whom one has a special connection. Still, Stan must step out of his "narrative" in order to make a legitimate judgment on that.

In sum, the conclusions liberals and communitarians reach need not always diverge to any great extent. It is important that we not underestimate the importance of that. As with the other tensions we've encountered, it is not clear that we are faced with an either/or choice here. Similar to what I suggested in regard to the ethic of care and the ethic of duty, we can think that liberals and communitarians emphasize different aspects of ourselves and our relationships, rather than two things radically at odds. Still, these views do provide importantly different ways to think about ethics, and that can make a difference for that persistent question Brown asks: "How to live by one's principles in a world that doesn't necessarily share them?" Certainly this is a political question that extends beyond this case and the liberal-communitarian dispute. But the liberal-communitarian debate has some major political implications. We will get into some of those in Chapters 6 and 7. In the remainder of this discussion I will not emphasize those issues. Instead, I'll take a brief look at the broad notion of politics as Brown and Pendlebury present it.

Ethics, Prudence, and Politics

It's often said that teachers should not be political. For instance, their job is to be experts in their curriculum and in instructional techniques, but decisions about educational policy should be left to others. Also, they should not be political in the sense of taking a partisan stand on issues. (Brown warns against such partisanship but does not say it is totally out of bounds). Teachers should present information and leave their preferences out of it. But, as Brown asks, can teachers really afford to stay out of policy making? Don't they have a legitimate political role in defending certain values, such as democratic values? After all, even an evenhanded treatment of a controversial issue can be highly political itself.

Whatever their differences on these issues, communitarians and liberals can (and often do) concur in the sort of broad conception of politics Brown and Pendlebury develop. It is a conception that challenges a notion of politics separate from ethics. Speaking of ethics and politics in the same breath may seem pretty odd. Often, these realms are thought to be about as far apart as you can get. Politics is sometimes thought of as the art of manipulation. "Politicians" in this sense would agree that getting people's trust is important but that the end justifies the means. Contrary to what Pendlebury thinks, "winning trust" *is* what is important, however that might be achieved.

Liberals are sometimes accused of fostering that attitude, and the charge is accurate to some extent. Thomas Hobbes's liberalism was grounded in his famous view that "during the time men live without a common Power to keep them all in awe, they are in that condition which is called Warre; and such a warre, as is of every man, against every man."[12] In this state of war, "every man has a Right to every thing; even to one anothers body."[13] Politics becomes the art of exercising power to compel people to surrender their "right to every thing," so that they can live in peace. This sort of theme has been echoed on down to our own time, particularly the idea that politics is a matter of power rather than rational argument and persuasion.

However, there is no necessary connection between liberalism and Hobbes's image of persons and their values. Hence Brown's beliefs about the importance of democracy and rational dialogue. (What sort of dialogue might be helpful in this case? Conversation? Argument? Thinking back to earlier chapters, should Andre Taylor be political? How about Lucy Williams?) Still, even if Hobbes is wrong about people being naturally selfish and competitive, that does not mean they are always reasonable and cooperative, and so Brown's ideas about politics and prudence, which are quite similar to Weber's. There is a place for principles (an ethic of intention). There is a place for trying to persuade people to share one's point of view. There is even a place for "going to the mat." Yet there is also a place for sensitivity to the reality of living with people and all their differing values, hang-ups, and infirmities (an ethic of responsibility). In Brown's hands this is hardly a lesser form of action; by being accommodating one can "rise above" one's principles. Self-righteousness is no virtue.

This view of politics can be traced back to Aristotle. For Aristotle, politics is not a retreat from ethics but an advance from ethics. For him, politics is putting ethics into action in the everyday world. This connects with Brown's point about politics and growth. Whereas Plato saw politics as a necessary burden, something educated people might have to turn to after their education, Aristotle saw it as an important part of education, indeed the culmination of human development. Politics was not just about governing but about wrestling with fundamental questions of human existence and realizing human well-being in the real world. Perhaps we do not want to give politics the status Aristotle gave it. Nevertheless, neither should we look at it as antagonistic to ethics.

The virtue political activity calls for is prudence. Perhaps that claim calls for some further thought, too. As I noted in Chapter 3, prudence sometimes is contrasted with ethics. Prudence can be understood to be cowardly, or merely expedient, which need not be a criticism. As we keep asking, is an ethical response always the correct response? James Griffin says, "it is sometimes better to fail morally and stay alive than not to fail and thereby lose one's life."[14] On the other hand, for Aristotle, prudence meant "practical wisdom," and that is not the same thing as cowardice or expedience. Nor is it the same thing as mere cleverness. Aristotle says that practical wisdom involves cleverness, but they are not the same, since mere cleverness need not have noble aims, whereas wisdom does.[15] Yet Aristotle did emphasize *practical* wisdom, practical in the sense that it had to take account of the "real world" and not just the ideal world. Thus, prudent persons are persons of integrity, but they are also persons sensitive to the complexities and particulars of the world, and they are willing to engage fairly and openly with other persons in order to make the world a better place. Far from being ignoble, they are persons to be admired.

Conclusion

We will see later that the communitarian-liberal debate about community and freedom has significant implications for thinking about teachers' involvement in politics. But whatever our conclusions regarding communitarians and liberals, there is a need for teachers to be political. Perhaps you still have doubts about just how politically involved teachers should be. That is not unwarranted. Even so, the political question of how to respond to ethical disagreements is inescapable. Avoiding a response is still a response. That puts teachers in a tough spot, ethically. As Pendlebury, Brown, and some of the other writers did and will show, politics is shot through with ethical difficulties. It may be wise to suspend trust, Pendlebury warns; dialogue is not something to just dive into. Recalling Weber, we have to remember that politics may require ethically dubious activities. However, the point here is to challenge the claim that that is all politics can ever be. There is a politics based in genuine trust and respect. Politics of this sort doesn't just happen; it is something people need to work on. But, if Brown and Pendlebury are right, it is something that is achieved in politics, not separate from it.

Once again, though, we may ask what really is achieved. Pendlebury and Brown present the possibility of people arriving at some justified conclusions, even in the face of disagreement. (Are they too optimistic? What might Sichel and Burbules say?) One standard Pendlebury explicitly appeals to is "excellence" in teaching. "Excellence" might seem to be a standard everyone can agree upon, a "common meaning" that is an aspiration for all. What sort of standard is this, though? The next chapter explores the notion of excellence. In particular, it examines excellence in conjunction with equality. Equality must be a concern for people interested in the sort of political community Brown and Pendlebury describe. Can teachers serve both excellence and equality? Susan Laird and Paul Farber will answer yes. But how should teachers try to do that? What does commitment to these ideas imply for teaching and the broader politics of schooling? These will be central issues in the next chapter.

Notes

1. Alasdair MacIntyre, *After Virtue*, 2nd ed. (Notre Dame, IN: University of Notre Dame Press, 1984), p. 220; emphasis added.

2. Charles Taylor, *The Ethics of Authenticity* (Cambridge: Harvard University Press, 1992), pp. 38–39; emphasis in the original.

3. Margret Buchmann writes of "role orientation" in teaching. The notion of "orientation" suggests that the role does not provide answers to teachers, but does tell teachers what questions are important and where to look for answers; for example, to the demands of their discipline rather than to their personal preferences. See Margret Buchmann, "Role over Person: Morality and Authenticity in Teaching," *Teachers College Record* 87 (1986): 529–43. On the other hand, Noddings says that teaching is not a role. See Nel Noddings, *Caring: A Feminine Approach to Ethics and Moral Education*, (Berkeley: University of California Press, 1984), p. 175.

4. I am not using "liberal" in the popular sense that distinguishes it from "conservative." I am using it in the philosophical sense that identifies a political stance that emphasizes things such as individual liberties and some form of state neutrality toward particular ways of life. In this sense, many contemporary "conservatives" are quite "liberal."

5. Will Kymlicka, *Liberalism, Community and Culture* (Oxford: Clarendon Press, 1989), p. 50.

6. John Dewey, *Democracy and Education* (New York: Macmillan, 1916), pp. 86–87.

7. Michael J. Sandel, *Liberalism and the Limits of Justice* (Cambridge: Cambridge University Press, 1982), pp. 148–50.

8. Ibid., p. 150; emphasis in the original.

9. Robert N. Bellah, Richard Madsen, William M. Sullivan, Ann Swidler, and Steven M. Tipton, *Habits of the Heart* (New York: Harper and Row, 1986).

10. MacIntyre argues against the idea that the situations of other persons can always be translated to fit into our own scheme of things, but he also holds out the possibility of understanding others in the way that we learn a second language. See Alasdair MacIntyre, *Whose Justice? Which Rationality?* (Notre Dame, IN: University of Notre Dame Press, 1988).

11. R. S. Peters, *Ethics and Education* (London: George Allen and Unwin, 1966), p. 225.

12. Thomas Hobbes, *Leviathan*, ed. C. B. Macpherson (Harmondsworth, UK: Penguin Books, 1968) p. 185.

13. Ibid., p. 190.

14. James Griffin, *Well-Being* (Oxford: Clarendon Press, 1986), p. 69.

15. Aristotle, *Nicomachean Ethics* 6.12.

5

Excellence and Equality

CASE

What a twisted situation it is, Connie Nakamura thought to herself, when a teacher dreads recognizing a student for excellent work. But dread is what Connie felt as she made ready to announce to her fifth-grade class the results of their unit spelling test. Once again Steven had earned a perfect score on the four weekly tests and final comprehensive test in the spelling unit. When Connie made the announcement a clearly audible groan came from the class. Steven had now received a perfect score for each of the five spelling units they'd covered so far this year, something none of the other students had managed.

Perhaps this wouldn't have been such a big issue if the top speller for each unit hadn't been rewarded by having the privilege of helping students in Ed Shapiro's third grade with their spelling. This was a plan Connie and Ed had worked out several years back. Ed's students really needed the help, and Connie was happy to have a way of recognizing excellent achievement in a way that was meaningful and motivating for her students.

The problem was that Steven had been top speller for all five units so far, and that pattern might well continue throughout the rest of the year. There were other good spellers in the class. On several occasions, other students missed only one or two words during the unit. But Steven had not missed any. He was intellectually gifted to start with, plus he worked hard at his spelling and took great pride in it. There was no doubt that he had earned his honors, but the other students were beginning to say that the system was not fair, that the privilege of tutoring the third graders should be more equitably distributed.

Connie wondered whether the students were right. She asked Ed about choosing a new tutor after each spelling test rather than at the end of the whole unit. There were times when other students besides Steven got perfect scores on the weekly tests. Connie would not have to choose Steven every time then. But Ed liked having the same tutor for a month at a time. There was more continuity for his students that way. It was much easier for him because he didn't have to brief the tutor anew every week.

Connie thought about making the criterion for tutoring passing the third-grade spelling test. But that would defeat the purpose of the reward, she thought. Her purpose was to reward excellence; passing the third grade test did not seem to be a sign of excellence. On the other hand, for some of her students, that *would* be an excellent achievement. Those students needed recognition too. But Ed did not like this idea. He needed a really excellent speller to help his students, someone who could model for them good study skills and habits, not someone who was just getting by.

Connie then had the idea of giving Steven a tougher spelling curriculum. Maybe then he would not always get a perfect score. Maybe he had an unfair advantage over the other students. Maybe giving them different curricula would put her students on an even footing so far as how much they would be challenged. But Connie was uneasy about this. Even if Steven would begin to miss spelling words on his test, would that mean that he wasn't still the best speller in the class? Was it fair to him to change the rules of the game at this point? He was the best speller in the class; why should he not be recognized as such?

But Connie had heard from Steven's fourth-grade teacher that it might be in Steven's interest to be "brought down a notch." Steven had always had an easy time in school, she said. It would do him good to struggle a bit. Besides, there was the ever-present danger of the other students being resentful of his success. Perhaps his success shouldn't be emphasized. Why not go to him and ask him to let some of the other students have a turn? That would be a good lesson in generosity and equality. If he refuses, just drop the whole idea of the tutorial.

To Connie, this seemed to put an unfair burden on Steven. He had earned his honor. How could she ask him to give it up now? Perhaps the other students were getting resentful, but maybe they were the ones that needed to change their attitude, not Steven. Maybe they needed to learn that excellence is important and that excellence cannot always be equally distributed. Ending the tutor program would be one way to end the problem, but that would be letting Ed down. Besides, it wouldn't really get at the root of the problem.

Connie did talk to Steven. She tried to gauge his feelings about the spelling situation without letting on about the problems she was encountering. Although Connie tried to be very careful, Steven clearly was uncomfortable. He didn't say so, but Connie got the definite impression that he knew very well what was going on.

The next week Connie graded the week's spelling test and found that Steven had spelled every other word incorrectly. It was obvious that Steven had purposely misspelled the words. After she passed back the papers it quickly spread through the class that Steven had not achieved a perfect score. A number of the children seemed pleased; Steven was close to tears.

Connie blamed herself for the situation. She guessed that her talk with Steven had prompted him to do what he did, but perhaps there was a silver lining to this situation. With this one "failure," maybe the pressure would be off and Steven could go back to doing his best. But then again, maybe he wouldn't. It seemed wrong to Connie that she should let Steven sell himself short this way. She was tempted to have him retake the test, but realized that that might create even more problems. Connie felt she had to find out what Steven was thinking. She tried to talk to Steven after school that day. She began by telling Steven how proud she was of him and his work. He avoided looking at her and evaded her questions about the test, murmuring something about having a "bad day" and asking her to please leave him alone. Connie didn't press. She feared upsetting Steven even more than he was already.

The next week, Ed asked Connie what was wrong with Steven. He had shown up late and unprepared for the tutorial session with Ed's students and had no explanation when Ed asked about it. And when Connie graded the week's spelling tests her head drooped onto her hands as she saw that once again Steven had misspelled every other word. It appeared that this was a problem that was not going to go away by itself. But what should she do? Clearly, Steven was suffering. Perhaps she should initiate a class discussion of the issue, but would that only add to Steven's suffering? Maybe she was focusing too much on Steven. All of her students needed encouragement. Some had begun to give up because they felt they had no chance of being spelling tutor. But they had been more enthusiastic this past week, and on the latest spelling test a couple had their highest score ever. Perhaps in her zeal to praise excellence she had lost sight of the need for equality. Perhaps Steven was hurt, but more than likely he'd get over it. Wouldn't he?

The more Connie thought about it, the more she wished she had never started the tutoring. Ed's students did benefit, however, and again, is it so bad to recognize excellence? Increasingly, Connie felt that she was at a loss about what to do. What would you recommend?

Reflections on "Excellence and Equality"

Literacy Learning as Moral Learning: Excellence vs. Equality?

BY SUSAN LAIRD

Heinz's wife needed an expensive drug in order to survive a disease, but the druggist refused to lower his prohibitively high price: Should Heinz therefore steal the drug?[1] Connie Nakamura's students need to be the top speller for the unit in order to qualify for the coveted privilege of tutoring Ed Shapiro's third graders in spelling, but only the exceptionally gifted Steven seems able to accomplish this feat every time. Should Connie therefore give Steven a tougher spelling test or withdraw from him the privilege of tutoring Ed's third graders so that other students can have turns at tutoring, too? The content of Connie's moral dilemma is nothing like that of Heinz's moral dilemma, a life-or-death matter made famous by developmental psychologist Lawrence Kohlberg. Yet, in its form, Connie's dilemma does superficially resemble Heinz's dilemma. We should note one key formal difference between Heinz's and Connie's dilemmas, however. Unlike poor Heinz's dilemma, hers is largely of her own making.

Connie blames herself for having started the tutoring arrangement—wrongly, I think. Teaching others is such an excellent way to learn that she should be delighted so many of her students want to do it. Steven might thus overcome any inclination toward arrogance that his giftedness may tempt in him, especially if Ed is as intent upon Steven's moral development as he is upon his own students' scores on spelling tests. Oddly, however, Connie has brought no seventh-graders into her classroom to help her own struggling spellers, nor has she considered how tutoring younger children in spelling might provide a more meaningful context for her own less-favored students' learning to spell. Spelling tests are all we know of her fifth graders' literacy curriculum. Connie seems to believe, as I suspect many teachers and parents do without a second thought, that competitive spelling tests are as natural to elementary schooling as strong winds are to the Great Plains.

Could this latter assumption, though seemingly devoid of ethical content, be one cause of her moral dilemma, the fatal flaw in this case? Like the druggist who does not exercise his power to reduce his price in Heinz's dilemma, Connie will have some power to transform her own dilemma to a less problematic situation for her students if she is willing to question the taken-for-granted necessity of competitive spelling tests for elementary school children. For I believe that her dilemma demonstrates how well-meaning teachers can suddenly find themselves in moral quagmires if they take for granted common schooling practices, such as spelling tests and competitive reward systems, without careful reflection upon the moral purposes of their teaching.

A Different Understanding of Connie's Dilemma

In Carol Gilligan's replication of Kohlberg's psychological study, Heinz's dilemma seemed to eleven-year-old Jake a straightforward conflict between the competing principles of law and life, logically resolved by his moral claim that "a human life is worth more than money."[2] Similarly, Connie's dilemma seems to her a straightforward conflict between the competing principles of excellence and equality, perhaps to be logically resolved by teaching her students "that excellence is important and that excellence cannot always be equally distributed." I do not share this facile view either of her dilemma or of excellence and equality.

What does "excellence" mean? Perfect scores on spelling tests? Such scores may provide an apparently reasonable way of qualifying Connie's fifth graders for the job of tutoring Ed's third graders in spelling. But if teachers themselves are seldom credentialled solely on the basis of their subject matter knowledge, why should peer tutors be? Perhaps a student's generous helpfulness to others, cheerful humility, perseverance and playfulness in overcoming difficulties, diligence and resourcefulness in learning, and ability to engage other children's curiosity and interests in activities would be more relevant qualifications. Could peer tutors not work in pairs, matched so that all appropriate strengths, academic, moral, and social, are brought to the peer tutoring situation? In any case, should perfect scores on spelling tests be regarded as a symbol of "excellence" in literacy learning or in fifth-grade learning generally?

You may protest that I am evading Connie's dilemma by asking questions about the context that gave rise to that dilemma rather than addressing the dilemma itself. My response may resemble eleven-year-old Amy's response to Heinz's dilemma in Gilligan's study, insofar as Amy responded "in a way that seemed evasive and unsure."[3] Amy considered Heinz's dilemma in terms of various consequences that possible actions might have upon the relationship between Heinz and his wife, and she faulted the druggist for his unfeeling response to their situation. Insofar as Connie expresses concern about hurting Steven, about the competent help and continuity that Ed's third graders need, about her own other students' needs to have their achievements recognized, about causing either Steven or the other students to give up learning, her own increasingly evasive and unsure response to this dilemma does resemble Amy's response to Heniz's dilemma and does seem entirely appropriate. But Connie never pauses to think, as her case provokes me to think, about the consequences that her actions can have for relationships between Steven and the "other" students, between each student and the class as a whole, between each student and the written English language, between each student and her or his world, between each student and her or his developing self-concept, even between each student and Connie herself. Indeed, I am inclined to fault Connie for her unfeeling response to Steven's classmates and the fullness of their relational lives.

In focusing so centrally upon Steven and his gift for perfect spelling, Connie has made Steven "other" to his classmates, and she has made his classmates and their particular gifts and challenges "other" to his standard. Connie does not name any student other than Steven; she does not seem to enter into any other student's feeling about learning. Nor does she pause to reflect upon what either "excellence" or "equality" might mean within the context of her students' own daily lives as one another's classmates or friends, or as daughters and sons, much less as speakers and writers of so-called "standard" English or of "other" languages or "nonstandard" English dialects. I do not think Connie can morally resolve her own dilemma without rethinking her moral purposes and relationships as a teacher of children.

Gilligan interprets Jake's and Amy's different approaches to Heinz's dilemma thus:

> *Both children recognize the need for agreement but see it as mediated in different ways—he impersonally through systems of logic and law, she personally through communication in relationship. Just as he relies on the conventions of logic to deduce the solution to this dilemma, assuming these conventions to be shared, so she relies on a process of communication, assuming connection and believing that her voice will be heard.*[4]

In relying on spelling test scores as indicators of her students' "excellence" or lack thereof, Connie has relied on a nineteenth-century pedagogical convention to establish her own impersonal system of logic and law. Steven's deliberate failures and his classmates' resentful complaints are obviously personal attempts to be heard, attempts to set aside or even disrupt that system of logic and law that rules the distribution of "gifts" and goods in their classroom.

If only Connie could find a solution to her dilemma just like Jake's solution to Heinz's dilemma, keeping that system of logic and law intact, how convenient and easy would everything be for her! Then she would not have to find out what the "other" students are going through; she would not have to find out what difference spelling does or does not, could or should make in each of their lives beyond her weekly tests; she would not have to find out how Steven and the "other" students think, feel, and act toward one another. She would not have to ask herself tough questions about the assumptions on which her curriculum and her classroom system of logic and law are based. In the absence of Connie's communication with the "other" students and with "other" ideas about elementary education, I find responding to her dilemma difficult. Before giving her any advice, I want the impossible: I want to have a long conversation with her. The conversation I want would range widely over all these considerations that have not yet entered into Connie's thinking.

Excellence: Spelling Tests or Literacy Learning?

The case does not give us much sense of Connie's knowledge or thought about excellence in the subject matter she is teaching, whether it be construed narrowly as spelling or more broadly as literacy. In considering her dilemma she does not even consider her curriculum's possible effects upon her students' moral and social learning. Yet what is literacy about if it is not about self-expression, self-examination, communication with others, and the mutual construction of thoughtful and good human relationships? What meaning and value can "excellence" in literacy learning, including its mechanical aspects like spelling, have apart from such moral and social purposes?

Does Connie know that there was no such thing as perfect spelling before the dictionary's invention in the eighteenth century? Indeed, Shakespeare spelled his own name numerous ways and is still regarded, rightly or wrongly, as the reigning genius of English letters. Today, even fifth graders should be able to understand that different standards exist for spelling in English. Such different standards highlight the social purposes they serve. For example, you would *practise* your spelling in Canada in order to earn the *honour* of tutoring, but *practice* it in the United States in hopes of earning the same *honor.* What is spelling but a social and political marker, its perfection a historical product of technological progress, that is, of industrialized publishing? Did not the now taken-for-granted notion of "the dictionary spelling" create a new "objective" (even if petty and arbitrary) means of bestowing cultural condemnation or authority after the demise of "the divine right of kings" who spoke "the King's English"?

If Connie's fifth graders cannot fully comprehend such questions, she herself could nonetheless think about their moral and social relevance to her students' situations. Difficulty with correct spelling today can make some persons more vulnerable than others to employers' unfair discrimination on the basis of disability or race, and some disabilities can make perfect spelling a nearly impossible goal to achieve. Moreover, an excess of spelling errors can make one's writing seem nearly unreadable in our contemporary context. For while telephones have diminished the necessity of our daily writing to one another, our industrialized print media have demanded our standardized spelling. Of course, most word-processing software can check your spelling for you; in fact, my own computer just informed me that *practise, honour,* and *genious* are misspellings. Meanwhile, electronic mail may lead us to reclaim writing as a medium of daily communication with one another along with our culture's lost tolerance for spelling errors.

How relevant to Connie's dilemma is this contemporary context? Will Connie's school district have sufficient resources to give all her students equal access to computers? If so, will she teach them how to do desktop publishing in class, how to use the spell-check feature, and to use it whenever they are writing for classroom publication? Will she teach them how to make "pen pals" (perhaps an outmoded term) across the U.S.–Canada border on the World Wide Web? Will she habituate them to writing and reading electronic mail, which may be full of misspellings or simply of variant spellings—perhaps even to send E-mail to and from Ed's third graders? If not, will Connie continue to use spelling tests that teach those with disabilities or chronic spelling difficulties only to feel bad about themselves and their inability to spell? Or will she teach them how to use inventive spelling in tandem with dictionary work whenever they are writing—while also actively protesting, in writing, those inequities in school funding that deny her students access to technology and up-to-date literacy education? If she must teach within a context of comparative technological deprivation, will she trouble herself to think about what classroom writing and reading situations and practices—perhaps even ones of students' own invention, such as "passing notes in class"—might best prepare her students' literacy skills and values for a more advanced technological context?

No such contextual considerations about the ends and means of her students' perfect spelling, or about their possible need for strategies to cope with misspellings and variant spellings, seem to plague Connie's mind as she invokes the notion of "excellence." If such considerations did give her pause, she would probably have questioned the short-sightedness of teachers and parents who equate excellence with perfect spelling-test scores, even as she might still reasonably have attached some importance to all her students' learning correct spelling, albeit by various means. Could such a limited view of excellence not shortchange Steven as well as the "other" students in Connie's fifth-grade class? Rare is the high school English teacher who can honestly claim never to have encountered those quiet, passive, docile students who have emerged from their elementary schooling with picture-perfect handwriting and perfect grammar and spelling, but still somehow write essays that express and communicate nothing of meaning to themselves or anyone else. I have witnessed students who could spell *their* perfectly on tests, but still consistently wrote *thier* on their papers. If students cannot or will not spell correctly in their writing, where's the point of their spelling correctly on tests?

One way Connie might resolve her dilemma would be to reconstruct her literacy curriculum so that her students could approach spelling and misspellings more pragmatically, with reference to their own unique and shared contexts as readers and writers in meaningful interaction with one another, with Connie herself, with Ed's third graders, with children in other classes, schools, states, and countries. Within such a new curriculum, continuous with students' lives and structured by their language interactions, she could develop a more generous and variegated notion of "excellence" through which all her students, albeit variously, could learn to take pleasure and pride in their developing communicative and expressive abilities. And Steven might be less inclined to take excessive pride in, or feel undue embarrassment at, his own achievement of such a stunted excellence.

Equality through Competition or Community?

If Connie embarked with her fifth graders, Ed, and his third graders upon the adventure of making literacy learning into a living experience, she might find that learning to spell correctly need not be such a socially divisive activity for children as spelling tests often make it. For example, students could make their own individual lists of spelling words, cited in their writing rather than competitively tested. Thus, Connie could engage all her students equally in learning tasks to which their individual abilities are equal. Rather than singling Steven out as an exception to the rest of the fifth grade, she could recognize that every child is equally worthy of her recognition as an individual with particular gifts and challenges.

Such a solution still leaves open the question of what Connie should do about her arrangement with Ed. He could have a list of third-grade spelling words and rules that fifth-grade tutors for his third graders must minimally know; however, fifth graders who don't know those third-grade words and rules might benefit from doing the third-grade spelling lesson, and some third graders may be ready for learning fifth-grade words. Therefore, perhaps a more reasonable solution would be for Connie's and Ed's classes to divide, trade teachers, and mix with one another regularly for interactive and playful literacy activities that might include writing to one another, helping one another identify misspellings and learn correct spellings as well as new words. Connie might initiate a similar exchange with the seventh grade as well, if that is possible. Through such mutual exchanges with older and younger students, Connie's students could develop their own individual spelling lists and in the meantime experience the social value of literacy.

Some difficult-to-spell words may emerge as demons for particular groups of students within a grade or even across grades; those students could then form cooperative learning groups. Some words may even emerge as demons for a whole class, including Steven. Rather than engage such groups in competitive drilling and punitive testing, Connie could use the commonly shared demon words for building school and class community. Students could learn to use song, dance, comedy, art, rhyme, games, and other such memorable aesthetic activities in the rote-memory work of learning to spell words that conform to no rules. The more that Connie and Ed treat error and difficulty as causes for their students' coming to work and play together, rather than causes for their competition and mutual resentment, the more equally will their students be able to share in the joy of learning even when what must be learned is as tedious and boring as spelling.

Therefore, Connie and Ed will need to think especially hard about how they will go about teaching their students ways of working and playing together, ways of helping one another. In making that move to include moral and social learning within her notion of "excellence," Connie may discover that students who cannot spell may be able to teach Steven a few things that he now finds difficult. Maybe he is shy and self-centered, and a bad speller in his class has the gift of helping shy children relax with others and take an interest in their activities. Maybe he is clumsy and weak, and a bad speller in his class has the gifts of patience and grace to share in helping Steven learn physical skills that are difficult for him. Rare is the child who needs no help in any aspect of life, but focusing on a child as "gifted" can have the effect of making that child anxious about her or his imperfections and difficulties to the extent even of being unable to admit them, of becoming arrogant. Or it can have the reverse effect of making the child feel compelled to feign ignorance and lack of curiosity and accomplishment in order to appear "normal." The more attentively and deliberately Connie works to ensure that all her students have ample opportunities to learn to give help and to receive help with grace, whether the help be academic or not, the less likely she will be to encounter again a dilemma such as that which her spelling tests have posed for her, Steven, and the "others."

When she does encounter moral dilemmas in working with her class, however, she will at least have constructed a classroom ethos within which all children could sit in a circle and, one by one, air troubled feelings and thoughts about a problematic situation and afterwards together work conversationally through those feelings and thoughts toward a solution that seems fair and appropriate for all. I myself have seen preschoolers do this, resolving bitter playground disputes and other problems while passing from child to child a piece of driftwood that they had all decorated and called their "talking stick," knowing that they must not interrupt the child who holds it. If Connie's classroom is to be a place where all her students feel at home working through their difficulties with one another honestly, Connie may be wise to provide them with a ritual through which they can observe, practice, and learn the skills for such working-through. Perhaps Connie, Ed, Steven, and the other fifth graders could form such a "talking circle," as I have heard Native Americans call it. Connie could begin by admitting that she has made some mistakes, which she knows have made some of them feel angry, hurt, resentful, discouraged, or embarrassed. She could tell them that she is sorry about their pain, that she wants all of them to have a chance at helping Ed's third graders, that she wants all of them to be recognized for their good work and to enjoy learning. She could inform them of how they will on that very day start to do spelling differently and invite them to talk, one by one without interruption, about how they feel about making her proposed change now. Afterward, she may negotiate with them about some aspects of the new plan. She could repeat this ritual on a weekly basis, especially while she is changing their literacy learning routines, and also use it whenever problems arise. She could combine use of this ritual with another ritual in which students write letters to her. Thus, she could model and invite that "excellence" in clear and thoughtful communication (which, after all, is the purpose of correct spelling) and communicate that she values all her students' learning equally, not just Steven's perfect scores on spelling tests.

Notes

1. All references to this dilemma come from Carol Gilligan, *In a Different Voice* (Cambridge: Harvard University Press, 1982).
2. Gilligan, p. 26.
3. Ibid., p. 28.
4. Ibid., p. 290.

Excellence, Equality, and the Scope of Connie's Concerns

BY PAUL FARBER

This case centers on Connie's concerns, first about reactions to Steven's success, then about her own responsibility to respond in a suitable way to Steven's willful withdrawal. Taken on this level, what is needed is to reflect on a certain moral tension Connie feels regarding the balance of excellence and equality in her efforts to manage this situation with care. So it would seem, but I think there is reason to examine the case from an alternative perspective. Given Connie's evident concern to handle things with care, she might find that Steven has presented her with an opportunity to confront a deeper problem than the one we see her inclined to face.

Alternative Interpretations

Connie's Perspective

In responding to this case, a great deal turns on how the matter is understood. It is fitting to begin with Connie's interpretation of events, for her view has been instrumental in what has occurred. As Connie sees it, Steven' s particular excellence has generated two distinct results. The first is his consistent success as a student in her class and as a speller in particular. The second, a consequence of the first, is the simmering resentment of other students to Steven's success.

What Connie faces as a result is the problem of how to reconcile two values that are central to her interpretation of events. She believes that it is desirable to encourage and reward individual excellence of the kind Steven has exemplified. She also believes that it is desirable to foster greater equality of results of the kind she had in mind as she fretted about the possibly discouraging impact on others of Steven's consistent success. She sought by talking to Steven to explore this delicate balance. His reaction compels her to go further. But to what end?

Some implicit details are worth noting. There is little question that the gaining of recognition for things like good spelling can in fact be strongly valued and enviable for children the age of Connie's students. Such recognition can be made a reward, one that teachers can manipulate and distribute in various ways. Furthermore, as all teachers know, certain ways of granting positive recognition can be effective in stimulating academically productive student efforts. But as a motivating technique, it is also the case that special recognition for success is the kind of good that derives its power from scarcity; recognition and the status that comes with it decline in value as the number of people entitled to claim them rises. This is why, in this case, a tension exists with regard to the prize: what makes it an honor, and Steven enviable, is the notion of being *the* best. There would be no case if, say, all the students passing the tests were enlisted to aid the younger ones. And this fact structures Connie's challenge as she sees it. She seeks to keep at her disposal the tool of closely monitored, highly rewarding kinds of public recognition for excellent work, while managing the unpleasantness that comes when the necessarily unequal distribution of such recognition comes into view and causes hard feelings.

An Alternative View

Few aspects of social life are more familiar than the way, in diverse settings, particular individuals manage to attain honored status, recognition, and privileges. Steven's case is utterly ordinary in that regard. As the comments above suggest, however, we need to be alert to the fact that settings that generate rewarding forms of recognition typically are contrived to do so. Status and recognition are built-in features of various practices and patterns of activity contrived over time (however ignorant we may be of the contriving or even of our own tacit participation in keeping various practices going). Some kinds of activity are especially conducive to promoting claims to such status in that they provide, by way of forms of competition or hierarchical structure, an unmistakable emphasis on position and standing among participants.

The structure of meaningful activities, and the frames of reference they provide for gaining various kinds of recognition, exhibit an important characteristic. They typically precede the individuals who find themselves within them and are in that sense a "given" feature of experience. But their continued presence requires in turn that individuals choose (or are induced) to remain involved over time; we can modify the rules, or even, by mass defections, shut down particular practices and forms of activity. The point is that in the course of living we locate ourselves in patterns of activity that are at once a given feature of our experience and subject to our inclination to attend to and care about them.

Those who actively promote and govern particular patterns of activity have a greater degree of responsibility regarding them. This is because they have taken it upon themselves not only to take part in some pattern, but to induce others to do so as well. Teachers are a prime example. They are participants in certain domains of learning and activity who take it upon themselves to initiate others into that domain, with all its attendant features, benefits, and constraints. Teachers attempt to see to it that certain patterns of social activity endure so that they may be a given feature of still others' lives in the future.

Our culture features multiple variations of a common pattern involving activities designed to reward particular forms of high performance with recognition and enviable status. Broadly speaking, such activities are familiar, easily recognized, widely acceptable or even positively expected; and they are common in our experience of school practices. However commonplace the pattern, instances of it are nonetheless chosen or adapted for particular settings. This is just what Connie has done. A common pattern of trumpeting high-status academic performance was drawn upon in executing the design of a classroom activity. She led her class in reiterating a deeply familiar sort of game, descendant of the first spelling bees.

Viewed in this way, Connie's own account of the case is faulty. If we may speak of the spelling contest as a game, Connie's interpretation seems to take no account of the artificial nature of the game itself. I do not mean to imply that this game contrasts with "genuine educational activities" of some description that are not artificial; all classrooms are artificial through and through in the sense of being designs for generating particular kinds of responses, understandings, forms of expression, patterns of interaction, and so on. The acknowledgment of artificiality is not a criticism, but a fact of organized social life. The problem is Connie's apparent belief that whipping up student interest in spelling lists of words is simply a given and not a matter of decision. This represents a blind spot with regard to her role in perpetuating such a pattern, with its winners, losers, motivated efforts and frazzled nerves.

This observation presents us with a problem different from the one Connie conceives. Instead of the question of how best to reconcile the "demands of excellence" and the "demands of equality" within the context of an unexamined school practice that seems to put them at odds, we may examine that practice itself. In doing so, excellence and equality may be freed from the meanings they have in the patterns of artifice and activity that Connie, Steven, and the rest are caught up in, and they may be used in turn to critique those patterns.

Two Arguments for a Wider Scope

At this point, we have done little to arrive at a judgment or weigh in as to what should be done. Indeed, the reader may be asking whether the messy inquiry hinted at above might not merely complicate things. How would it help Connie decide what to do in real time? Certainly one can engage in endless analysis, but what about Steven, today?

I would argue that despite such understandable concerns, there are reasons to believe that it would be beneficial to inquire further in terms of the larger frame of reference I have sketched above, that it would be right for Connie to alter the interpretation that has thus far structured her understanding of this case. There are two arguments to consider in this discussion.

Meaning What We Say: The Erosion of "Excellence" and "Equality"

If Connie proceeds with her inclination to balance the demands of excellence and equality in practice, she would in effect reaffirm two things. First, she would reaffirm the view that (1) excellence is suitably recognized (perhaps even best recognized) in terms of high performance on narrow, explicitly framed, and easily assessable tasks. She would also reaffirm the view that (2) "equality" can be taken to mean maximizing the number of contestants capable of competing for scarce rewards.

In the case of (1), this view trivializes the educational meaning of "excellence" by reducing it to quantifiable distinction (a winning score). In life, if not often enough in school, many truly valued, deeply appreciated, forms of excellence are recognized by way of sensitive, holistic judgment. Discrete skills and techniques serve, but do not constitute in themselves, the kinds of excellence we truly applaud. It is not the great writer's repertoire of basic skills that confirm her or his excellence, however much those skills are required in the achievement of the art. The same is true in the many other domains of excellence we can appreciate, whether art or science or meeting the highest standards of friendship. Whatever the category, we can distinguish the necessary skills from the fully integrated achievement of meaningful excellence. Think of what it would mean if we could not routinely make this vital distinction between performable, even essential skills, and the purposeful accomplishment of the kind of excellence that matters: we would be forced to make room for idiots savants alongside Nobel laureates, great artists, and loved ones in the book of those we most admire.

The distinction turns on the question of whether something that one can do is worthwhile on its own account, such as spinning a yarn or being a friend, or only when done in service to other valued ends, as are such things as typing, calculating, or, in the current instance, spelling. Speaking broadly, we can be trained to perform with more or less excellence in the latter kind of skills, those that are of a subsidiary kind. And with some degree of trained facility, we can, sometimes, succeed in using such skills to do what the idiot savant cannot do: pursue meaningful goals in complex, sometimes ill-defined but often richly rewarding domains of activity. A large part of what excellence means is, it seems to me, bound up in learning to discern what is possible to achieve in these many domains and why it is worthwhile to strive to do so.

That is the first reason it worries me to think that Connie may set herself the task of finding a way to repair things enough so as to go on with a practice that so elevates the importance of a subsidiary skill. Further determined efforts to reward excellence of that kind seem to me misguided.

In the case of (2), her worry about the demands of "equality" likewise threatens to enshrine a degraded notion of that term. We live in a world in which various talents and competencies are widely valued, and various individuals—whether by dint of hard work or natural ability or carefully cultivated upbringing or some combination of these—display superior levels of performance. There are of course profound questions of equity here with regard to what sorts of talents are socially valued and whether levels of performance are fairly or unfairly compared, cultivated, and assessed. But even if all the fairness questions were somehow settled, the deeper problem of equality would remain. Equality calls us to the task of maintaining a full measure of respect for all persons regardless of the way different situations channel attention, rewards, and recognition—however equitably—to an elite group.

To see this, consider the way equality quietly functions in the context of healthy family life. However proud its members might be about the accomplishments of kin, everyone has a place at the table. As an ideal, equality calls us similarly to recognize each person's belonging at the table, her place in the conversation there, his being in the circle.

Back in Connie's classroom, even with Steven out of the picture, it is doubtful that most students could compete for the prize. What would Connie's efforts likely achieve? The many students who never dreamed of competing with Steven in all likelihood cannot compete with his closest rivals either. But these noncontestants were probably not complaining about Steven either; they are second-class students to begin with insofar as this high-profile game is concerned. This means that the kinds of things Connie might bring about with adjustments made in the name of equality would aim at the nearest rivals of Steven, and she would gauge her success by the quieting of their complaints about Steven's consistent success.

Is this what equality should mean in school, that a rough parity exists among those competing for the honors, while everyone else looks on from the sidelines? The ideal should rather lead us, and Connie, to question whether classroom practices ought to be designed in ways that reinforce the category of the elite (and its companion, the losers, however they are dubbed or disregarded). It is true that school practices have emerged over many years to perform such a function, drawing permanent distinctions between the educated elites and those learning the lesson of their lesser standing. But this is no argument for the rightness of such discriminations, just as it was no moral argument for slavery to say, truly, that the economy of the South depended on that division of labor for a long time.

While one might find the analogy extreme, it still may be true that in schools the time has come to move beyond the sort of ranking we have come to expect and toward an ethic of greater mutual respect and care, more like the ideal of family life in certain crucial respects. These might include seeing to it that invidious distinctions threatening the equal respect of all members are not welcome and that no patterns of activity that threaten to undermine any participant's place and full standing are tolerated. It is possible to radically reconceive the classroom concerning those aspects of its design that reinforce rigid distinctions between categories of students.

But is that a fair burden to place on Connie? In her defense, one might argue that she is, after all, in tune with the expectations of the larger society regarding student achievement and the hierarchy of accomplishment. Isn't Connie correct in striving to promote high levels of achievement on the part of as many of her students as possible? What's wrong with equalizing the chance of success (and the recognition and status it brings) for as many as she can?

The problem as I see it is that while Connie may succeed in extending the number competing for the prizes on display, in doing so she reaffirms the sense in which it may appear natural, a given, that particular individuals shall be anointed successors to the successful, and others shall hear, even if it is spoken in euphemism, the clear signal of their shortcomings.

Equality need not be subservient to hierarchy in this way. As an ideal governing school practices, it can do more than urge a widened competition for positions of respect. Indeed, there are few elements of school life more hostile to the ideal than the continued presence of high profile practices reaffirming social status on the basis of narrow-gauged academic performance. Connie's ruminations on equality should take account of this.

Selling Steven Short: Respecting the Integrity of Steven's Decision

It may be that other aspects of Connie's classroom practice more than compensate and fully retrieve the deeper sense of excellence and equality that ought to govern school practices. Still, there is another quite different argument for urging Connie to examine her interpretation of this case.

Put simply, Connie's interpretation suggests that what is needed is some adjustment that encourages Steven to resume and maintain his honored position while quelling the unrest and stimulating the interest of others in the game. But Connie may be wrong to assume that Steven would welcome this. It is possible that however inchoate his feelings might still be on the matter, he is coming round to a different conclusion altogether. Having gotten caught up in problems concerning his position as top student, he may be sensing that what is at stake for him concerns something more dear: worrying about his honor may assault his dignity. How so?

The issue stems from a fundamental distinction between "honor" and "dignity," the former term connoting one's superior standing or rank while the latter adheres to what in all persons alike is worthy of respect. Consider how Connie's interpretation leads one to view Steven. The assumption is that Steven feels wronged by having the rules of the game, and his undeniable success to date, questioned, that he is feeling punished for his excellence and has dropped out for spite. This leaves him outside the game, pouting and a little pathetic. His apparent spitefulness suggests that he is as petty as the game itself—indeed, that as his former teacher hinted, he needs to be "brought down a notch." Furthermore, we are given to understand by Connie's earnest desire to restore Steven to a happier state of mind, that what he needs most is to again display the talents that brought him honor. She is inclined to use her skill toward that end. But what sort of end is that for her to have in mind for Steven? Doesn't Steven deserve a teacher whose energies are directed beyond helping him to rack up of points and win contests? The dignity of all students is diminished to the extent that teachers regard them primarily in terms of narrow accomplishments, rank, and the pursuit of honors.

Sensing this, Steven may be questioning the point of such displays. Steven, a "born winner," has something to lose if important adults in his life center their dealings with him on the varieties of his victories, especially when honors result from the exercise of subsidiary skills. This is why his decision to withdraw may be something more noble than Connie assumes it to be. Rejecting the narrow competition for honors, Steven may be engaging in what Herbert Kohl has called willful "not-learning," dropping out to protect one's dignity. Instead of seeing this as a ploy to have Connie stop messing with his winning ways, it may be a call for her to focus on things that he can take some fuller satisfaction in.

This may or may not be the case; perhaps Steven really is being petulant and petty. Nevertheless, he deserves the benefit of the doubt. Indeed, all students deserve to be treated in a way that respects the fact, and presumes that, their dignity matters to them. This point closely relates to the earlier concern about equality of respect, and it indicates why it matters very much that Connie reconsider her interpretation. If she carries on assuming that Steven has no cares beyond regaining his honored ways, she risks selling Steven short where his dignity is concerned.

Thinking about the Next Steps

I am urging that Connie adopt a different perspective than the one she has exemplified thus far in this case. Such a perspective would lead her to address three matters in greater detail. First, because immediate harms should be avoided, I think that Connie should give Steven room. I see little harm in him performing poorly on a few spelling tests. Greater harm could come from efforts to manipulate his compliance regarding the game. Such efforts would deny the possibility of a deeper insight on his part and therefore may represent for him an inadvertent insult. Such efforts might also succeed, and his incipient criticism of narrow tasks and invidious distinctions might not develop further in ways that lead him to seek more from education than winning recognition. She needs to take up the conversation with him without the ulterior motive of getting him to win honors again.

Second, Connie should call herself to account for the way notions such as "excellence" and "equality" are applied in the educational settings she governs and for promoting designs in practice that limit or distort their meaning. Excellence can be sought in activities more attuned to the dignity of all learners than to the determination of academic honors, and equality can focus attention on ways to recognize the diverse talents, interests, and characteristics of all the children in her care. Equality and excellence so conceived are not necessarily at loggerheads, and they need not require trade-offs that diminish them both. While it is not possible to explore this idea in detail here, perhaps some brief comments might serve to underscore the point. If good spelling is a goal to be served, Connie could strive to embed spelling in activities that encourage student expression through stories, projects, plays, or the like. Students could edit their own or others' works that have been written to include particular words (if the spelling of those words could be deemed to warrant such requirements). The work involved in creating such texts or projects could integrate the efforts of students with diverse talents in ways that would allow, in principle at least, all students to contribute in meaningful and valued ways to the life of the classroom. By striving to bring about something excellent, whether individually or in concert with others, each person would have opportunities over time to affirm his or her standing as a valued member of the class. Ideally, each student would receive the full measure of equal respect. Learning to spell words with precision in the process would be a part of it, but not the (only) point.

Finally, at least a word is in order regarding those other students who have a stake in all this, the younger ones whom Steven has been tutoring. We do not know whether Steven's absence represents a real loss to them, however convenient it may have been for Ed to have him come. Be that as it may, it is in keeping with the broader purpose above to see to it that those who have a talent for helping the younger children be encouraged to do so and not allow this inherently worthwhile possibility to be held hostage as a prize in a game. Don't the younger ones deserve something more than this? Or perhaps they are undergoing preparation, learning to see that the point of school activities is gaining the mark of success. If Steven's withdrawal helps put a halt to that sad notion, he will have done far more for them than he could ever do by helping them to spell.

Further Reflections on "Excellence and Equality"

More Than a Rejoinder to Paul Farber

BY SUSAN LAIRD

However differently we have formulated our responses to Connie Nakamura's dilemma, Paul Farber and I generally agree that she may be mistaken to see it as a simple moral tension between excellence and equality. We also agree that Connie's competitive reward system, which singles Steven out from the rest of the fifth grade, may be the primary cause of her dilemma. Whereas Paul has explained why the patterns of classroom life implicit in Connie's taken-for-granted reward system are harmful, I have attempted to demonstrate other possible patterns of classroom life that might accomplish her claimed purposes of teaching spelling and of mediating the defensive standoff between Steven, her "other" students, and herself. Both Paul and I have questioned the simplistic meanings that Connie attaches to "excellence" and "equality." I have offered an alternative practical view of the case premised on less legalistic, more contextual understandings of excellence and equality than Connie's, whereas Paul has usefully offered explicit formulations of both the meanings that Connie attaches to them and the meanings implicit in my own account. Thus my rejoinder to Paul is largely a statement of agreement with him.

Yet I think both his response to Connie's case and my own response to it fall short of capturing what that case has to teach educators about the topic of this book, ethical judgment in teaching. Perhaps Paul would agree with me on this point as well. Neither his response nor mine sufficiently emphasizes the fatuousness in any notion of an educational ethics predicated solely on responsiveness to particular problematic situations as they arise. Implicit in both Paul's response and my own is the notion that dilemmas such as Connie's may arise on account of taken-for-granted teaching practices premised upon missing, shaky, or too-rigid philosophical foundations—in this case faulty understandings of excellence and equality. Although correcting those conceptual misunderstandings may do much to redirect Connie's teaching toward resolving her dilemma, I am not convinced that such corrected understandings constitute the whole lesson Connie might learn from her dilemma. Ethical judgment in teaching must include teachers' everyday thinking about their students' moral learning and moral curriculum in every subject and every aspect of their lives, if ethical judgment in teaching is not to be reduced to classroom crisis management.

I have faulted Connie's notion of excellence as a miseducative distortion of the relationship between her students and a specific subject matter (spelling, literacy), whose moral purposes and historical context she does not seem to have considered. But, in more general terms, Paul has faulted her notion of excellence for its failure to distinguish between a "subsidiary skill" and a meaningfully "integrated achievement." His formulation maps easily onto my own account of Connie's failure to consider her students' spelling in pragmatic relation to their literacy and its moral purposes in their lives, which might differ from one student to another in profound ways. At the same time, however, Paul's formulation has the virtue of adaptability to subject matters other than spelling and literacy. If Connie's case involved arithmetic quizzes about reducing fractions, for instance, rather than spelling tests, Paul's argument would still apply insofar as reducing fractions is only a subsidiary skill, just as spelling is. In such a case, a larger notion of meaningful excellence as integrated achievement might involve the intelligent marshaling of that skill for immediate and worthwhile practical purposes: for example, using arithmetic operations in cooking or woodworking or working with textiles or metals, perhaps, just as children did at the University of Chicago Laboratory School under Ella Flagg Young's and John Dewey's leadership at the turn of the last century. Paul's distinction is thus useful to extend thought about Connie's case to other cases involving different subject matter contexts that may or may not be so obviously laden with moral purposefulness as I think literacy almost always is, or at least should be.

In responding to Connie's dilemma, I envisioned a literacy curriculum that would displace Steven from his exclusive status and central location in her thinking by aiming to improve all her students' spelling skills as writers and readers interacting with themselves and others and to reward them all with the experience of mutual helpfulness as a social good rather than an academic prize. Paul has constructed a compelling argument to justify such an effort by considering what a hard place

Connie's classroom must be for Steven. Indeed, he has formulated a notion of equality implicit in my little thought experiment envisioning alternative moral-pedagogical possibilities for Connie's classroom. For Paul conceives equality not as equal opportunity to compete for scarce honors, but as equal respect and dignity. He explains, moreover, that this understanding of equality derives from the best possible family life.

Yet, even as he has argued that Connie needs to rethink her conceptions of equality and excellence and, furthermore, has sensitively recognized Steven's possible virtue in resisting them, Paul has not considered the challenge to moral learning that his own different understandings of those concepts may place upon the students in Connie's class, especially after years of schooling guided by understandings of equality and excellence similar to Connie's. Paul acknowledges that Connie will have to rethink her literacy pedagogy if she takes his critique of her case seriously. Yet her moral dilemma also challenges her to think constructively about her students' moral learning—even if the subject is only spelling. The question here is not just the morality of Connie's actions, not just whether she does right by wronged Steven and the third graders who may or may not miss his tutoring; her dilemma also poses a challenge to educate all her students' moral actions and attitudes in response to everyday conflicts and misunderstandings. How will they learn to help one another graciously rather than eye one another jealously and defensively? How will they learn to communicate with their teachers openly and honestly rather than cryptically and manipulatively, to reflect carefully upon their daily difficulties, accomplishments, attitudes, and habits rather than continue as if the only alternative, when things seem amiss, were to act out?

I am not suggesting that Connie should add the subject "Ethics" to her fifth-grade curriculum. Rather, I want to emphasize the importance of her thinking about that context from which Paul has derived his notion of equality—the best family life—and the sort of moral education appropriate to it. If Dewey were alive, I have no doubt he would heartily approve of Paul's reference to that context, for he argued in *The School and Society* that "What the best and wisest parent wants for his own child, that must the community want for all its children."[1] Recognizing that any children's parents fall short of being the best and wisest (often not for lack of either trying or talent), Jane Roland Martin would approve of Paul's reference also, insofar as she has suggested that schools should be redesigned to provide children "a moral equivalent of home."[2] In the most educative homes, adults listen to children and learn from them. Connie should remember that Jake and Amy were only eleven years old when they responded to Heinz's dilemma, yet Gilligan seems to have learned much from listening to them. And Paul is surely right that Steven's withdrawal from Connie can be instructive for her. So might the "other" students' complaints if she has the courage to listen to them. But toward what ends?

American domestic autobiographical fiction written for girls coming of age to womanhood gives us many accounts of educative family life. Connie could find such narratives helpful to her thinking about what teaching might mean if she were to approach it from Paul's, Dewey's, and Martin's moral perspective. In my own reading of such fiction, especially by Louisa May Alcott and Ntozake Shange, I have found several exemplary maternal figures who have approached childrearing as teaching—teaching explicitly intent upon the achievement of children's growing capacity and responsibility for learning to love and to survive despite their pains, conflicts, and difficulties, especially including their mother's absence.[3] In making my response to Connie's case, I thought about what teaching spelling might be like if Connie approached that pedagogical task with such an intention explicitly in mind. I thought about what teaching fifth graders might be like if she recognized that literacy learning can be one means for their learning to love our language, themselves, and one another and for their learning to survive in a world with an ever more rapidly growing dependence upon written communication. Surely, Connie could also rethink the teaching of arithmetic intent not only upon the development of subsidiary skills such as reducing fractions, but upon a larger notion of excellence that includes a moral teaching achievement such as I have drawn from my philosophical readings of domestic fiction. She could, indeed I think she should, do likewise with the teaching of other subjects, such as health and pubescent sexuality.

Aiming for such a teaching achievement would require her to engage her own ethical judgment along with her students' developing ethical judgment in many aspects of her teaching, not just in response to crises, but in the making of their classroom rituals, routines, and special events from day to day, hour to hour. The chief risk in considering ethical judgment in teaching through case studies of dilemmas is that one may overlook other vital aspects of moral teaching in the absence of crisis. Such an approach risks overlooking those cases (such as those I have found in domestic fiction) that demonstrate what teaching can mean when it purposefully leads children to learn everyday habits, dispositions, attitudes, and skills for joyful living even when living is hard.

Nonetheless, Connie Nakamura's dilemma could teach her that any classroom crisis can be more than just a teaching trouble with which she must grapple alone. Classroom crises may present both Connie and her students real opportunities for shared moral reflection, courage, and growth through which they might learn more about surviving their difficulties in ways that strengthen, rather than diminish, their capacities for loving one another with all their many imperfections and differences. One advantage of considering ethical judgment in teaching through case studies of dilemmas is that it may underscore how moral crises are everyday events in classrooms, not just life-or-death dilemmas like Heinz's. Thus, classroom rituals and routines for responding to crises as special events for moral learning may be vital sources for ethical judgment in teaching and for moral education generally.

Notes

1. John Dewey, *The School and Society and The Child and the Curriculum* (Chicago: University of Chicago Press, 1990), p. 7.

2. Jane Roland Martin, *The Schoolhome: Rethinking Schools for Changing Families* (Cambridge: Harvard University Press, 1992).

3. Susan Laird, "Who Cares about Girls? Rethinking the Meaning of Teaching," *Peabody Journal of Education* 70 (1995): 82–103.

Response to Susan Laird

BY PAUL FARBER

Reading Susan Laird's remarks, I began to think of her as if she were directly involved in the case. I hope that readers, and especially Susan Laird, will forgive me for asking, What if she were Connie's principal? How might things go for "Principal Laird" if she were to follow the recommendations she proposes?

From my perspective, the first observation is that we evidently share a great deal of common ground. Nothing is more striking perhaps than the fact that we both refuse to accept the terms of the current dilemma. As principal, Susan Laird would be in an excellent position to work on what we both see as the possibility of resolving the dilemma by way of changes in practice that integrate excellence and equality at a higher level. Both terms currently mean something different—and less—than they could in an enriched classroom environment. Additionally, we both believe that it is desirable to reflect on Steven's problem in the context of what other students face and derive from the current situation; that all are shortchanged by a curriculum that focuses on achieving a narrow band of skills at the expense of higher-order, expressive and integrative activity; and that the current competitive-individualistic ethos is both unnecessary and undesirable. In short, Principal Laird could help Connie strive to generate more fully satisfying forms of interaction, integrating the efforts of all students, while downplaying forms of activity that emphasize inequality and confine excellence to coming out on top.

In addition to supporting this very comprehensive agenda, Principal Laird would be in a position to promote further reflection on her valuable ideas about curriculum matters. In particular, I think that her comments about the way spelling as a subject has come to us forged by particular social-historical processes is important to understand. As Jane Roland Martin has written, school subjects are not God-given, nor are "the basics" fixed for all time.[1] Practitioners must continually take responsibility for the way subjects and definitions of the basics are defined and change. In this respect, Susan Laird's comments about the current context in which students find themselves as language users, and the consequences attached to the attainment of certain kinds of skills, are important considerations in the planning of curriculum. It would be reassuring to know that educational leadership everywhere was inclined to encourage, as it currently does not widely do, the kinds of inquiry Susan Laird would promote as principal in Connie's school.

But two issues cloud this prospect. The first concerns the application of critical judgment regarding Connie and her work. Professor Laird's remarks convey the clear impression that Connie is blameworthy for the current state of affairs. She says early on that Connie's dilemma is "largely of her own making," comments on her apparent thoughtlessness, and concludes with a suggestion that Connie should initiate the desired transformative process by "admitting that she has made some mistakes." Now while I think teachers do carry a heavy burden of responsibility in practice and I am not against anyone owning up to their errors, I think this overstates Connie's culpability. As with all practitioners, Connie has stepped into patterns of activity deeply institutionalized in entrenched habits, norms, and expectations. To declare that individuals are culpable for the problems and dilemmas that bubble up from the collectively generated institutions they find themselves in seems to me problematic, potentially unfair, and unnecessarily punitive. For most of us, and Connie included, our powers to know what is best to do in practice—let alone to figure out how to do it—develop but slowly as we reflect on the patterns of social life in which we are engaged. Connie might be credited instead with acknowledging that something is amiss and challenged to find ethically and educationally worthy ways to redirect her teaching practices. I believe this orientation is more fair, but apart from that I think it better serves the practical purpose of realizing the kinds of principled commitments Susan Laird articulates. For while such normative ideas can be wielded to frame criticism of the shortcomings of current school practices and practitioners, their greatest power comes from their being applied prospectively, framing new goals for educational practice to achieve.

Perhaps this turn toward a prospective orientation would quite naturally occur if Susan Laird's conversation with Connie could in fact take place. Such a setting, unlike the writing of a formal response to the case, would after all allow for the kind of interaction that she praises as central to "Amy's way" of moral reasoning, generating the fabric of relation-sustaining communication. In conversation, the articulation of critical judgments, which is akin to "Jake's way" of drawing impersonal, principle-governed decisions about states of affairs, might well be suspended, left unsaid. But a second concern bears on just that eventuality. Susan Laird suggests that Connie's problem is likely bound up in a faulty approach to practice, a misguided tendency to think in Jake's way and thus to discount those goods valued by Amy, such as communication, connection, and voice. Connie, she suggests, seems committed to rules over relations, and this is at the heart of the problem. The image of Connie in the conversation circle, the "new" Connie, derives its power from this, that though she has made a wrong turn she can still turn round, join her students, and begin anew. This way of putting things underscores the suggested dichotomy between Jake's and Amy's way of proceeding. But thinking about the matter in terms of such a dichotomy is, I believe, misleading and possibly counterproductive.

Consider the case unfolding now with Principal Laird on the scene. While we can imagine everything working out as hoped, it might not go that way. What if Connie is in fact stubbornly committed to her current methods and she defends them, saying that while in this case things are troublesome, by and large her teaching is effective and widely appreciated. Most of her students are inclined to work hard and learn, and parents of her students have mostly been well satisfied over the years. So she thanks Susan, a principal she knows to be a respectful listener, and determines that she will ride this out with Steven, making at most some minor adjustments. Such a discussion might have served in fact to reaffirm her commitment to the way she has learned to teach.

A new dilemma arises, this time for Principal Laird. Her vision of what an appropriately changed classroom would be like and why it is important has not changed, but she must acknowledge the extent of her differences with Connie. She now faces the question of whether to place greater stock in respecting Connie's professional standing as equal to her own or to assert the authority her standing as principal gives her, for the sake of pursuing her vision of excellence. Shall she abandon or shelve her commitments to change in order to show respect for Connie's judgment or use her position to apply further pressure in order to effect change?

Letting that scenario rest for a moment, here is another. Principal Laird has the same conversation with Connie, but this time Connie "comes around," following Susan Laird's suggestions to the letter. Unfortunately, Connie's plans do not go as she had anticipated. Many students rally around the traditional spelling contests, a few even expressing their grudging admiration for Steven, the recognized champ. Little enthusiasm is expressed for pursuing very different ways of learning, and Connie cannot seem to spark the kind of interest she had hoped for. The prevailing view seems to be to do the kinds of things everyone is used to. This is amplified over the next days and weeks as a few parents express curiosity tinged with misgivings. The conversation Connie promotes seems most of all to have revealed the depth of expectations and allegiance to the prevailing, traditional approach.

So what is to be done? Connie wonders whether to abandon the guiding ideas for a transformed classroom or to contest what she is hearing, perhaps even disregarding the voice of resistance she has encountered regarding her new ideas. Should she emphasize her educational commitments concerning excellence in practice, or emphasize the value of giving the views of the recalcitrant students and parents a standing equal to her own, thus in effect yielding to the prevailing sentiments?

A number of things may be noted about the scenarios. First, they show how efforts to eliminate or overcome particular dilemmas in practice can sometimes generate new ones, a fact that neither Susan Laird nor I noted in our initial, fundamentally optimistic responses. While many dilemmas regarding excellence and equality may be resolved, educators can hardly expect to succeed once and for all; the two ideals are both so bound up in competing conceptions of good educational practice that it is scarcely conceivable that they won't at times collide.

But more than this, what these scenarios suggest is how problematic it would be to presume one ought to approach such problems committed to the characteristic features of either Jake's or Amy's way of proceeding exclusively. In both instances above, it seems clearly abhorrent to select either of the options in opposition to the other. In the first, the principal needs to press on in keeping with those educational principles believed to be truly important but needs to find ways to do so that preserve, even deepen, the relationship with Connie. A genuine respect for her judgment, as a moral equal, does not require settling for a truce in which each gets to hang onto his or her options unchanged. If the matter is important—as it clearly is here—the principal is obliged to struggle for the educational principles she believes in, struggle to see them inform and direct future practices as fully as possible. This can be done while granting Connie the opportunity to modify either her or the principal's thinking about the merits and applications of the principles in question and revising them further as subsequent experience in modified practices begins to add its testimony.

The same is true in the last scenario. The revitalized commitments Connie has developed are next to worthless if too easily abandoned. If the principles of good teaching she now holds mean anything they must be faithfully explored over time. But that does not mean shutting off the contrasting views of others with a stake in her work. If they express what she sees as an underdeveloped set of ideas about what might be the case in her classroom, only Connie's principled perseverance will make it possible for them to come round to a better view, understanding what is short-sighted or deficient in their current conceptions.

These possible scenarios show why, in my view, it is important to depart from those of Susan Laird's observations that urged both Connie and the reader to be wary of Jake's way of thinking about dilemmas in practice. What is misleading about this is not that features constituting Jake's way—such as the application of abstract reasoning and impersonal analysis—do not lead to trouble sometimes; they do. But so too are the features characteristic of Amy's way of proceeding uncertain and ambiguous in practice, leading up worthwhile avenues and down blind alleys in turn. Neither way does alone what their union allows to be done, and that is to address practical dilemmas, such as those that arise when excellence and equality pull in different directions, in a way that builds educationally meaningful relationships in and by way of the process of clarifying educational principles worth struggling for. Perhaps we can think of Jake and Amy as representing not a pair of ways to choose between, but two overlapping and linkable vocabularies to employ in the interests of reconstructing the institutions we find ourselves in (indeed, despite what is suggested about the dichotomy, Susan Laird's response exemplifies just such an integration). Seen in this way, we can note also the risks that arise: it can be handy to stress impersonal reasoning just when necessary personal dealings become difficult or to think relationally just when principles seem to demand more than we would prefer to give; the full array of resources can be employed to avoid responsibility as well as to take it. This risk, however, is unavoidable in the domain of practical judgment, a basic test of moral decency. With no sure formula to guide them, Principal Laird and Connie would have no choice but to carry on the interplay of their principled commitments and open relations, seeking to discern how best to nudge along better paths the evolving practice they share.

Notes

1. Jane Roland Martin, "Two Dogmas of Curriculum," *Synthese* 51 (1982): 5–20.

Discussion

In his second essay Paul Farber identifies a couple areas where he and Susan Laird appear to disagree. Connie's blameworthiness is one. (Is Connie blameworthy? Here Laird and Farber take us into issues of institutional context once again. Is it important to assign blame in this case?) Ethical perspective is another, even more fundamental, issue. Recalling the ethic of caring–ethic of duty continuum, we would place Laird toward the "caring" end (Amy's way) and Farber (a bit? a lot?) more toward the "duty" end (Jake's way). (How does the discussion in this chapter add to your thinking about the caring-duty debate?) Yet despite these differences, there are considerable similarities, as both writers note. Particularly, Laird and Farber agree that Connie needs to broaden her ideas about excellence and equality. They have quite similar visions of a richer, more holistic conception of educational excellence that highlights equality, community, and cooperation as opposed to difference, individuality, and competition.

In this discussion I will try to keep the dialogue alive by offering challenges to some of Farber's and Laird's key claims about excellence and equality. Two distinctions are central. One is between *dignity* and *honor*. The other is between two sorts of equality: *simple equality* and *complex equality*. Laird and Farber emphasize the first element of each pair. I will try to show how the second elements may be worthy ideas. In the end we still will have plenty of grounds for questioning Connie's current approach, but I also think we will have reason to believe that difference, individuality, and competition might have some proper place in the pursuit of excellence in schools.

Excellence

Nowadays there is a good deal of talk about the need for excellence in schools (often with the further explicit or implicit claim that schools are failing on that score). Sure, excellence is desirable. The problem is we do not just pursue "excellence" but rather excellence in particular things. For example, excellence might be conceived in terms of mental proficiency or preparation in an academic discipline or self-actualization or social responsibility.[1] (Can you think of other possibilities?) These conceptions clash in our case. Connie's approach to spelling does more to emphasize mental proficiency and academic discipline. Laird and Farber argue that those are not enough, at least not the way Connie is thinking about them. Even if excellence in literacy as an academic discipline is important, Connie needs to see it in a more integrated and meaningful way and do less to stress mere proficiency in subsidiary skills such as spelling. Beyond that even, excellence in the academic discipline should be connected to self-actualization of students and, above all, social relationships.

This view has a good deal to recommend it. But there are questions we ought to ask. Even if this vision is a good one, there is the issue of self-determination for individuals and communities. Farber himself raises this issue when he stresses respect for Steven's wishes and when he points out that people simply may not want the sort of changes Laird recommends. That isn't the end of the issue, of course. It may be that people should want those changes and perhaps should be convinced or even compelled to accept them. (The next two chapters delve into these questions.) But there is a prior question: Is Farber's and Laird's vision a good one? Should a school really be modeled on a family, for instance? Don't teachers have to be judgmental in a way parents do not? Parents' first obligation may be to their children, but should teachers give their students similar priority? Teachers may have obligations to the wider society that parents do not have. For the sake of the common good, might teachers need to foster competitions among students that help identify and develop those most able to perform certain tasks or fill certain social roles, even if parents should not?

The point is, even if we agree that social responsibility is an important excellence, we still must ask what excellence in social responsibility involves. This is a central question in this case. What attitudes and actions best contribute to the life of the classroom and to life beyond? Answers to this question will depend on people's broad understandings of what is worthwhile and important. Certainly, our understanding of the nature and value of equality will play a role. Obviously, equality is very important for Laird and Farber, and their concern for equality is clearly reflected in their understanding of excellence. Let's think more about equality and its connection to excellence.

Dignity and Simple Equality

In this section and the next, I will present a distinction between two sorts of equality: simple equality and complex equality.[2] Laird and Farber stress simple equality, but if we think about equality as complex equality we might reach somewhat different conclusions about our case. In this section I'll focus on simple equality.

Simple equality is equality understood as sameness. If we are talking about equal treatment, for instance, what we mean is same treatment. How important is this sort of equality? I will call the position that it is of overriding importance *egalitarianism*.[3] This view says that for some important goods, such as educational opportunities, rewards, or recognition, all people are entitled to equal shares of them. (Here I gloss over an important issue: What goods are the important ones? An egalitarian need not seek equality in absolutely everything.) If some people have more, then those who have less are entitled to more until they have the same as everyone else. If it isn't possible to raise everyone up, then some should be taken away from people who have more until equality is achieved. This position has some disturbing implications. Let's imagine that the good at stake is the intellectual talents children have. Assuming for the moment that Steven really is intellectually gifted, he would have more of this good than some other children. From the egalitarian point of view, efforts should be made to bring other children up to Steven's level. Since it seems unlikely if not impossible that all can be brought up to that level, efforts should also be made to bring Steven down. Perhaps egalitarians would not go so far as to take away Steven's abilities by excising parts of his brain, but they might say that little if anything should be done to cultivate them. It would be better to waste his talents than allow inequality. This is a problematic stance, to say the least, but perhaps not uncommon. Could it be behind the fourth grade teacher's idea that Steven should be "brought down a notch"?

Egalitarianism raises questions of justice. Yes, treating people differently can be unjust, but injustice can result from same treatment as well. R. S. Peters puts the point this way: "The notion basic to justice is that distinctions should be made if there are relevant differences and that they should not be made if there are no relevant differences or on the basis of irrelevant differences."[4] Just as we do not want to make distinctions between people when that is not warranted (when there are no differences or when the differences are irrelevant) neither do we want to ignore differences that are relevant. A learning disabled student may need more time to complete an assignment than other students. To that extent, it would be unfair to treat that student the same as other students. That is different from saying a girl should have more time merely because she is a girl. Unlike the learning disability, sex would seem to be an irrelevant factor when deciding how much time students should have for completing their work. Of course, this issue can be complicated. Proponents of same-sex schools and classes for girls argue that sex is relevant for at least some educational policies. Advocates for disabled students argue that disability is not relevant for some central educational purposes; that is the basic idea behind mainstreaming. The issue is what student characteristics are relevant. In our case, if Steven really is relevantly different from other children, justice requires that that be recognized.

Is Steven relevantly different from the other students? Farber and Laird stress that Connie's students are not relevantly different, at least so far as the activities in question are concerned. They still value differences. Yet the similarities should take priority; they are what is relevant for the particular purposes at hand. (The further question is Supposing we do identify relevant similarities or differences, what do we do about them? For example, even if we agree that Connie was wrong to treat Steven differently, it does not follow directly that something should be done about it. There may be values besides equality and justice to think about. In his second essay Farber shows how judgment should take account of contextual factors.)

Why should similarities take priority? We can begin to understand where Laird and Farber are coming from by looking at the distinction between honor and dignity that Farber mentions. The problem with the "honor" view is that it is tied to hierarchy and privilege. As Farber visualizes it, the elite compete for honors while everyone else looks on from the sidelines. In contrast, in the dignity view all people possess dignity simply because they are human beings. Thus, people should have "a place at the table" regardless of their particular achievements or abilities.

This suggests an egalitarian view, but it need not be the extreme position described above. Commitment to the basic similarity of human beings as human beings does not require simple equality in all the significant rewards and status schools and society distribute. But if there are differences in distribution of these goods, it must be shown that the advantages certain people have work to the advantage of *everyone*, not just the elite. In this way everyone shares a basic equality. John Rawls presents this idea in his "difference principle."[5] This principle asserts that the justice of the basic structure of societies should be judged in relation to the position of the people who are worst off. If it can be shown that in a particular social structure reducing the advantages of the better off would increase the advantages of the worst off, then the structure is not just; the people who are worst off could be doing better. (Again, what to do about injustices is a further question.) While it is not clear that Laird and Farber take Rawls's view, Rawlsian arguments could support their recommendations against the criticism that they are too focused on the welfare of Steven's less advantaged schoolmates. (Rawls does not support an extreme egalitarianism that would require hindering Steven's achievement as long as inequality exists. It could be that lowering the expectations of the better off, say by reducing the financial rewards they would get from development and exercise of their talents, would work to the disadvantage of people less well off who benefit from those talents. And Rawls could say that Steven has some claim to deserve his honors, though this issue is complicated.[6])

Honor and Complex Equality

Concern for dignity is an advance over concern for honor that denies the basic equality of persons. Yet some communitarians wish to rehabilitate the idea of honor.[7] They do not deny a place to dignity and simple equality, but they do question their priority. In terms of Peters's conception of justice, we might interpret the "honor" view as putting at least relatively more emphasis on relevant differences than on relevant similarities. Since Farber and Laird want to distance themselves from the "honor" view, looking at honor and what it implies for equality will help us get some critical perspective on their views.

As you might suppose from our discussion in Chapter 4, communitarians endorse honor because it is linked to social roles and practices. As we saw there, appeals to current practices can be problematic. Farber criticizes Connie for accepting as given a practice (competitive spelling tests) that is merely contrived. Communitarians could concur. But they could continue on to argue that there is a deeper social practice, for example democratic dialogue and deliberation—which both Laird and Farber would appear to endorse—in which citizens have particular roles to play and for which we can and should recognize superior role performances. Farber is right that honor suggests "superior standing or rank," but communitarians could argue that there is nothing necessarily bad about that. They are not committed to saying rank or standing must be confined to some hereditary or educational elite. But it does mean we should value and encourage the quest for excellence and honor in the roles vital to democracy and other worthwhile things. (Here I'll make a distinction between "honor" and "honors." One can agree with Farber that emphasis on "narrow accomplishments, rank, and pursuit of honors" diminishes dignity, yet say that is different than being concerned for honor. A grasping quest for mere honors is dishonorable.)

Equality still is a concern here, but a different conception of equality is needed. Walzer offers a conception that he calls "complex" equality. This sort of equality does not require that everyone receive the same share of a particular good. The idea is that there are numerous "spheres" of activity. Each sphere has its characteristic excellences. In each sphere we recognize people who "win," who better attain its excellence than other people. Equality is achieved by maintaining an adequate number and range of spheres so that many people have a real chance for excellence. People may "look on from the sidelines" for some things, but be "in the game" for others. The person who excels in the literacy sphere may not excel in the mathematics sphere or in the athletic sphere. The point is not to withhold honors but to spread the honors around the various spheres. The lesson people need to learn, Walzer says, is that respect and dignity do not require "winning"—or at least "not losing"—in all important spheres; "losing" in one sphere is not an affront to one's dignity because one can win in another and have that honored.

But what about the person who does not excel in any of the spheres? What would happen to the least advantaged persons whom Rawls is concerned? Walzer admits that competition may be keen and that there may be some people who never "win." He has a couple responses, however. One is that status in a particular sphere should not be transferred to status in another. Likely, he would second Farber's criticism of "reaffirming social status on the basis of narrow-gauged academic performance." But his point would be that honoring narrow-gauged academic performance is not the main problem; the problem is allowing this performance to determine status in a different sphere, the social sphere. Walzer agrees that the educational elite should not dominate the social and political spheres. (Of course, the heritage in the United States endorses the notion that education *should* count toward political and social status. What do you think about that issue?) The other, related response is that there are certain areas where simple equality is called for. Educational opportunity is one of these areas, Walzer says. Just because students do not excel in the educational sphere does not mean that they aren't entitled to an adequate education.

This may be of little comfort to some people. For example, someone coming from Laird's caring perspective might still object to the difference, individuality, and competition Walzer's view countenances, and even encourages. It is fair to ask what benefits Walzer sees in all this. A principal benefit he sees is plurality. (The subtitle of his book is "A Defense of Pluralism and Equality.") Having a number of distinct spheres of activity simply is a good thing. Society is enriched and invigorated by having a range of such spheres to participate in and deliberate about. Doing too much to emphasize sameness threatens plurality. (Do Farber and Laird support plurality? Is plurality a good thing? Could it threaten communities by leading to fragmentation? This issue is central in the next two chapters.)

So, in their response to our case, proponents of honor and complex equality could agree with Laird and Farber that Connie's spelling program does not provide the rich literacy experiences students need and does not provide enough "spheres" of activity for the children. They could also agree that fostering feelings of community and mutual respect is vital. But likely they would have more sympathy than Laird and Farber for Connie's competitions and for her notion that her students' attitudes about excellence and equality need to be changed so as to be more accepting of differences in talent and achievement, more willing to value "winners" than to resent them.

Conclusion

All children have basic ethical rights to simple equality in respect and education. Nothing in our discussion has challenged that. But there are issues about how or whether we should go beyond that basic equality. Beyond what's required by basic equality, should we push for ever greater equality as an egalitarian would tend to suggest? Or should we do more to acknowledge and reward excellence differentially? Based on our discussion, it would seem that ethical theory is not decisive on this question. Perhaps this is as it should be. Amy Gutmann argues that so long as the basic education all children need for citizenship is not hampered, allocating resources for education beyond that "threshold" is a matter for democratic deliberation, not theory.[8] If that is so, Susan Laird's statement that "Ethical judgment in teaching must include teachers' everyday thinking about their students' moral learning and moral curriculum in every subject and every aspect of their lives" makes a great deal of sense. Theory cannot tell educators and society how to balance the demands of excellence and equality. What's needed are reflective people attuned to the full range of complex ethical issues that must be confronted. We need educators thinking beyond "crisis management" to deeper, more encompassing issues of human well being and how those issues are played out in the day-to-day activities of people's lives.[9]

So, again, we come back to the need for politics. In this chapter we see once again some of the issues we have encountered before. Like Sichel and Burbules, Farber and Laird emphasize conversation. However, is conversation appropriate or helpful? Perhaps argument is needed. But then Laird prompts us to ask whether this is really a good idea or just a prejudice of people disposed to "Jake's way" of thinking. And this question can be broadened to a more general caution about claims to "truth." For example, some of the "truths" of good spelling may be relative to particular historical and/or political contexts.

So, surprise of surprises, our issues keep bubbling. But note, too, how the familiar themes of agreement and dialogue surface again. While the views we've explored here clash in some important ways, they also converge, in their common aspiration to excellence and equality as aims that need not be in competition, for example. Again we see caution about dialogue but also a sense that reasonable, sensitive dialogue is somehow fundamental to teachers' and students' ethical project.

But we also see something rather new added to our understanding of that project. Largely, we have discussed the ethical growth of teachers. Laird, however, more clearly than anyone to this point perhaps, has placed the ethical growth of students before us as a (the?) fundamental aim of teaching. This points us in a direction we will follow in our next two chapters. Farber anticipates the basic issue in his second essay—ethically, should schools, particularly public schools, get into that business? Isn't this an area where we must give students and their parents extensive freedom for self-determination? But then we must ask, how important is diversity in ethics? All along our writers and I have tried to make the case that unity and agreement (of some sort) is desirable. Is it really? What sort of unity? At what price? We confront these questions in Chapter 6.

Notes

1. Madhu Suri Prakash and Leonard Joseph Waks, "Four Conceptions of Excellence," *Teachers College Record* 87 (1985): 79–101.

2. This distinction is made by Michael Walzer in his *Spheres of Justice* (New York: Basic Books, 1983).

3. This discussion is drawn from Joseph Raz, *The Morality of Freedom* (Oxford: Clarendon Press, 1986).

4. R. S. Peters, *Ethics and Education* (London: George Allen and Unwin, 1966), p. 123.

5. John Rawls, *A Theory of Justice* (Cambridge: Harvard University Press, 1971).

6. For a discussion of Rawls's views on desert see Thomas Pogge, *Realizing Rawls* (Ithaca, NY: Cornell University Press, 1989).

7. For discussions see Peter Berger, "On the Obsolescence of the Concept of Honour," in Michael Sandel, ed., *Liberalism and Its Critics* (New York: New York University Press, 1984), pp. 149–58; and Charles Taylor, *Sources of the Self* (Cambridge: Harvard University Press, 1989).

8. Amy Gutmann, *Democratic Education* (Princeton: Princeton University Press, 1987), p. 136.

9. Again, for discussion of how ethical values are played out in the details of schooling, I refer readers to Philip W. Jackson, Robert E. Boostrom, and David T. Hansen, *The Moral Life of Schools* (San Francisco: Jossey-Bass, 1993).

6

Unity and Diversity

CASE

Smithville is one of those small, agricultural towns common in the Great Plains states of the United States. It is a homogeneous community, its people descendants of settlers from western Europe. Everyone knows everyone else, and they look out for each other. There's a thriving local culture, built around participation in traditional pioneer handicrafts, church, and activities in the one K–12 school the community's children attend.

Sally Johannsen, the one math teacher for students in grades 8–12, grew up in a town much like Smithville, though in another part of the state. One of the main reasons she sought a teaching position such as she has was that she yearned to be part of a close-knit community like the one she grew up in. In her four years at the large state university she had experienced what it was like to be without such a bond. She wanted it back again.

Her nearly six years in Smithville had been happy ones. Yes, she sometimes missed the diversity and intellectual stimulation that she had in college. At times, she did get impatient with the narrowness of people's views. But in the end, she still felt that this frustration was outweighed by the sense of unity and security she felt in a community of people who cared for common values and for each other.

However, now her feeling of contentment was being shaken. Around the end of September, three Vietnamese families moved into the community.

Together they had bought a farm nearby, and they were all sharing the large farmhouse. From the start, some members of the community resented these people. For one thing, the sale of the farm had inspired bad feelings. The previous owner had been forced to sell the farm, which had been in the family for four generations, because he simply could not make a go of it. To some people, the Vietnamese families were taking advantage of the misfortune of their neighbor.

Also, the Vietnamese kept pretty much to themselves. Only one of the families spoke English, so it was difficult for most of them to interact with the community. The head of one of the Vietnamese families, Dr. Tran, had been a mathematics professor in Vietnam and spoke English quite well. He acted as a liaison between the community and the Vietnamese families, but even he did not seem overly anxious to interact. Smithville residents noted that the Vietnamese did not attend the annual Christmas program at the school, which was attended by everyone else in this thoroughly Christian community. They did not even go to the football games, another major community event.

Several of the Vietnamese children were in Sally's classes. She saw the problems and felt it was imperative to help these children become part of the community as quickly as possible. Language was a concern. Dr. Tran's senior daughter (who wished to be called Cathy rather than by her Vietnamese name) helped by acting as an interpreter for the other Vietnamese students. But Sally worried that this might keep the children from learning English as quickly as they should. Furthermore, many of the other students were becoming impatient with the extra time and attention the Vietnamese children received. And Cathy Tran herself was becoming increasingly resistant to her role as translator. She felt this was keeping her from being more readily accepted by the other high school students. It did too much to remind them that she was different.

Of course, Sally felt that her task was not just to work with the Vietnamese students but with the other students as well. She was disturbed by their lack of tolerance. She tried to help students learn to value the diversity the Vietnamese brought to the community, as well as to see things they had in common. So, she and the other teachers gave lessons on Vietnamese geography and history. Sally felt that, as a math teacher, she couldn't do as much of this as the history teacher could, say. But she did do some, and she felt she was in a good position to help students learn to get along because doing mathematics did not require as much English as other classes. The Vietnamese students did well. They showed a great deal of talent and enthusiasm for math (as for all their academics). However, the other students tended to be more lukewarm about it, and this became another source of friction. Sally guessed that this might have less to do with culture than with the fact that the Vietnamese adults had all had professional careers in Vietnam while the people of Smithville were farmers or had blue-collar jobs.

Sally sought out Dr. Tran to talk about the situation. He was a bit more open to Sally than others, perhaps because of their common interest in mathematics. They got along pretty well, and Sally enjoyed the intellectual stimulation Dr. Tran provided her. But Dr. Tran was not enthusiastic about Sally's plan to meld him and his people into the community. Indeed, he was quite upset by his daughter's eagerness to be an "American." He assured Sally that they planned to be cordial and courteous with other community members but that he felt no need to do more. He doubted that he and his fellow Vietnamese would ever be fully accepted. Besides, he and the others were concerned about preserving for their children the culture of their homeland and worried about community pressure to give it up. As devout Buddhists, they didn't want their children participating in the Christmas program at school, in which all the other children participated. Why not change this to a secular program of some sort? Even doing a little thing such as providing food in the school cafeteria that was more palatable to Vietnamese tastes would be appropriate. The Vietnamese probably had legal grounds for contesting some of the school's policies, but they were not going to press the issue so long as they were left alone.

Sally received a similar lack of encouragement from people in the community. They were not receptive to the suggestions Dr. Tran gave her. They too were devout in their religion; they too wanted to preserve their way of life. Plus, the community didn't have the economic resources to be all things to all people. They too were ready to live and let live, but little more than that.

In the meantime, the Vietnamese students in the school continued to be isolated. They appeared to prefer this. However, Cathy had begun to be excluded from this group, at least by the older Vietnamese students. This appeared not to bother her too much. But neither was she being accepted by the majority students. She had made a few friends, but she was definitely on the fringe. She seemed to have gotten herself in a place where she had *no* community to call her own.

Sally was deeply troubled by the situation. In Dr. Tran she thought she had an intellectual soul mate who would share her concern for diversity. In the community of Smithville she thought she had caring companions who would reach out to others in need. She was not sure what to do now to break down barriers. She wasn't sure on what grounds she might build unity. She wasn't even sure she should try. Perhaps there now existed a proper balance of unity and diversity. After all, everyone did seem to be tolerating everyone else. Still, Sally worried about Cathy. She felt that she had to intervene for her sake. What do you think?

Reflections on "Unity and Diversity"

Unity and Diversity: An Interpretation

BY MICHAEL S. KATZ

Like other professionals, teachers are influenced not only by the professional duties required of them in their roles in the schools but also by their own personal moral ideals. Sally Johannsen is guided by such an ideal—the ideal of community. She took her teaching position in Smithville because she "yearned to be part of a close-knit community." Moreover, she wants this sense of community not only for herself but for the new Vietnamese students and in particular for Cathy Tran. She feels that belonging to a community provides a person with a "sense of unity and security" among people who cared "for common values and for each other."

Sally appears to experience herself as having a duty both to her Vietnamese students and to herself to create a community in which her students will be able to experience a similar sense of unity and security among people caring for common values and for each other.[1] Her efforts and her accompanying frustration at their minimal results clearly grow from this sense of duty, a duty informed by her ideal of community.

In this regard, it is important to introduce the notion of self-respect in one of its central forms. According to Thomas Hill, self-respect is achieved when people live their lives in accord with personal standards by which they are prepared to judge themselves even if these standards are not extended to others. Hill writes that "the standards might be ideals for which one strives or merely a minimum below which one cannot go without losing face with oneself."[2] We are told that in facing her own disappointment both with Dr. Tran and the community of Smithville, Sally is not sure what to do to break down barriers and to build unity. She isn't even sure she should try. However, my own reading of the situation suggests that accepting the status quo is not a satisfactory resolution of the problem for Sally. It would lead to a diminution in her own self-respect, an abandonment of her own commitment to foster the sense of community that she feels makes life satisfying for her. Since Sally's professional and personal life seem to be informed by her ideal of community, to maintain her own self-respect she must do everything she can to translate this ideal into reality for herself and her students.

We are told that Sally still worries about Cathy Tran and feels she must intervene. What is this worry based on? Is it a legitimate worry? How can we characterize the way Cathy Tran is being treated and the way she is reacting to this treatment? What kind of treatment does Cathy Tran deserve morally, and is there anything that Sally can do to bring about such treatment? Since the case is written from Sally's perspective, we can only speculate about the answers to some of these questions. We are told the following about Cathy: (1) she prefers "Cathy" to her Vietnamese name; (2) she acts as a translator for the other Vietnamese students but she is becoming "increasingly resistant" to that role because it is keeping her "from being more readily accepted by the other high school students" and reminds them that she is different;

(3) she has begun to be excluded by the older Vietnamese students and is not accepted by the majority students; (4) she has made a couple of friends but is "definitely on the fringe"; and (5) she seems to have gotten herself in a place where she has "no community to call her own."

Is Cathy Tran experiencing prejudice and discrimination? Is she being denied basic respect and human dignity as a person? My guess is that Cathy Tran might answer these questions in different ways depending on when we talked with her, what her mood was, and how she viewed her struggle to become accepted as a minority person in a rather parochial small town where people had limited experience with "outsiders," particularly those from a very different culture. However, the surface appearance of things does not indicate that Cathy Tran is being violently harassed by other students, being insulted with regularity, or treated with contempt. She is simply not being welcomed with open arms into the dominant group. Such seems to be the case with many students who move to a new school in their junior or senior year, as students have already formed their friendship groups, and these are not easily broken into. How much an obstacle her ethnic background poses for her acceptance is difficult to determine. The fact that she made a couple of friends is a significant achievement to be noted, for it would seem to diminish the pain and suffering of being a total outsider in a new community. How dissatisfied Cathy is with not having more friends and receiving more acceptance is unclear, but the fact that the older Vietnamese students have excluded her appears "not to bother her too much." Her object of identification seems to be with the American culture.

What is also not discussed is any conflict Cathy Tran feels between her family culture and the culture of the school. Cathy's father, we are told, "was quite upset by his daughter's eagerness to be an 'American.'" Her father wants to hang on to and promote traditional Vietnamese values and his devout Buddhist religious practices. Cathy, like many other immigrant children, is caught living in two worlds with different value orientations and is probably struggling with how to maintain her filial respect for her parents and their traditions while still adapting to, or even embracing, some of the values of her new, American culture.

If Sally feels like intervening for Cathy's sake, it would make sense that she take Cathy's view of the world, and Cathy's feelings about herself and her situation, into account. Sally cannot appropriately care about Cathy *without understanding her*, and presumably Sally is interested in acting in ways that show she does care about Cathy. We are not told what kind of relationship they have and how much personal information they have shared, but Sally might be admonished not to keep pushing forward "in Cathy's best interest" without trying to find out how Cathy herself perceives her best interest.

What has just been said about Sally treating Cathy in a caring manner applies to her showing respect for Cathy. We can show respect for people in two ways: (1) by acknowledging their basic rights to be treated with dignity and not to be used or exploited by others; (2) by understanding and treating sympathetically their own projects, concerns, values, hopes, aspirations, and so on. The first kind of respect is respect for persons as generic persons with rights; the second kind of respect is idiosyncratic respect for persons as unique individuals in the world. Sally clearly has a duty to ensure that her students do not treat Cathy with disrespect in her classroom and at school, and she can achieve this, in part, by ensuring that her classroom is conducted in a respectful way. However, she can show respect for Cathy as an idiosyncratic individual only by coming to understand what Cathy values, hopes for, aspires to, wants to be seen as, and so forth. The next stage of Sally's intervention might be to create the trusting context in which Cathy feels comfortable sharing some things that are important to her.

It is also not clear to what degree Sally has trampled upon the cultural sensibilities of Dr. Tran. We are told that Dr. Tran is "not enthusiastic about Sally's plan to meld him and his people into the community." Clearly Sally's well-intentioned efforts were not seen as being respectful of what Dr. Tran wanted for his own family. The interactions between Sally and Dr. Tran have created some important issues, but it is unclear whether these issues can be resolved or even talked about with civility. The major issue is how the school's policies and practices can reveal a respectful attitude toward the culture of the Vietnamese families. This is not an issue that can be resolved without serious dialogue and an attitude of respectful accommodation. These attitudes do not exist at the present time. Whether Sally can promote the conditions for civil dialogue to occur is also unclear. And we should ask, "Who would be the relevant parties for such a dialogue?"

At the end of the case study we are asked to consider whether there is a proper balance of unity and diversity. We are told that "after all, everyone did seem to be tolerating everyone else." Does this represent a proper balance of unity and diversity? We can explain the problem in part by taking the two extremes. If there is only unity but no diversity, then everyone is forced or compelled to adopt the dominant cultural values of the majority or be rejected. Here we have "Americanization" at its worst, wherein a particular conception of what it means to be a "good American" is imposed on everyone, and no respect is shown for people with different values.

At the other extreme, we have diversity with no unity. Here we would celebrate all forms of cultural diversity equally, showing unqualified acceptance of all cultural value systems with no concern for seeking common values that would unite us as individuals in a community. This cultural relativism without a concern for unity would, at its extremes, be anarchic. The mosaic of American cultures might begin to unravel under this version of pluralism.

So what appears to be the case in Smithville? Smithville's condition will soon become an anomaly of history in most places in the world. Ninety-three out of every hundred children being born today are being born to Asians, Latinos, and Africans, or African Americans. In the world today, only whites have a declining birth rate. As Carlos Cortez puts it, whites in the United States are running out of space to keep "the others" out, and only head-in-the-sand attitudes toward the demographic changes in our world will prevent us from accepting the fact that our society, and all societies, will be darker and more multi-cultural.[3] Thus, a historical perspective indicates that Smithville's residents are atypical in one sense and typical in another. They are atypical in that they have maintained their very limited form of cultural homogeneity, but this cultural sameness will soon be much more rare. They are typical of many affinity groupings in that they do not want to let in outsiders. Thus, their response to the Vietnamese seems to be, "Americanize yourselves in our image or we will not accept you." The Vietnamese response seems to be, "Leave us alone and we won't bother you." This hardly seems to be an appropriate balance of unity and diversity.

The problem here surrounding the issue of finding a balance between unity and diversity is probably not a problem of "how should we act?" or "what is the proper moral thing to do here?" In my view, what is called for here essentially is not moral *action* but a change in moral *sensitivities* or *sensibilities*, a change from an "us versus them" mindset to something more inclusive and accommodating.[4] The question "Why should I be tolerant of people who do not share my values and life style?" is a question that people in the school and the town should be asking. Unfortunately, they are not asking it. Can we make people consider issues and problems that are alien to their existing moral sensibilities? Can we coerce them to consider what they would rather not consider? This is a troubling issue. Should people consider world hunger in communities where hunger is not an issue for them? Should they consider the world AIDS epidemic in towns where no one has ever had AIDS?

My own view is that they should. Smithville's residents cannot make the assumption that the Amish made in educating their own children, namely that their children would grow up in Amish communities, become Amish adults (swearing allegiance to Amish values), and never leave the Amish community, which prided itself on its separation from the larger secular society. Many of Smithville's children are going to leave the cultural homogeneity of their small community and enter the increasingly pluralistic culture of the larger society. So, facing the very complex issue of maintaining their own sense of cultural identity while tolerating and including others whose values are different is an educational necessity for the teachers and students of Smithville. The students need to face the realities and issues of a culturally pluralistic society if they are to learn to live sensitively in such a world. The alteration of moral sensibilities is part of what moral education of character requires.

Sally does not need to teach history in her math class to insist that the issue of balancing community with respect for diversity be considered seriously by her school staff and by all members of the school district she is in. This is not a battle she should be waging alone, but an issue that should be confronted by the whole educational community of which she is a part. Sally cannot single-handedly change the attitudes and beliefs of the Smithville residents or the Vietnamese families, but she might be able, with some help, to initiate a thoughtful dialogue among members of the educational community and/or the larger community. If that is her orientation, the problem shifts from "What can I do to intervene for Cathy Tran?" to "What can be done to promote genuine dialogue about developing an inclusive, tolerant community that is respectful of different cultural traditions while maintaining a sense of unity or collectivity?" Developing such a constructive dialogue seems to be a necessary precondition for changing the fundamental sensitivities that exist in the town and the school.

The responses of both the community and Dr. Tran to their new situations have been, it appears, acutely defensive; defensive adaptations of two groups to each other does not promote the kind of mutual respect and concern for the other's well being that should characterize a moral community. However, developing a larger sense of "moral community" where "the others" are not seen as "other" but as part of the group is not an easy task. Sally Johannsen has committed herself to the ideal of "community," but she does not appear well equipped to promote the kinds of cultural conditions that will allow new sensitivities to emerge among students, parents, and other members of the community. Her efforts, so far, have been well intentioned, but modestly successful. She needs to rethink what she is really trying to accomplish here. What kinds of conditions will be necessary to develop an appropriate balance of unity and diversity? However much Sally needs to rethink the basic problem here, one thing does seem clear. She cannot afford to stop with what she has done. She cannot afford merely to accept the status quo. Such a response would do serious violence to her own self-respect, to her ideal of community, to her efforts to establish a respectful, caring relationship with Cathy Tran, and to the educational needs of the students of Smithville, many of whom will emerge into a world very much unlike their present community.

Notes

1. The sense of "duty" imposed by self-defined ideals is not similar to the kind of duty imposed by laws or other moral standards. It is the duty imposed by the ethical ideal on oneself only and not something that can readily be extended to others. Thus, if one asked a very caring teacher why she felt that she must give extra help to all of her neediest students, she might answer, "I simply must do it to be true to myself." This caring conduct might be viewed as supererogatory conduct by others, that is, beyond the call of duty, but as dutiful conduct by the person holding the ideal.

2. Thomas E. Hill, Jr., "Self-Respect Reconsidered," in William H. Shaw, ed., *Social and Personal Ethics* (Belmont, CA: Wadsworth, 1993), p. 215.

3. Carlos Cortez, "Multiculturalism in the 21st Century," lecture given to the faculty in the College of Education, San Jose State University, December 9, 1994, Assilomar, California.

4. For an interesting discussion of why certain "sensitivities" are critical to ethical judgment, see Julius M. Moravcsik, "On What We Aim At and How We Live," in William Shaw, ed., *Social and Personal Ethics*, pp. 65–78.

Unity, Diversity, and Identity

BY EMILY ROBERTSON

I employed a couple of strategies in thinking about this case. First, discerning a good response to moral questions depends on knowing the particulars of the context: a helpful action in one situation might not be so in another, superficially similar, situation. Because the case study itself is limited in the details it can provide, I frequently found myself wanting to know more. As I cannot investigate this hypothetical community or interview Sally, Cathy, or Dr. Tran, I tried to supplement the case study by bringing other experiences to bear on it. I consulted my memories of growing up in a small town rather like Smithville. I took note of the reported experiences of the substantial Vietnamese community in the medium-sized metropolitan area where I currently live. I read interviews with Vietnamese students in our local, quite diverse, high school. And I drew on the experience of international students at my university. Secondly, I thought about the issues suggested by the chapter title, "Unity and Diversity." Here I drew upon ideas gleaned from the current debates on multiculturalism and diversity. And I asked myself whether this was indeed the best way to frame the moral issues in this situation.

Exploring the Context

The following are some of the elements I thought about in considering the context.

Smithville

The town is presented as a homogeneous community, where everyone shares the same values and looks out for each other. But recent discussions of diversity have led us to see differences among people presumed to be homogeneous. These observations are consistent with my own experiences growing up in a town similar to the one described. The "unity" experienced in such a place may not be entirely voluntary and community opinion can be hard on those who challenge the "consensus." Some people may hold different views but be reluctant to express them openly when they run contrary to the majority opinion. Thus, I'd like to know more about the people in the town. The Vietnamese are unlikely to be the only source of diversity, and their presence might seem less threatening to the presumed unity if the differences already present were more visible. Perhaps there are some whose own views, long kept under wraps, might be encouraged to blossom from the example of the Vietnamese.

Sally

In some ways, Sally is presented as someone made uncomfortable by diversity, having sought her current position in this town because it promised the unity and security she had experienced as a child. Apparently, she feels that the arrival of the Vietnamese families challenge this unity, and that is part of her motivation for wanting to encourage stronger relationships between the new arrivals and the locals. Several of the people I discussed this case with saw her as a "busybody" trying to enforce her conception of a good life on others. How open is she to having her own views challenged and altered by the experience of the newcomers? Is she really in a position to be leading others in this cross-cultural exchange? How reflective is she about her own role in this situation? For example, although she is said to miss the diversity and intellectual stimulation of her college days and to sometimes grow impatient with the narrow views of the townspeople, there's no suggestion that she's tried to act on these feelings during her six years in Smithville. To what extent are her own needs framing the moral situation through her projection of these needs on others?

Cathy

Since Cathy is Sally's most immediate concern, I would particularly like to know more about their relationship and about Cathy herself. Cathy is presented as wanting to fit in and as trying to downplay her own culture and language in order to do so, even changing her name to an "American" one. Some of the Vietnamese students in our local school report more complicated attitudes toward their situation. Recently, the student newspaper included an interview with Anh Ly, a sophomore, who feels a responsibility based in Vietnamese tradition to set the example for her younger brothers and sisters. She reports that she finds this a hard job and that she is confused, but that she is trying her best to be a good sister and daughter. She also expresses gratitude for being in the United States, for the freedom she has experienced here, and for the help she has received from fellow students and teachers. Anh Ly appears to be trying to honor Vietnamese traditions while also appreciating and becoming part of her new environment. Cathy, too, has to reconstruct her identity in her new situation and seems to be feeling caught between two worlds. Unlike Anh Ly, Cathy appears to feel that she must reject one in order to enter the other. How helpful Sally can be to Cathy depends on the depth of their relationship and the opportunities Sally has to support Cathy, as well as on Sally's ability to help Cathy consider the range of choices she confronts in defining herself.

Framing the Moral Questions

What are the ethical issues in this case? Is unity and diversity really what is at issue here? My local high school is quite diverse, yet the Vietnamese students there experience many of the same issues that emerged in Smithville: language (they are there because our high school has the city's only English as a Second Language program); differences in cultural attitudes toward school (in general, they work very hard and find it difficult to understand the less-engaged attitudes of other students); helping others in their families and community (those who have expressed a view take it as their responsibility to do well and help others do well). This suggests that the alleged prior unity of Smithville may not play a central role in the problems the Vietnamese face. (There is a difference for their parents: in a city of the size and diversity of the one I live in, the adults are under no pressure to participate in the community, nor are they under special observation or scrutiny.)

The Vietnamese adults are described as not "overly anxious to interact" with the townspeople. Dr. Tran is not interested in being "melded" into the community. He does not want his daughter to become a cultural American. The Vietnamese, too, are interested in unity, that of their own cultural group. They want their children to remain Buddhist. They cannot be expected to attend Christmas programs in order to become part of the community, Sally's goal for them. The Vietnamese students are said by and large to want to remain a separate group. Neither are the townspeople anxious to increase their interaction with the Vietnamese families. Each group seems willing to maintain civic decency, to be cordial and courteous, to live and let live. (From an American perspective, it seems remarkable that the Vietnamese do not wish to take legal action concerning the Christmas program.) Nevertheless, no one seems interested in closer relationships except Sally. She is said to want to help students from the town value the diversity the Vietnamese have brought to the community, but this goal seems almost inconsistent with her previous motivations and stance. No one seems to be a clear advocate of diversity.

Sally's brand of unity, becoming one community in a robust sense, may not be an appropriate goal here. Yet Sally is right that having some sense of an appropriate outcome is important, since that helps determine what actions it would be best to take. Ideally, what would be the most desirable relationship between the Vietnamese community and the other residents of Smithville? From the perspective of multiculturalist movements, the end to be avoided for the Vietnamese is forced assimilation, the cultural hegemony of the majority, the marginalization and oppression of the Vietnamese minority, treatment of them that shows disrespect. From another perspective, there is an issue of the moral obligations of voluntary immigrant groups to the country of immigration. What can the townspeople rightly expect of the Vietnamese as citizens of the community? And what are their obligations to these new immigrants as part of a country that has seen itself as a nation of immigrants? And what about Cathy? What role should others such as Sally play in Cathy's struggle to develop her own identity? And how should we frame the relationship between Cathy's efforts to define herself and the Vietnamese community's desire for collective self-definition?

Conclusion

I believe that in a multicultural, democratic society such as the United States, immigrant groups can be expected to enter the political culture, for example, to support constitutional principles and the democratic process itself. But they should not be required to abandon their cultural form of life, unless it is incompatible with their political socialization. Individual immigrants and their descendants have the right to appropriate their cultural heritage without suffering discrimination because of it. Thus, both ethnic groups and individuals claiming an ethnic identity have rights to respect and nondiscrimination. The main issue in this case study, I believe, is increasing the inclusiveness of the school and community to avoid marginal status for the Vietnamese without expecting cultural assimilation from them as the price of their inclusion.

The Vietnamese of Smithville wish to survive as a cultural group (at least, some of them do). No one can *ensure* the success of this project: a culture has to make its case to each generation. Cultures survive by shaping the characteristic forms of thought, feeling, and action of their members. At some level, the assent of individuals is required and cannot be compelled. Later generations have the option of following a different path. And typically, the cultures that survive in changed circumstances do so only by self-transformation.[1] But the school and the town can make survival more or less possible through the alternatives they provide and by their attitudes. Acknowledging the Buddhist religious traditions of the Vietnamese in the public events and rituals of the town and school, for example, allows the Vietnamese to participate in the life of the community while retaining their religious perspective.

Individual Vietnamese such as Cathy must construct their unique individual identities from the resources at hand. Vietnamese traditions, the cultural expectations of their communities of immigration, and majority group stereotypes of what the Vietnamese are like compete as partial "scripts" for their lives.[2] Multiculturalists hold that it is oppressive to require minorities to *deny* their ethnicity in defining themselves, as that is part of who they are. However, it also can be oppressive to require that their ethnicity be central to their own self-definitions. Collective definitions of what it is like to be "authentically" Vietnamese, produced by immigrant groups resisting cultural assimilation, also can restrict an individual's choices. Cathy should have the right to affirm her Vietnamese identity without suffering discrimination, but she should also have the opportunity to confront aspects of Vietnamese traditions and break with them, if she chooses. Anything else would place unwarranted constraints on her autonomy. Making such choices is not, of course, a simple matter. Since one's culture partially constitutes one's identity unconsciously through the process of socialization, to confront aspects of it is simultaneously to confront aspects of one's self. And while the potential to define one's self should be respected in all, no one creates themselves de novo; selves are developed through interaction with the significant others around us.

What should Sally do? First, she should reflect on her own motivations and perspective. She should consider whether her own experiences and predilections are distorting her moral perception in this case. In particular, she should not assume a responsibility to forge a new unity, with the same homogeneity and common values that she believes previously existed. Such a unity cannot be forced or orchestrated by a single individual, and, in any event, is probably not the appropriate goal here, or so I've argued. Sally should work toward mutual respect and sensitivity, drawing on the civility that currently exists.

Sally is right to see her role as working with the other students as well as the Vietnamese students. The school has made some efforts to become more inclusive through teaching units on Vietnamese geography and history. The spirit in which these curriculum changes are made matter, as well as the changes themselves. They should be viewed not simply as concessions to the Vietnamese, but as recognition of their new citizenship: American history now includes them. She would be right to work on making the changes Dr. Tran suggested—school programs that all can attend without offense to their religion, appropriate food in the cafeteria, and so on. In trying to bring about these changes as well as other appropriate ones, Sally should seek out other teachers, students, and members of the community who might be interested in becoming more inclusive.

Sally's role in helping Cathy develop her own identity can only be a rather modest one, in my view. She can offer Cathy a friendly ear, if Cathy chooses to confide in her, but the choice of how Cathy positions herself with respect to her Vietnamese heritage and the American culture she has entered is not Sally's to make. These actions aim at more modest changes than Sally wants, although they go further than either Dr. Tran or other citizens of Smithville presently desire, but they have the virtue of giving others the space to define themselves, both collectively and individually.

Notes

1. For further discussion of this point, see Jurgen Habermas, "Struggles for Recognition in the Democratic State," in Amy Gutmann, ed., *Multiculturalism: Examining the Politics of Recognition* (Princeton: Princeton University Press, 1994), pp. 128–35.

2. K. Anthony Appiah, "Identity, Authenticity, Survival: Multicultural Societies and Social Reproduction," in Gutmann, *Multiculturalism,* pp. 159–60.

Further Reflections on "Unity and Diversity"

Unity and Diversity: A Response to Emily Robertson

BY MICHAEL S. KATZ

To extend my commentary on the ethical issues raised in the case study, I shall comment upon several important points raised in Professor Emily Robertson's thoughtful interpretation. In this regard, I shall focus on three particularly important issues raised by Dr. Robertson: (1) whether the approach of Sally Johannsen is actually, or potentially, misguided in her effort to create a sense of "unity" in the community; (2) what is at stake in showing respect to the Vietnamese both collectively and individually; (3) what is involved in an individual's effort to define her own cultural identity, especially when caught between the cultural world of her parents and the world of the larger society.

Several excellent preliminary points made by Dr. Robertson bear noting before I discuss the three issues I mention above: (1) a case study does exclude much interesting contextual detail, and it would be helpful to know more to make an adequate interpretation of what is given; (2) there may be a good deal more "diversity" (or at least "heterogeneity") behind the surface appearance of unity and homogeneity in this small town; indeed, as Dr. Robertson correctly notes, the surface appearance of unity and homogeneity may be quite misleading; (3) consulting one's own experience in these matters can yield important insights, and Dr. Robertson has illustrated the value of doing so in her essay.

The first issue I would like to discuss is whether Sally Johannsen is actually or potentially misguided in her efforts to create a sense of "unity" in the community. Dr. Robertson notes that several people with whom she discussed the case saw Sally as a "busybody" who was "trying to enforce her conception of a good life on others." Dr. Robertson also questions, perhaps correctly, whether Sally can really lead others in this cross-cultural exchange. She also questions how "reflective" Sally is about "her own role in this situation." She asks "to what extent are her own needs framing the moral situation through her projection of these needs on others?" Since I had expressed much sympathy with Sally's effort to be true to her own ideal of community and to how this ideal was central to her self-respect, I found Dr. Robertson's questions appropriately unsettling but critically important. In my own essay, I indicated that Sally "cannot single-handedly change the attitudes and beliefs of the Smithville residents or the Vietnamese families, but she might be able, with some help, to initiate a thoughtful dialogue among members of the educational community and/or the larger community." What Sally should or should not do, of course, does depend mightily on the nature of her ethical motivations, the clarity and value of her vision, and her sense of her limitations.

Dr. Robertson raises the real possibility that Sally is self-deceived about her motivations: Sally sees herself as acting altruistically to help others respectfully accommodate conflicting value systems, but she may be acting selfishly to satisfy her own needs to live in a community in which there are no value conflicts and minimal tensions between different cultural groups. As Albert Camus reminded us in his wonderful novel *The Fall*, self-deception is like the dawn; its possibility is with us every day. What Dr. Robertson's essay has made me see is that my sympathy for Sally Johannsen's motives may be unwarranted, especially if I have read them inappropriately.

However, even if Sally's motives are appropriate, Dr. Robertson raises an important point about her vision. Is it appropriate to try to develop a sense of unity in the larger community? Dr. Robertson writes: "Sally's brand of unity, becoming one community in a robust sense, may not be an appropriate goal here." This seems to me to be a telling objection, if correct, to Sally's entire project. However, we need to be clear about the kind of unity Sally is seeking and how we can assess it. Is it the kind of unity that does not allow two different cultural groups the opportunity to preserve and sustain their own distinctive cultural identities? If so, it is a wrongheaded kind of "unity." We are told that Sally values "the sense of unity and security she felt in a community of people who cared for common values and for each other." This statement may mean that Sally is not comfortable with a community in which different cultural groups choose to value different things and choose to maintain different cultural traditions. However, we can ask whether Sally actually envisions an enlarged sense of "unity with diversity" wherein the community acknowledges its multicultural nature and respects the rights of individuals to pursue, both individually and collectively, their own versions of happiness. This enlarged sense of community might require a broadened tolerance of the townspeople toward the Vietnamese and a sense that people who are different deserve to be included, respected, and not discriminated against. Nevertheless, the question remains: What kind of "unity" is Sally seeking and is it ethically desirable? As Dr. Robertson points out, it is not culturally or ethically desirable to purchase unity at the cost of forced assimilation and a denial of one's ethnicity or cultural heritage. Thus, we are reminded of Sally's doubts at the end of the case study: "She wasn't sure on what grounds she might build unity. She wasn't even sure she should try. Perhaps there now existed a proper balance of unity and diversity."

My own guess is that these doubts are the right kind of doubts. It is not clear what kind of "unity" is possible or desirable here. Moreover, it is not clear whether one individual should try to build it. This is an issue that needs further discussion. Yet it does seem to me that one central value underlies any sensible version of "unity" in a liberal democracy: the right of all individuals to equal liberty and respect as human beings who are valuable in themselves independently of their beliefs or achievements or ethnic identity. Implicit in this right to equal liberty is the opportunity to pursue one's own conception of the good life. However, the universal right to equal liberty and respect is not the focus of the cultural conflict here, for the case study presents a condition in which two incompatible cultural traditions are seeking to perpetuate themselves. In this context it is not clear whether it makes good sense to talk of an enlarged cultural community that can readily accommodate both cultural traditions. It is in that sense that Dr. Robertson very wisely questions Sally's pursuit of "unity." Moreover, it is in that sense that this essay poses the problem of "unity" for all who are considering what would be an "appropriate balance of unity and diversity" in American culture.

A second issue that Dr. Robertson's insightful interpretation raises is the following: What is at stake in showing respect for the Vietnamese individually and collectively? First, what is at stake in showing any cultural group collective respect? Dr. Robertson makes many helpful points about this in her concluding section. She says that immigrant groups "should not be required to abandon their cultural form of life unless it is incompatible with their political socialization" (the meaning and justification of the qualification might require some explanation). Moreover, she states that "individual immigrants have a right to their appropriate cultural heritage without suffering discrimination because of it." Thus, she argues that ethnic groups (and individuals within them) have "rights to respect and nondiscrimination." Later she suggests that "the school and the town can make survival more or less possible through the alternatives they provide and by their attitudes." She offers as an example of cultural respect "acknowledging the Buddhist religious traditions of the Vietnamese in the public events and rituals of the town and school."

These comments are richly suggestive and valuable. Yet there is much to be discussed here. How far must the larger cultural group go to accommodate a subculture's desire for self-preservation? How much acknowledgment or recognition of the subculture is warranted in public events? In the school curriculum? Is noninterference sufficient in some cases or must the public do more? These are complex issues, and they are made more complicated when one considers communities in which many subcultural groups coexist side by side. How much recognition in the curriculum can be shown to a wide range of different cultural groups all present in one school? How will teachers overcome their limited knowledge of the various subcultures and their traditions? However we answer these questions, we should note that the failure to do anything to acknowledge a cultural group's distinctive heritage within the school curriculum and/or within the larger cultural community may be interpreted as a sign of "disrespect" even when no such disrespect was intended.[1] Thus, it does seem appropriate that Sally and other teachers have given lessons on Vietnamese geography and history. It also seems appropriate that Dr. Tran would like to see the school accommodate his culture's religious traditions in the holiday season and would like to see Vietnamese food in the school cafeteria. Such accommodation would acknowledge the legitimacy of the Vietnamese culture, even if only in a minimal way.

For some multiculturalists, respect can only be shown by celebrating the other cultures' traditions and contributions. However, there is a range of legitimate options between celebrating a culture and ignoring it. The Smithville community, in my view, needs to travel some distance toward acknowledging the legitimacy of the Vietnamese culture; and in regard to that, Sally's initial steps at the school have not been unhelpful. What remains open to question is how much the Smithville community must do to show respect for the Vietnamese culture, either in school or in its larger cultural milieu. Tolerance is certainly one form of respect. For some it may not be enough, but this case study suggests that the Vietnamese are not asking for too much more. However, they are asking for something.

As for showing an individual respect, I think Dr. Robertson and I share similar views. As I stated in my first essay, respect has two versions: (1) respect for a person as a bearer of generic rights (including the right not to be discriminated against, used, or exploited for others' purposes) and (2) idiosyncratic respect for a person as a distinctive individual with his or her own goals, values, hopes, aspirations, and so on. Dr. Robertson and I would agree that Cathy Tran can be best shown respect if she is allowed the opportunity to define her own cultural identity for herself.

Therefore, let me comment briefly on my final issue: What is at stake in an individual's effort to define her own cultural identity, especially when she is caught between the cultural world of her parents and that of the larger society? Dr. Robertson appropriately suggests that Cathy "should have the right to affirm her Vietnamese identity without suffering discrimination, but she should also have the opportunity to confront aspects of Vietnamese traditions and break with them." She is also quite right in suggesting that individuals do not create themselves de novo; "selves are developed through interaction with the significant others around us." All individuals are psycho-cultural beings, influenced by their early cultural upbringing but free to make sense of their experiences in their own way. Education, both formal and informal, should include the opportunity to grow in self-knowledge through reflection upon one's past and upon the values that make the most sense to one. Cathy's struggle with her identity, like that of other immigrant children, is one that may leave her feeling conflicted, unsure, and confused at times. Nevertheless, as Dr. Robertson wisely points out, it is a struggle that Cathy must undergo on her own terms. She must figure out how to be the person she chooses to become, but this pursuit of her own identity is one that can be aided by caring, thoughtful, and sensitive friends and teachers. Sally Johannsen can help, but only by respecting Cathy's privacy and only through establishing a trusting relationship with her that shows both caring and respect. Because Cathy must decide what she can reveal in her relationship with Sally, Dr. Robertson sums up Sally's proper role well: "She can offer Cathy a friendly ear, if Cathy chooses to confide in her, but the choice of how Cathy positions herself with respect to her Vietnamese heritage and the American culture she has entered is not Sally's to make." Amen. Another thing. If Sally really cares for Cathy, she can let her know that if Cathy ever needs someone to "be there for her," Sally will be that person. It will be Cathy's decision to accept or reject such an offer.

Notes

1. See Charles Taylor, "The Politics of Recognition," in Amy Gutmann, ed., *Multiculturalism: Examining the Politics of Recognition* (Princeton: Princeton University Press, 1994), pp. 25–73. Taylor's essay expands on this important point.

Response to Michael Katz: Community and Autonomy

BY EMILY ROBERTSON

On reading Michael Katz's analysis of our common case, I was struck by the many areas of agreement between us. We share a similar perspective on Cathy's situation as, in Katz's words, "caught between two worlds with different value orientations." We agree that Sally should not continue to try to act in what she sees as Cathy's best interest without finding out what Cathy herself wants. We each believe that achieving community is not a project that Sally can undertake alone. Both of us hold that neither unity without diversity nor the converse are appropriate solutions for Smithville (or elsewhere) and that Smithville does not now have the appropriate balance of unity and diversity. Finally, we agree that Sally needs to rethink her framing of the problem.

We do, however, approach the problem from somewhat different perspectives. For example, I say that Sally may be "framing the moral situation through her projection of [her own] needs on others." I enjoin her to show more respect for the rights of Cathy and Cathy's community to define themselves and their own needs. Katz, on the other hand, says that Sally's self-respect may depend on her trying to enact her personal ideal of community. He says that "to maintain her own self-respect she must do everything she can to translate this ideal into reality for herself and her students." However, Katz also holds that Sally (and everyone else) should respect others' projects as unique individuals in the world. It's this latter point that I've emphasized and extended to groups as well as individuals. Since Sally's personal ideal of community requires the cooperation of others, whose projects and ideals may be different from hers, Sally, I argued, should resist attempting to enact her project whatever the attitudes and wishes of others.

Noting this difference led me to reflect on the role of personal moral ideals in making moral judgments. I think of personal moral ideals as standards one holds for oneself without expecting others to adhere to them. For example, I learned punctuality from my father, a railroad worker for whom it was a professional norm. I strive to be punctual even in contexts where I fully realize that being "on time" means I'll be the first one there. I don't blame others for behaving differently; they know they'll wind up wasting five or ten minutes waiting for others to arrive, so why be on time? Yet I am my father's daughter, and I show up at the appointed hour.

Sally's ideal of community is not like my commitment to punctuality, because enacting her ideal requires the cooperation of others. Sally can be successful only if she persuades others to share her ideal. In an important sense, community is a social, not merely personal, ideal. While Sally's self-respect may require her to make the *attempt* to achieve community, surely it cannot turn on the *success* of that attempt. And respect for the autonomy of others places constraints on the methods Sally can choose for translating her ideal into realty. I do not think she "must do everything she can" to actualize her ideal without the qualification that her actions must be consistent with the self-determination of others, with respect for their projects as well as her own.

Furthermore, while Katz focused predominantly on Sally's problem, I placed the situation of Cathy and the Vietnamese community at the center of my deliberations. I argued that we can evaluate Sally's goals only in light of some conception of the right of Cathy to construct her own identity and the right of the Vietnamese community to seek its own survival as a cultural group. Also, I argued, we must consider the obligations of immigrants to the country of immigration and the reciprocal obligations of that country to them. Only then can we determine what Sally may legitimately do in seeking community.

Mary Catherine Bateson expresses a view similar to the one I took with respect to the situation of Cathy and the Vietnamese community. Commenting on her observations of American women living in Iran as wives of Iranian men, she writes:

> *It is not sufficient to reject one tradition and embrace another—this is the convert's danger, involving an oversimplification of both. It is also not sufficient to camp out in a new tradition without commitment, taking refuge in relativism to avoid responsibility and using distance to avoid the need to criticize the culture one comes from.*[1]

Cathy appears to be trying to convert, while the adults in the Vietnamese community may be hoping to camp out. My point was that in the long run neither is likely to be a good solution.

I gave greater weight to the obligation to allow others to be self-determining than to the good of community. There is, however, a tension between respect for the autonomy of children and the need for adults to help children develop their identities. The education of children cannot proceed without the transmission of cultural values; they cannot be left to decide entirely for themselves what their fundamental commitments will be. The development of individual identity requires primary socialization in cultural communities. As K. Anthony Appiah notes, there is a "deep problem" here about "how respect for autonomy should constrain our ethics of education":

> *We have to help children make themselves, and we have to do so according to our values because children do not begin with values of their own. To value autonomy is to respect the conceptions of others, to weigh their plans for themselves very heavily in deciding what is good for them, even though children do not start out with plans or conceptions.*[2]

Thus Cathy's emerging conception of herself should be respected, although both her Vietnamese community and the American culture of Smithville will rightly play a role in shaping her commitments. In my view, respect for Cathy's autonomy places constraints not only on Sally's actions, but also on the Vietnamese community's efforts to perpetuate themselves through her. But the Vietnamese community (and the other residents of Smithville) are entitled to respect for their plans and projects as well. Showing proper respect for them requires proper recognition of their cultural identities in public life, including public schools. I have argued that changes need to be made within the school in order to show proper respect for all. But whether Smithville will develop a rich and robust common community through the interactions of all citizens over time is not for Sally, or any individual, to determine.

Notes

1. Mary Catherine Bateson, *Composing a Life* (New York: Plume, 1990), p. 66.
2. K. Anthony Appiah, "Identity, Authenticity, Survival: Multicultural Societies and Social Reproduction," in Amy Gutmann, ed., *Multiculturalism: Examining the Politics of Recognition* (Princeton: Princeton University Press, 1994), p. 158.

Discussion

Michael Katz and Emily Robertson agree with Sally Johannsen that something needs to be done about the situation in Smithville—right now there is not a proper balance of unity and diversity. Yet they also have doubts about Sally's aims and actions up to this point. Their concerns have several sources. They question Sally's motives: Is she merely interested in her own comfort? They ask whether she really knows enough about the situation: Has she really listened to Cathy, for instance, or is this simply a personal crusade? Does Sally have a right to push people toward an idea of a good community in the first place, or is she just being a "busybody"? Finally, Robertson and Katz wonder about the quality of Sally's vision for unity and diversity.

Perhaps we should think more about these issues. In light of our discussion of self-interest and integrity in Chapter 3, why *shouldn't* Sally be concerned for her own comfort and personal commitments? A possibility neither Katz nor Robertson explore is that Sally leave Smithville. Similar to Lucy in the "Self and Others" case, leaving Smithville may not be the ideal option for Sally, yet if her commitment to her vision is strong enough, maybe leaving Smithville and sticking to her ideal is preferable to staying and compromising (if indeed it is compromise that is actually called for). Or, supposing for the sake of argument that Sally is motivated by caring, should we fault her for not knowing more about Cathy? Must she justify her caring? Besides, how decisive are Cathy's views? Just as Sally might be self-deceived, couldn't Cathy be self-deceived as to her own true desires and needs? Regarding the busybody charge, perhaps there is the danger of paternalism here, but I'm reminded of the reply Marley's ghost gave to Ebeneezer Scrooge when Scrooge tried to console him about attending to "business" during his life—"Mankind was my business!"

How much of a "hands-off" attitude should people take when they honestly believe other people are mistaken?

While these are all good, tough issues I am not going to pursue them further here. In this discussion I will concentrate on the question of what sort of balance of unity and diversity is desirable in Smithville. While passing judgment on Sally's conception of community will not tell us what she should do—even if her vision is the right one, for one reason or another it might not be proper or wise for her to pursue it—certainly it is a central issue for Sally (and all educators nowadays). Few issues prompt as much controversy today as do issues of unity and diversity.

To get at the issues I will start off by considering what a communitarian might say about the case. I think it's fair to characterize Katz and Robertson as liberals, and so a communitarian critique might help us think about the significance of their views on unity and diversity and what problems their views present. But there is also dispute within liberalism as to the proper balance of unity and diversity, and I'll present a liberal view that challenges some of Katz's and Robertson's claims. Finally, I'll say a bit about the ideas of pluralism and relativism that come up in this chapter. They are helpful for thinking about the issues of truth and human relationships with which we have been wrestling.

A Communitarian View

Neither Robertson nor Katz is much impressed with Sally's vision of a "close-knit community" based on "caring for common values." A communitarian, however, would be rather more sympathetic to Sally's aim of "robust" community. Recall that communitarians desire communities that share "thick" ethical values. For one thing, these values provide a firmer basis for interpersonal solidarity than the "thin" liberal concerns for freedom, respect, rights, and so on. One can respect the rights of others without having much regard for the people themselves, and focusing on one's rights can actually fragment communities by putting people in competition. Often, if not typically, people appeal to rights in an effort to advance their claims against those of other people. In contrast, some communitarians endorse "decency," which involves willingness to refrain from asserting one's rights for the sake of community coherence.[1] So, for instance, if it seems strange that the Vietnamese do not sue over the school's religious Christmas program, a communitarian might attribute that to our all-too-frequent inclination to assert rights rather than do what is good for the community. Does civic decency exist in Smithville? In one place Robertson suggests it does, but communitarians are after more than the "live-and-let-live" attitude she identifies with decency. Even if the Vietnamese are not suing, it is not clear that they refrain because of regard for the community, and it is not clear that decency reigns in the wider community.

Furthermore, people's rights can be scrupulously protected yet not result in much benefit for those people. People's rights to vote can be protected while they still are allowed to live in poverty. Communitarians argue that we need a thicker shared idea of what is good for people if we are to adequately judge their well-being and what we as a society should be doing about it—what are people able to do as a result of their rights, and are these good things? It may be that the Vietnamese are not being exploited or insulted. But are they adequately able to move about, enjoy recreational activities, have social interactions?[2]

Critics of communitarianism often claim that it threatens group and individual freedom and diversity because it stresses "common values." This criticism may have particular weight in our case as differences in values seem so obvious and important. But just because cultures differ on some values does not mean they cannot share some. For instance, Martha Nussbaum claims the "functional capabilities" I identified above are human capacities all people have and which need to be exercised if any life is to be a good, full one. (Can you think of other candidates for universal values?) She describes these values as "thick but vague," suggesting that there still is proper room for particular cultural groups and individuals to determine their own ways of making use of those capacities. Thus, they do not pose an unreasonable threat to freedom and diversity. Of course, communitarians have another reply: What is the point of freedom and diversity if nothing good comes of it? Communitarians might want to protect Cathy's freedom to the extent of agreeing with Katz and Robertson that Sally must not be too quick to foist her ideas of community on Cathy or that Cathy should not be confined to the Vietnamese community against her will. Yet they might be concerned that Robertson and Katz go too far to stress Cathy's self-determination. If Cathy is to have a full and meaningful life she needs to be guided by the thick values that can only be had through close identification with a particular community. If she is encouraged to make her own way will she lose her identification with her Vietnamese heritage? Will she ever be able to really identify with the majority community? (Recall Pendlebury's discussion.)

To sum up, communitarians might share some of the concerns Katz and Robertson have about our case. They certainly would be concerned about the integrity of Cathy Tran and the groups in Smithville and so want to know more about the particulars of Sally's vision of community. They might also question whether schools are a good place for forging community, and so question Sally on that basis. Still, they do pose some basic challenges for us to think about. First, they suggest that the state has an interest and obligation to guide its policies by particular conceptions of what is good (even if these are vague). So, at least in principle, Sally, as a public school teacher, did not err in advocating a conception of a good community (although there still are questions about her conception and how she went about advocating it). Second, while communitarians might endorse the change in moral sensibilities Katz calls for, just what those sensibilities should be, what the basis of community unity should be, is another matter. And last, Katz and Robertson may place too much emphasis on Cathy Tran's self-determination. While they clearly assert the importance of the Vietnamese community in Cathy's ethical life, a communitarian might say they do not go far enough. (What do you think about these communitarian claims?)

The Liberal View

I have characterized Katz and Robertson as liberals based on such things as their concern for Cathy's autonomy and, as Katz puts it, the liberty "to pursue one's own conception of the good life." These are standard liberal concerns. Yet within liberalism there are different views on these, which involve differing views on diversity and unity.

A basic liberal concern is that the coercive power of the state (as exerted through laws and regulations regarding schooling, for instance) should not be used to advance or hinder particular conceptions of a good life. But clearly Robertson and Katz want to put some ethical constraints on what Sally and the Smithville community can do, and they even are willing to use state coercion to get people to consider changing their "moral sensibilities." This appears to be a contradiction (assuming I'm right in identifying them as liberals). What's going on?

Here is where liberals sometimes appeal to a distinction between morality and ethics or right and good. The idea is that while people may differ in their notions of what is good (that is, their "ethics"), these are different from what is moral or right, which is binding on everyone. We should not put too much emphasis on the terms "ethical" and "moral." Robertson's distinction between "personal moral ideals" and other moral values gets at the same point. The important thing is not the terms used but the idea that some things can rightfully be required of people whereas others cannot. Thus, we might stress "respect" as Katz does, arguing that this is a moral duty all people have to everyone else, regardless of their more particular ethical ways of life. (Although, according to Katz, there is a sense in which we need to respect the latter too.) By securing respect and rights, we provide the conditions in which people can pursue their own personal ideals of a good life. Of course, communitarians say this is not enough. To some extent, a liberal might agree. Some argue that a positive regard for people is also needed. (We'll get to this below). Still, rights are basic. A modern, diverse society cannot rely on fellow-feeling. Even if we want to be "decent" we also want a scheme of basic rights to protect us when people aren't willing to be decent.

In any event, liberals claim that state agencies such as public schools are not in the business of shaping students' conceptions of a good life even though they may have a role in supporting morality. But, so the argument continues, morality does not hinder or support any particular conception of the good life. Again, the aim is to secure the freedom, respect, rights, and so on that allow for that pursuit.

But does this really represent no particular ethical viewpoint? Noddings and Laird might say it represents an ethic of duty, which is a particular ethical view. There are two broad liberal responses to this sort of criticism. One is to concede something to the charge of particularity yet maintain that that is all right because it is a proper ethical view. This sort of perspective has been called *comprehensive* liberalism to reflect the claim that liberal values have a comprehensive place in human life. (Kant is sometimes associated with this sort of liberal view.) On this view, teachers still should not dictate what is good. They should engage students in thinking critically about what is good, though, for freedom of thought is important for everyone everywhere. (This is a theme you will see in the essays in Chapter 7.) So, a comprehensive liberal might take exception when Robertson says that "Sally's role in helping Cathy develop her own identity is a rather modest one." Yes, Sally should not impose a conception of identity upon Cathy. Yet teachers can have (at least in principle) a significant and legitimate role in helping students actively and critically examine differing conceptions of a good life for the sake of making intelligent choices for a fulfilling life.

Other liberals, on the other hand, give more credence to the charge of ethical particularity in liberal values. So they look for a nonethical basis for those values. For example, they might look for instrumental reasons for teaching them. Katz hints at something like this when he argues that Smithville youngsters need to be more sensitive if they are going to "live in the real world." (There may be truth in this, but, considering Sandel's comments about an "instrumental community" from Chapter 4, how much should we rely on this kind of argument?)

Another major liberal view that seeks a nonparticularistic basis for unity, but one that is not simply instrumental, is *political liberalism.* Unlike comprehensive liberalism, which asserts that liberal values are appropriate to *all* areas of life, political liberalism asserts simply that liberal values are justified and applicable in the *political* realm. In answer to the charge of ethical particularity, a political liberal does not argue that liberal values are ethically superior; however, they are *politically* superior. For example, it could be argued that in the public political realm an ethic of duty is a better stance than an ethic of care—impartiality, rights, and so on have legitimate priority there—without arguing the particular ethical view that an ethic of duty is better, period. Caring might still be better for nonpublic, private matters, say. This answer might be challenged. Feminist ethical theory often takes issue with this appeal to a public-private split. It is seen as ignoring the political significance of what goes on "in the home," for example, relationships between husbands and wives. Those relationships are public business, involving issues of social justice. Political liberals could agree, at least to some degree. Their key point is that if caring or other perspectives are appropriate to the public realm, they must be justified on political grounds.

Although it is difficult to say exactly where Robertson and Katz might be placed in this scheme of liberal positions, we see some hint of a political liberal's argument in Robertson's point about immigrants entering the "political culture." If we can show that certain ethical values and dispositions such as respect or caring are requirements of liberal democratic citizenship, then teachers are justified in challenging the "existing moral sensibilities" to which Katz refers, even if some people may not like it. (Thus, we might still talk of morality or ethics here, although it is a "political" morality and not a "comprehensive" morality.)

This assertion, however, raises another point of contention: What are the requirements of liberal democratic citizenship? Even if we agree that teaching liberal democratic political values is appropriate, there are differing conceptions of what these values are, and, of special interest to us here, differences regarding how much diversity is permissible or desirable in a democracy. Communitarians would have their views on this issue, but rather than pursue that angle, I'll look at a further debate *within* political liberalism.

I mentioned above how liberals value autonomy. Commonly, liberals stress the need for personal and group self-determination, not only for individual well-being, but for democratic purposes. If a democracy is to work, people need to be able to make up their own minds about things, to use good judgment about what is in their and their society's best interest, rather than simply follow the crowd or charismatic leaders. From this point of view, it's pretty clear that teachers have a right and obligation to challenge people's moral sensibilities.

However, William Galston questions the idea that autonomy must be a liberal value, and in so doing wants to give more weight to diversity than other advocates of liberalism.[3] He is not against unity, but he does challenge a liberal unity built upon autonomy. He suggests a contrast between two sorts of liberalism that I'll call *diversity liberalism* (Galston's preferred sort) and *autonomy liberalism*. Because Katz and Robertson can be seen as leaning toward autonomy liberalism (perhaps not to the same extent), taking some time with Galston's argument might help us think about their claims.

First, what does this liberal dispute imply for our relationship to groups such as those in our case? Galston agrees that "[t]he liberal state has a legitimate and compelling interest in ensuring that the convictions, competencies, and virtues required for liberal citizenship are widely shared."[4] Therefore he can agree that schools are justified in having people "consider alien issues and problems" if they lack the proper convictions, competencies, and virtues. But what are the proper convictions, competencies, and virtues? For Galston, a central virtue is *tolerance*. Now tolerance is another standard liberal idea; Katz stresses it. But what does it mean? Galston says that the tolerance needed "is the refusal to use state power to impose one's own way of life on others."[5] This sort of political tolerance of diversity does not require or justify that schools foster students' skepticism of their own ways of life. They do not need to question their own way of life; they simply must not impose it on others. However, this sort of skepticism might be just what Robertson wants, as shown in her criticism of people "camping out" in another culture without being critical of their own. Galston takes exception with autonomy liberalism because it aims to generate this sort of skepticism and in doing so advances a particular ethical stance—one that emphasizes autonomy—and thus, ultimately, is hostile to diversity.

Autonomy liberals might counter, however, that there are certain forms of diversity toward which liberal democrats *should* be hostile. In their eyes, Galston's toleration is not strong enough. Amy Gutmann argues that "mutual respect" is needed for democratic citizenship, over and above tolerance.[6] (At least over and above Galston's sort of tolerance. Katz links his notion of tolerance to respect. Would even his idea of tolerance be strong enough from Gutmann's point of view?) By "mutual respect" Gutmann means "a reciprocal positive regard among citizens who pursue ways of life that are consistent with honoring the basic liberties and opportunities of others."[7] Toleration does not imply this sort of positive regard, and that's a problem because it does not do enough to counter discrimination. A person may tolerate other people's ways of life while still believing those ways to be wrong or worthless or depraved and so do nothing to include those people in social and political life or to look out for their well-being. Galston does say a state is within its rights to forbid and punish discrimination. An autonomy liberal, however, would reply that it is not enough to just punish people; if political life is to be stable and cooperative we also need to foster within people a disposition of actual positive regard of others. Regarding Galston's skepticism charge, Gutmann denies that the reflection an autonomy liberal wants requires students to doubt their parents' or culture's way of life. Yet she does say that schools are within their rights to promote reflection on things that are relevant to social justice, even if parents protest. So, for instance, Sally need not challenge students' Christian faith in order to foster proper respect for Buddhism. However, she does need to challenge any beliefs that the difference in faith is *politically relevant*, for example, that being a Christian should be a requirement for holding public office or receiving public benefits such as schooling. After all, it is not at all clear that being a Buddhist is inconsistent with the political need for "honoring the basic liberties and opportunities of others." Lest we be too glib about how far Gutmann's distinction gets us, she also notes that fostering critical thought about political matters will very likely promote critical thoughts about other things, such as parents' ways of life. However, for an autonomy liberal such as Gutmann, that is a risk that needs to be taken.

Often in the background of the autonomy view is the belief that the sort of interaction they recommend is beneficial to groups at risk of discrimination. But is integration into this sort of liberal culture really so beneficial to those people? Clearly, the groups in our case are suspicious of it. They fear that aspects of their cultures will be lost, and that is just the sort of concern Galston has. Even liberals who value autonomy can say we should do more to safeguard the integrity of some groups. Will Kymlicka argues that the existence and stability of certain cultural groups that are at risk is so important that these groups should have the right to resist forced integration and to restrict the mobility, residence, and political rights of their group members and members of other groups.[8] Hence, perhaps Dr. Tran is right about not wanting to meld. (Kymlicka talks about native peoples in the United States and Canada in this context, and so we need to wonder about the applicability of his arguments to the situation of the Vietnamese in our case. Arguably, their culture is not at risk in the way Native Americans' is. Similarly, members of the majority group would not be able to claim special treatment.)

On the other hand, one might argue, as Robertson does, that groups cannot demand guarantees that they will survive. Kymlicka agrees on that. But as both our writers recognize, there is an issue of how far teachers (and the state generally) should go in helping or hindering survival. One thing Kymlicka insists upon is that it is not the state's business to change ways of life (beyond what citizenship requires). Sally may be within her rights to try to influence Dr. Tran and other citizens of Smithville toward her vision of community, so long as she is not acting *as a teacher*. She can have conversations, write letters to the editor of the local newspaper, or do other things as a private citizen. Similar to Arthur Brown's point about Stan Stankowski, Kymlicka might say Sally needs to keep her public and private roles more clear and distinct.

Before we leave this issue, we should think about one other major theme in Katz's and Robertson's essays, namely what should be done for Cathy Tran. Up to now, in trying to judge the merits of diversity and autonomy liberalism I've focused on the attitudes of these schools of thought toward groups, but what about the implications of these views for individuals? Robertson and Katz emphasize Cathy Tran's freedom to chart her own course in life. Cathy has a right to affirm her identity with the Vietnamese community but also a right to break with it. As Robertson says, "respect for Cathy's autonomy places constraints . . . on the Vietnamese community's efforts to perpetuate themselves through her." This is a characteristic theme for autonomy liberals.

Liberals such as Galston and Kymlicka do not deny that Cathy should have certain freedoms. They do question what those freedoms should be, however. Galston complains that the autonomy view typically secures individual freedom by prompting individuals to challenge group views. For Galston this is an unwarranted threat to diversity. What we should do instead, he says, is protect people's "rights of exit" from groups.[9] Let us suppose, for example, that Dr. Tran restricts Cathy's freedom and choices, say by forbidding her to attend school dances. A diversity liberal could say this is something that Sally must tolerate. It is not her business to promote Cathy's freedom by challenging Dr. Tran, at least not as a teacher. Cathy can exert her freedom by leaving home when she is of age.

This approach prompts some concerns, as Galston himself recognizes. Will Cathy be prepared to live in the "outside" world should she eventually exit from her Vietnamese household? Will she be welcomed in the "outside" world? Will she have a place? (How might issues of equality enter into the case? Where might we need to seek simple equality? Complex equality?)

Cultural Relativism and Ethical Plurality

These liberal and communitarian views give us a range of options for thinking about unity and diversity. In closing this discussion I'd like to suggest a way of understanding them as sharing a common orientation and extend this orientation to the other perspectives we have discussed in this book. To do that I'll expand on the notions of relativism and pluralism presented in this chapter.[10] Defenders of cultural diversity sometimes justify diversity by appeal to cultural relativism, saying different cultures have their own values, which we should respect. That sort of relativism is perfectly reasonable. However, sometimes the claim continues on to assert that any attempt by one culture to impose particular values on another must be considered a form of homogenizing oppression. Along with Robertson and Katz, I wish to challenge this sort of relativism.

A form of relativism is consistent with the view of objective ethical judgment I have tried to describe and defend throughout this book. There may be times when people can correctly justify their beliefs and actions with a relativist reason of "that's just the way *we* do it, even if others do differently." Thus, to the suggestion that they should sue the Smithville school district because of its policies, the Vietnamese might justifiably say, "That would be the wrong thing for us to do; we do not do things that way." At the same time, bringing suit might be the right thing for someone else to do. Thus, cultural relativism can be a legitimate source of ethical diversity.

Yet, this is not the end of the story. All the views described in this book can be read as holding, in one way or another, that there is some basis for critically evaluating the beliefs and actions of cultural groups, whether this basis be ethical or political, thick or thin. We do not tolerate or respect Vietnamese beliefs just because they *say* their beliefs and actions are worthy of tolerance and respect. They can be *shown* to be worthy of tolerance and respect. They are consistent with democratic principles, for instance, and they manifest other admirable values, even if we ourselves would not wish to live that way. To be clear, I am not saying we should respect *people* only if their *beliefs* pass muster. As Robertson and Katz suggest, the United States is changing; Vietnamese and other immigrants simply are here now and so deserve a "place at the table." "We" are no longer the same "we" that might have existed before. Still, to respect people does not imply that their beliefs cannot or should not be challenged. Charles Taylor argues that we owe people a presumption "that all human cultures that have animated whole societies over some considerable stretch of time have something important to say to all human beings."[11] The Vietnamese culture certainly qualifies for such a presumption. Yet it is a presumption. Even things we admire can be criticized. Indeed, as I've suggested before, to argue about them can be a sign of respect.

Now this still appears to leave a good deal of room for ethical relativism. After all, even if we agree that there is some objective ground for arguing about ethical values, there still is a lot of disagreement. But not all the disagreement should be explained by relativism. As I have argued, much of the plurality in our writers' views stems from the nature of the issues themselves. There is dispute between comprehensive and political liberals because democracy is a complex issue, not because the meaning of democracy is all a matter of individual or group opinion. It may be that once a range of justifiable understandings is identified, choice among those comes down to particular personal or group ideals. But that is quite different from saying the decision is relativistic through and through. As it sometimes is stated, a value such as democracy may *under*determine correct choices, that is, leave room for some range of differing conclusions. However, that is very different from saying the correct choices are *un*determined, are completely a matter of relativistic decision. If this prompts visions of intolerance, we should recognize that this pluralistic view provides reason to endorse the accommodation Katz and Robertson advocate. It holds that views can differ and yet all be right. We need to tolerate and respect these views, not just for the sake of tolerance and respect, but because those views are good. On the other hand, if this prompts worries about being too accepting, we need to understand that even if in some situation there is no one right answer, there still can be wrong answers. Someone might claim Nazi Germany was democratic, but that claim simply is false. (How can we say such a thing? The next chapter deals with the question of ethical truth.) This sort of pluralism is not the anarchic pluralism Katz rightly attacks. Appeal to it does not solve the dispute about unity and diversity (and our other issues), but it does present the possibility of fruitfully arguing about it. (Should Sally argue? Would conversation be better?)

Conclusion

From our discussion it seems that unity is not something we should rush headlong to embrace. But neither should we unthinkingly embrace diversity. In Katz's typology of respect we see concern for people's generic rights as human beings and also for their particular values and goals (this is reminiscent of the dual concern for universals and particulars we have considered before). In Robertson's discussion of Cathy's personal identity, we see the significance of belonging to particular groups, but also of belonging to no group in particular. Katz and Robertson echo our by now very familiar refrain against an either/or view. Too, we see once again the view that certain virtues or "sensitivities" need to be cultivated in and for civil, and civic, dialogue, even while we clearly see the difficulty of achieving that.

It is important to respect cultural differences in this dialogue. However, the mere fact that some of the ethical ideals of people clash does not mean that they can share no basic ethical commitments, even if these are vague. Indeed, in our case, the actors would not have deep ethical disagreements, at least not ones that would concern them, unless they had a common understanding of what was at stake. If the Vietnamese had a value system that valued deference to state authority over individual freedom, then there likely would not be a disagreement about current school practices in Smithville. But because both community groups value freedom similarly, and see it at stake in the case, they recognize that they have a significant issue to deal with. Perhaps this provides little solace, given that there is a sharp and seemingly intractable dispute. But it is a considerable achievement to recognize oneself and others as sharing fundamental values. Some people may refuse to recognize that. However, ethical pluralism provides that there may be ethical or political grounds for acting against people's preferences, as careful as we may need to be about that.

Coercion may be an ethical response. It may not be ideal, but politics (in the good sense) may require it. But if we are to do that, what is our justification? We may appeal to common meanings, but is something stronger needed? Is it enough, for example, to say that democracy requires certain policies in Smithville schools? What is the ethical status of democracy itself? Can it be justified in turn? Is it an ethical truth, for example, or is it simply a faith of a particular group?

Ethical pluralism as I have described it holds that while the mere fact of divergent views does not show that someone *must* be mistaken, someone still *could* be mistaken. So it is consistent with ethical pluralism to say that there is a truth to at least some of these ethical issues. But is truth really possible in these matters? Is truth really that important? As an "arbitrator" might ask, is the pursuit of truth more divisive than helpful? Should people have the right to be wrong? The next chapter confronts these questions. In some ways, our preceding chapters have all been building to the point where we can explicitly take on the issue of truth; it seems an appropriate issue for the last in our series of cases.

Notes

1. See John Kekes, *Moral Tradition and Individuality* (Princeton: Princeton University Press, 1989).

2. These are just a few of the "basic human functional capabilities" Martha Nussbaum says are essential for judging the quality of a human life. See her "Aristotelian Social Democracy," in *Liberalism and the Good*, ed. R. Bruce Douglass, Gerald R. Mara, and Henry S. Richardson (New York: Routledge, 1990), pp. 203–52.

3. William Galston, "Two Concepts of Liberalism," *Ethics* 105 (1995): 516–34.

4. Ibid., p. 529.

5. Ibid., p. 524.

6. Amy Gutmann, "Civic Education and Social Diversity," *Ethics* 105 (1995): 557–79.

7. Ibid., p. 561.

8. Will Kymlicka, *Liberalism, Community and Culture* (Oxford: Clarendon Press, 1989), pp. 145–46.

9. Galston, p. 533.

10. This discussion is based upon Susan Wolf, "Two Levels of Pluralism," *Ethics* 102 (1992): 785–98.

11. Charles Taylor, "The Politics of Recognition," in Amy Gutmann, ed., *Multiculturalism: Examining the Politics of Recognition* (Princeton: Princeton University Press, 1994), p. 66.

7

Faith and Truth

CASE

"They'll keep making a stink about it, I'm sure." As she entered the teachers' lounge for her morning cup of coffee, Mary Ann Massaro caught Jan Wallace's comment to a couple faculty members sitting at the table nearest the coffee pot. As Mary Ann sat down with them Jan explained that she was reporting on the previous night's school board meeting, which she had attended. As Mary Ann knew, the main agenda item had been a parent-initiated proposal to require that creationism be given equal time with evolution theory in school science classes. The board voted unanimously against the proposal. This was not a surprise. Supporters of the proposal were quite visible and strident, but they were only a small minority of the community. Jan was speculating on those supporters' response to the vote. "Just wait and see," she said, "those Bible thumpers will be worse than ever. Thank God the board has the courage to stand up for what's right."

Mary Ann was happy to hear the result of the vote. As a biology teacher in the high school she would have been affected by the proposal, which she did not support. Her opposition to creationism was not that it was a religious doctrine. As a scientist, she felt that any theory of genesis, including a creationist one, could be explored and judged on its scientific merits, and to that extent would be appropriate for discussion in public school. Her opposition was based on the prevailing opinion among scientists that current creationist theories were not plausible enough scientifically to merit equal time with evolutionary theory.

She was ready to discuss the creation-evolution issue with anyone interested in honest pursuit of the truth, realizing that no scientific theory can lay claim to being the final truth. As far as she could tell, however, supporters of creationism were not interested in truth, being willing to ignore or distort facts for their own purposes. Mary Ann was pleased that her faith in the democratic process was vindicated; regard for the truth had won over dogma.

As Mary Ann gulped the last of her coffee on her way to her first-period biology class, it occurred to her that she might have to face the "stink" firsthand. Jeff Becker and Beth Knopf were students in her first-period class whose parents had been active supporters of the defeated proposal. The issue had not come up in class yet. Would they bring it up now? Jeff wasn't the sort of person to initiate something like that, but Beth surely was. Mary Ann had heard that Beth was active outside of class handing out literature and talking with (some said "haranguing") other students. Mary Ann was not eager for the issue to come up. Not the least of her anxieties was Jeff. While Mary Ann felt that Beth could handle any attacks upon her faith, she was more concerned for Jeff. Jeff's mother had just died of cancer. Religious faith had helped sustain Mrs. Becker during her illness, and it was a principal source of her family's strength for facing their grief. Was this the time to attack that faith?

In the minute it took Mary Ann to reach her classroom she decided to let things take their own course, trusting to her students' good sense and her own control to keep things from getting out of hand. She wouldn't raise the issue, but if it came up she would set aside the scheduled material and allow students to discuss it. Consistent with her belief in the value of honest inquiry, she didn't feel she could squelch such a discussion.

When Mary Ann entered the room Beth was passing out some creationist pamphlets. Mary Ann was not pleased that Beth did this without first clearing it with her but let that pass. It seemed that now the issue needed to be met, so Mary Ann asked Beth and the other students whether they wanted to talk about it. There was nearly unanimous desire to do so. (A couple students felt that the issue was getting the class off track. Jeff didn't express an opinion one way or the other.) Beth spoke first, going through the several points offered in the pamphlet, which attacked the scientific credibility of evolutionary theory and offered empirical support for creationism. Students attacked Beth as trying to impose her religious beliefs on them. She denied that, saying that she only wanted her beliefs to get a fair hearing. She also claimed that secular science was a religion that was being imposed on her and other students.

To Mary Ann, this line of discussion seemed unproductive. What counted as "religion" was a philosophical discussion that could go on forever. She broke into the discussion to refocus it on the issue of scientific credibility, an issue that she felt more appropriate to the class and one in which some real progress might be made. Beth responded quickly that religion was a central issue and Mary Ann's evasion of it showed she was biased against religion as a source of truth. She also challenged Mary Ann to say how the claims made in the pamphlet were incorrect. Mary Ann was taken aback by the directness of Beth's challenge. As she tried to respond, Mary Ann realized that she did not have the expertise to refute all the pamphlet's claims or even speak knowledgeably about them. Beth realized it too. She said that the inadequacy of Mary Ann's response showed that Mary Ann's belief in evolution was as much a matter of faith as Beth's belief in divine creation. She continued on to say that it was a weak faith at that, given that Mary Ann had not bothered to defend it publicly before the board or be more informed about it.

Mary Ann felt herself trembling with a mixture of anger and self-doubt as she listened to Beth. Beth's charges hit hard. Thankfully, other students took up the discussion, for Mary Ann feared she could not find her voice to speak. But the students did not address the substance of Beth's charges so much as tell her to "chill out." By this time the class period was over and Mary Ann had pulled herself together enough to say that they had to stop for the day.

Now she had to decide what to do next. It seemed to her that truth was not well served in the discussion. Most of the discussion had not gotten at the central issues, and when it had, Mary Ann felt she had not done well to contribute a sound scientific perspective. She felt she shouldn't leave the issue. On the other hand, if she pursued it, would she do better? What would the other students think if she was unable to give a better response to Beth? With study, she probably could present a better case. But then she thought of Jeff. Was rebutting Beth so important as to risk Jeff's perceiving it as an attack upon his faith? She could explain that to attack the scientific credibility of current creationist theories did not imply an attack on the idea of creation. But would Jeff see it that way? However, the issue might go beyond just a few individuals. Mary Ann felt the sort of activist religion espoused by Beth and others, which, by all indications, they would continue to fight for, was dangerous. But could she be so sure about the truth of her cause as to justify a crusade against these people? The large majority of the community shared her beliefs, apparently. But what does the majority opinion show? Mary Ann knew how accepted opinion had sometimes been an obstacle to scientific advances.

As Mary Ann thought about it, weren't many of her own actions and beliefs based on particular "faiths"? Were those faiths so very different from Beth's and Jeff's? What sort of "truth" could Mary Ann claim in her beliefs about science, evolution, and teaching? What role should faith and truth play in the lives of teachers? What advice would you give Mary Ann?

Reflections on "Faith and Truth"

Ethics, Education, and the Creation/Evolution Controversy

BY HARVEY SIEGEL

My initial advice to Mary Ann would be to study the creationist literature and think through the issues confronting her, her students, and the broader community. Questions concerning the nature of science and religion—What distinguishes one from the other? In what ways are they alike? Different?—are central to these issues. While science teachers don't routinely address such questions systematically in the course of their teacher education, they should. That is to say, they should become familiar with the philosophy of their subject (as all teachers should be familiar with the philosophy of their subjects). In Mary Ann's case, this means that she should become familiar with the philosophy of science.

Beth is arguing that "religion is a source of truth." Is it? The answer depends, in part, on how we understand "truth." How do Beth, and creationists more generally, understand that notion? Interestingly, they typically interpret it in the same way that scientists do. Beth claims that creationism is a *viable* biological theory—at least as good a theory as evolutionary biological theory—and that creationism gives us an accurate depiction of *the truth,* that is, the way the biological world actually is and has been. Creationism holds that organisms and species did not evolve in the manner described by the theory of evolution; that God created the species as "fixed kinds," which cannot change from one kind to another; that these "kinds" are not closely related to one another at the molecular level, and, indeed, that molecular biology is essentially irrelevant to the scientific understanding of interrelationships between and among organisms and species; that the history of life on Earth extends over only a few thousand years, rather than the millions of years that current scientific theory takes to be the period of the history of life on Earth. On these and many other issues, creationism and evolutionary theory disagree: what one holds to be true, the other rejects as false. Both sides take the relevant sort of truth to be *scientific* truth, that is, accurate depiction and explanation of the phenomena that both sides agree is the proper subject matter of biological science.

Insofar as creationists and evolutionary theorists understand their views to be rival scientific theories, both sides should agree that both views should be subject to the same standards of scientific adequacy. How is scientific adequacy, or truth, judged? Standard criteria include those of testability, descriptive adequacy, explanatory adequacy, and predictive power. On these criteria, evolutionary theory does exceedingly well. Creationism, on the other hand, does very poorly. It fails to explain almost all relevant biological-biochemical-genetic phenomena; it fails utterly to predict, and therefore is not testable; it even fails adequately to describe biological phenomena.[1] In this respect, Mary Ann's belief that creationism fails as a *scientific* theory, in that it fails to offer a defensible understanding of biological phenomena, is well justified. Creationism does not offer the sort of truth concerning actual biological phenomena that it claims it offers.

But Beth also claims that *religion* is a source of truth. Here it seems that Beth has shifted her notion of truth. Truth now is not that which is revealed by proper scientific inquiry, but rather that which is revealed by divinely inspired texts. This changes not only the relevant notion of truth, but also the relevant target of inquiry. For the "truths" now sought are not those most profitably and plausibly studied by biological modes of inquiry, nor are they to be assessed in terms of biological-scientific criteria. But why should religion be thought to be a source of *scientific* or *biological* (as opposed to some other sort of "revealed") truth? Neither Beth nor other creationists have provided us with any good reason to think that it should. So there is, in Beth's position, a dubious attempt to have it both ways: to regard creationism as a legitimate scientific theory able to identify and explain scientific truths, and for that reason deserving of equal treatment in the biology curriculum, and also—when confronted with the hard fact that creationism simply fails to meet minimum standards of scientific adequacy—to regard it as a religious rather than a scientific "source of truth." Being able to come to grips with this tension in Beth's creationist position is essential if Mary Ann is to be able to deal adequately with the challenge Beth has posed to her; to do so Mary Ann will, again, have to become more familiar with the philosophy of science. Hence my advice that she does so and help her students to do so as well.

Beth also claims that Mary Ann is "biased" against religion as a source of truth. How should we evaluate this charge? If Beth is claiming that religion is a source of scientific truth, then Mary Ann's rejection of religion as such a source should not be seen as biased, but rather as a straightforward invocation of the scientific criteria of evaluation of scientific claims, hypotheses, and theories that were mentioned earlier. If Beth thinks these criteria are defective for purposes of picking out scientific truths or warranted scientific theories, the burden is on her (and her fellow creationists) to explain why. Unless she can successfully do this, her charge of bias is unfounded.

But what about Beth's claim that Mary Ann too is resting her beliefs on faith: faith in secular science? Here everything depends upon what is meant by "faith." If by that term Beth means that Mary Ann has confidence in the ability of scientific investigation to establish scientific truths, but that that confidence is unsupported by evidence (or contrary to evidence), then Mary Ann should simply deny that her confidence in science rests on faith. For there is plenty of evidence—from the history of science, from the philosophical study of scientific methodology, from the scientific development of methodological techniques—that science *does* offer a broadly reliable, albeit fallible, way of establishing scientific truths.[2] Beth is content with the claim that her creationist belief rests ultimately upon faith, that is, upon accepting, despite lack of supporting evidence, that the Bible contains the inspired word of God. When she claims that Mary Ann's beliefs concerning science are also a matter of faith, she is out to establish that Mary Ann's confidence in science is similarly ungrounded in relevant evidence. But Mary Ann's beliefs concerning science needn't be ungrounded in that way; if she familiarizes herself with the philosophical dimensions of science we have been discussing, she will be able to rest her confidence in science's fallible ability to discover and explain scientific truths on relevant evidence rather than faith.

Now all this musing about creationism and science might seem to be beside the point: aren't we supposed to be deliberating about *ethical* judgments and about what Mary Ann ought *ethically* to do? Well, yes we are. But these points concerning the scientific status of creationism are important if we are adequately to come to grips with the ethical issues before us. They help to set the stage for our consideration of those issues, to which we now turn.

My only advice to Mary Ann thus far has been to familiarize herself with the relevant portions of the philosophy of science, since it is that familiarity that will enable her to deal adequately with the difficult issues Beth has raised. This bit of advice is in keeping with what I take to be one of Mary Ann's primary ethical obligations: as a teacher, she is ethically obliged to educate her students well. Because she is a biology teacher, she is obliged to have, and to convey to her students, an adequate understanding of her subject matter. By "adequate" I mean to refer here to *disciplinary* adequacy, and that is determined by the current status of the discipline of biological science. I offer this as a fundamental ethical obligation of any and every teacher: to teach well his or her subject, as measured by appropriate standards of disciplinary adequacy. According to this standard, creationism is an overwhelmingly inadequate scientific theory—more accurately, it does not qualify as a scientific theory at all—and Mary Ann has an ethical obligation to make this fact clear to her students.

That is not Mary Ann's only obligation, however. As a teacher, she has other ethical obligations as well. In particular, she is obliged to treat her students with respect and to treat them in such ways that they are not harmed, either psychologically or in any other way. However deficient Beth's creationist views are, scientifically, Mary Ann ought not to belittle them or make Beth feel inadequate because of them. Mary Ann ought not to ridicule Beth's (or any other student's) beliefs. She is obliged only to make clear to Beth and the other students that creationist beliefs are *scientifically* inadequate. This she should do sensitively and respectfully. To do this insensitively or disrespectfully would be to fail to treat her students with respect.

Mary Ann, like all science teachers, is obliged to maintain standards of scientific adequacy in her courses and to help students to see that creationism fails to meet minimum scientific standards.[3] To the extent that a student's religious beliefs contradict good science, the science teacher has an obligation to point that out to the student. Of course, the science teacher may not force the student to abandon the one belief and accept the other. Nevertheless, the student needs to understand that the religious belief does not constitute good science. Science teachers would do students a great disservice if they failed to make clear to them the unscientific nature of their religious beliefs (when those beliefs do in fact fail to meet standards of scientific adequacy). If the student who understands this continues to embrace the religious belief and reject the scientific one, the student should understand that he or she is not choosing one scientifically legitimate belief over another, but rather rejecting the scientific for the religious.

The task of science education is to give students an understanding of science—not only the content of current scientific theories, but the methods of scientific inquiry and the nature of scientific knowledge as well. I would go further and say that students have the *right* to a decent science education, where "decency" is again understood in terms of disciplinary adequacy. If so, then the suggestion that creationism be presented as a legitimate *scientific* alternative to evolutionary theory both denies to students their right to a decent science education and undercuts the purpose of teaching science in the first place. Students are entitled to their religious beliefs, of course; but these beliefs have no place in the science curriculum—*especially* when they masquerade as science. Creationism does not meet minimum standards of scientific adequacy; consequently, it should not be presented as a legitimate scientific alternative to evolutionary theory in the science classroom. The science course that rejects creationism is not telling students they cannot maintain their religious beliefs but rather that those beliefs are not acceptable *as science*.

None of this is meant to suggest that science teachers should callously disregard their students' deeply held religious beliefs. Teachers must treat students with respect and sympathy and be sensitive to the conflict some students may experience when they discover that their religious beliefs are not acceptable as science. But protecting students from such conflict shows no respect for students and fails to teach science as well. As long as we regard science as an important part of the curriculum, we must teach it—not callously, not insensitively, but well. Students' religious beliefs should not force us to abandon standards of disciplinary adequacy.

These reflections are especially relevant to Mary Ann's treatment of Jeff. She should of course be very sensitive to Jeff's psychological and emotional state. Jeff's mother's recent death, the fact that her religious faith sustained her during her illness, and the fact that the family's religious faith was a principal source of their strength in facing their grief, all suggest that Mary Ann might well harm Jeff if she belittled that faith. That she manifestly must not do. But she must, nevertheless, distinguish between Jeff's religious faith and his science education. Her obligation is to endeavor to enable Jeff to achieve a reasonable understanding of science—both the content of its current theories and the criteria of scientific adequacy against which such theories are judged. She is also obliged to do what she can to help Jeff cope in this difficult period. However, she shouldn't do anything to help Jeff cope that will harm his growing understanding of science.

Notes

1. See here Harvey Siegel, "Creationism, Evolution, and Education: The California Fiasco,"*Phi Delta Kappan* 63 (1981): 95–101; Siegel, "The Response to Creationism," *Educational Studies* 15 (1984): 349–64; and Mike U. Smith, Harvey Siegel, and Joseph D. McInerney, "Foundational Issues in Evolution Education," *Science & Education* 4 (1995): 23–46.

2. Consider the example of "double-blind" testing. In testing the efficacy of drugs, it first was realized that subjects' reactions to drugs was affected by their beliefs about the efficacy of the tested drug, and so scientists tested drugs without informing subjects whether they were receiving the test drug or an inert control substance. But then it became clear that the scientists' expectations were themselves communicated to the subjects, thus again interfering with the accurate experimental determination of the drug's efficacy. Therefore "double-blind" techniques were developed, in which both the subjects and the administering scientists were kept ignorant concerning which subjects received the experimental drug and which received an in-

ert control substance. This methodological advance provided a practical way of controlling for the "placebo effect," in which subjects' reactions were affected by their expectations as well as the biochemical properties of the experimental drug, and thus gave scientists a way to determine more accurately the real biochemical effects of experimental drugs. Here our "faith" in double-blind methodology is straightforwardly justifiable in scientific terms. There is nothing "faithful" about it, if by "faith" one means "belief contrary to evidence" or "belief held without regard to relevant evidence." For further discussion of double-blind methodology and its justification, see Harvey Siegel, "Laudan's Normative Naturalism," *Studies in History and Philosophy of Science* 21 (1990): 295–313, especially pp. 299 ff.

3. The following three paragraphs are adapted from Siegel, "Creationism, Evolution, and Education," p. 99.

Advice to Mary Ann Massaro: "Teaching" Evolution in the Schools

BY ALVEN NEIMAN

Students such as Beth are to be welcomed rather than feared. This is because they provide teachers such as Mary Ann, as well as Mary Ann's students, with the opportunity to engage in the kind of impractical, deep and broad inquiry I will refer to as philosophical. In my discussions with Mary Ann (and I hope that the discussion is ongoing, for philosophy must be continually practiced to be learned and utilized) I would, first of all, ask her to accept Beth's challenge as a means of leading Beth, and to the extent possible, the entire class into philosophy. I would try to show her how philosophical inquiry is in fact an important part of her work as a teacher. I would do this even though I am aware that she, like most of the teachers our educational system now produces, is quite likely to be unequipped to engage in philosophical inquiry and quite intimidated by the prospect of integrating philosophy into her curriculum. Part of my job, then, would be to begin the admittedly difficult task of making her full emergence as a philosophical practitioner possible.

What, then, is philosophy? Over two thousand years ago Socrates, the patron saint of philosophical inquiry, was charged with corrupting the young of Athens, found guilty, and executed for asking questions that most citizens felt should be avoided, questions thought by most to be at best frivolous, at worst corrosive of ordinary human value. What kind of questions? According to Alfred North Whitehead all of these questions reduce to a single one, "What is it all about?"[1] As Josef Pieper (whose account of philosophy I will rely on here) puts it: "[E]ngaging in philosophy means asking questions, reflecting on questions and ultimately asking one question only."[2] What's it all about?

But don't nonphilosophers ask similar questions? What's it all about? What's going on here? Isn't this the same kind of question police officers ask at the scene of a crime, stockbrokers ask as they puzzle over the ups and downs of the market, political scientists ask at political conventions, chemists ask in their labs? Not exactly. Philosophical questions are useless in ways these are not. Moreover, they aim at a breadth and depth of meaning beyond what is involved in these other questions. Let us examine these characteristics in turn so as to make the nature of philosophy clearer.

Socrates' opponents were quite right to suggest that his questioning was, in an important respect, of no practical value. Asking and trying to answer his questions won't rid you of your hunger, make you richer, or even help you get a more enjoyable job. In fact, for Pieper, philosophical questions are quite self-consciously meant to remove us from the ordinary world of work and practice where such concerns are of the essence, a world in which we ordinarily live as biological and social creatures confronting our day-to-day needs, earning our daily bread. But such questioning will, if Pieper is right, help us in one respect. It makes us free, if only for a short while, from the ordinary desires and needs that blind our vision, free to reflect upon the most basic aspects of things—our most basic rationales for living the kinds of lives we live, for valuing those things we explicitly or implicitly value most of all.

What's it all about? Or, What do I value most of all? How is my life, my various activities as a human being, to be understood? Why do I do what I do? Every life contains answers to these questions, even those lives that explicitly, on the surface, are clearly indifferent or even hostile to philosophy. Ask yourself just about any "why?" question: Why are you reading this book, taking this class? Why do you go to school at all? Why do you get up in the morning, even? In turn, ask "why?" of your answers until you reach "rock bottom," so to speak, until you can only say in all honesty, "just because." Isn't this just the kind of childish questioning parents aim to extinguish? Why? Why? Why? Perhaps, but this process can have value, for here one's life philosophy may be revealed. Here we may find an answer to *the* philosophical question applied to your life: What do *you* value most of all? What do *you* see as the goal or purpose or meaning of your life as a whole and of the individual practices that this whole contains? In a peculiar sense, perhaps such philosophizing isn't necessarily useless at all. Might it not be useful to reflect upon the values that for now are most basic in one's life? To reflect upon possible connections and conflicts between these values? To study the great philosophers in order to see what philosophies of life have in the past carried the greatest weight and why?

Here we find something of the depth and breadth promised by philosophy. The inquiry just described aims to uncover one's most basic, deepest values, motivations, desires. It aims at uncovering the *ultimate reasons* behind what we do; it also aims at *ultimate connections* or breadth of understanding. How do my various desires "hang together"? If I am a teacher, how does my rationale for being a teacher fit with other aspects of my life? Am I a coherent whole? Does my right hand know, and can it approve of, what my left hand is doing? Philosophy becomes a normative enterprise when I allow it to reach down into the depths of my life, and out to its breadth, in order to understand what I am ultimately or really all about, in order to ask whether I can in the end approve of what I have found there.

Let us return to Beth and Mary Ann. My suggestion here is that the best way for Mary Ann to comes to terms with Beth's indictment is to enter into philosophical inquiry into her own life and work and encourage Beth to do so as well. Most basically that indictment calls into question the validity of Mary Ann's commitment to the teaching of science within a democratic framework. The anger and self-doubt she feels seem to me to result from the absence of philosophical training. In what follows I want to imagine the sort of dialogue I might hold with Mary Ann, as well as the sort of dialogue Mary Ann might eventually initiate Beth into. Along the way I will suggest ways in which discussion on a philosophical level can enrich the teaching of any subject and is, in fact, an essential part of any process of education that imagines itself to be democratic.

So let us begin our questioning. What is science? And what is so important about it? And what does it mean to *teach* it, as opposed to indoctrinating or socializing one into it? In discussing these questions with my own liberal arts students I often begin with another: Why do so many of us today grant science such authority? Most of the students in Mary Ann's class (Beth and Jeff *may,* to some extent, be exceptions, exceptions worth discussing) go to medical doctors rather than witch doctors or priests or poets or someone else for help when they are sick. We trust scientifically trained technicians to build our cars and improve our foods and create ever-new means to master nature for our benefit. Why is this so? Why are we prone to think that someone good at science (e.g., Einstein) might have good ideas about politics or life in general? (We do the same kind of thing with generals, and sometimes even movie stars; why?) Why, finally, is it so important for our students to know something about science? Why is it required?

My favorite audio-visual aid in this regard is from an old *Saturday Night Live* television show starring comedian Steve Martin. (It gets the discussion going.) The skit is entitled "Theodoric of York: Medieval Barber." A shave and a bloodletting . . . two bits! After Steve-Theodoric kills off two or three patients, Jane Curtin's character says to him, "You charlatan! Admit it, you don't know what you're doing." Steve-Theodoric's response is funny but also "deep."

> *Theodoric: Wait a minute. Perhaps she's right. Perhaps I've been wrong to blindly follow the medical traditions and superstitions of past centuries. Maybe we barbers should test those assumptions analytically, through experimentation and a "scientific method." Maybe this scientific method could be extended to other fields of learning: the natural sciences, art, architecture, navigation. Perhaps I could lead the way to a new age, an age of rebirth, a Renaissance. (He thinks for a minute.) Nah!*[3]

Off he goes to prescribe more bloodletting and a good dose of boar's vomit to his next customer. But might we travel his road not taken? Perhaps the authority of scientific knowledge and practice has to do with *the* method of science.

What method? This question is worth discussing. At least several obvious answers are, on the surface at least, problematic. One answer is that science, unlike other methods, is based on experience. We have reason to believe that the next set of sinus infection symptoms will be cured by antibiotics because previous ones were. We know there are sunspots on the sun because we've seen them through a telescope.

Or *do* we really *know* these things? (What is knowledge anyway? How does it differ from mere opinion or (even) rational belief?) Some infections don't respond to antibiotics. We've seen (or "seen") the sun set and rise, but science tells us that it is the earth that moves, not the sun. Finally, scientists speak of a world (e.g., the microcosmic world of quarks, in which a table only appears to be brown, solid, etc.)

that no human eye, at least, has ever seen. (A question we will return to later: Does science really "get at" reality? Do quarks really exist? Are tables really just collections of quarks?) What is this method employed by the scientist, this scientific method? Why do we trust in it so?

If it is method (in some broad sense of the term) that distinguishes science from pseudoscience (astronomy from astrology, biology from creation science), no mere listing of results can qualify as science education. If it is (as I believe it is) the broaching and testing of hypotheses by particular flesh and blood individuals that makes the history of science unique, then this inquiry requires us to examine real scientists (not disengaged pure intellects such as *Star Trek*'s Mr. Spock) truly engaged in their work. Perhaps Beth's challenge could best be met, perhaps even disarmed beforehand, in a system of science education that travels as far from the mere tabulation of results as the one I merely intimate here.

I fear that too much science education in the schools is either mere tabulation or facile examination of an ersatz history of science populated by disembodied Spock types. A more adequate teaching would, I believe, involve discussion of how philosophers, asking philosophical questions, have come to see science. A key idea in this regard is that science (as well as history, poetry, art, philosophy itself) be seen as an intellectual tradition, an evolving community, a community in which basic hypotheses are confirmed and disconfirmed, in which the lower level of inquiry at which most science goes on is guided by certain higher-level paradigms provisionally accepted at one time or another as worthy of guiding that inquiry.[4] Within biology, Darwinian evolution is today taken by the overwhelming majority as paradigmatic for lower-level inquiry.[5] One may refer to such commitments as "faith" only as long as it is understood that even here evaluation and revision is ultimately possible. Science, the philosopher C. S. Peirce suggested, is fallible but self-correcting. Its faith commitments, its taking for granted some paradigm or other, is always provisional, open-ended. Thus it differentiates itself from ersatz intellectual traditions such as magic, astrology, or witchcraft.[6]

John Dewey, a philosopher who attempted to codify and extend many of Peirce's ideas, felt that an education or initiation into the various intellectual traditions was an essential part of American citizenship. How else, Dewey suggested, could citizens come to possess the critical autonomy and community-mindedness necessary for self-government? In such education there is surely an element of faith, or reliance upon authority. In math we cannot learn if at the beginning of instruction students demand a proof that 1 + 1 = 2; Latin language instruction goes nowhere if students can't, for a time at least, accept a teacher's word for how this or that verb should be conjugated. Democratic education in these areas may postpone aspects of philosophical questioning to allow for more fruitful questioning later on. (Can I, after years of Latin, read Cicero with benefit?) Democratic education, for Dewey, would allow all beliefs to be critically examined. But not all can be examined at once. There are nuances of "faith," reliance on authority, that Beth's charges miss completely. Yet her indictment requires Mary Ann to reflect upon these matters and hopefully to reflect upon them to some extent with her students.[7] Beth's concerns, then, allow Mary Ann, in fact force Mary Ann, to reflect upon several of her most basic values. These include not just her vocation as teacher of science but also as advocate of democratic education.

Here I can imagine Beth again raising her skeptical questions. What's so good about democracy? Why must we believe it is better than even the most benevolent dictatorship (especially when one of the greatest philosophers of all time, Socrates' student Plato, felt otherwise)? Isn't Beth right to suggest that Mary Ann's "faiths"—in science, in critical inquiry, in democracy—represent a commitment to a secular religion (of Enlightenment rationality, perhaps)? Should science supersede religion as a democratic value in schools? Don't public schools, in teaching science (even *if* evolution *is* more "scientific" than creation science) and democratic values simply indoctrinate, that is, inculcate views to be ultimately held without question?

Not without question. The problem here is to bring Beth in good faith to the enterprise of questioning I've referred to as philosophical. And here Beth's contentiousness may be an ally. There is in fact only a fine line between sophistry and philosophy. Both share a common lineage. Both grow out of a love of "argument." But will the "argument" be a fight, voices contending for power? Or will it be a dialogue aimed at discerning truth? The ambiguity signals the precarious ground upon which Beth stands but also marks Mary Ann's opportunity. Mary Ann's job is to cultivate a habit of dialogue with Beth in order to befriend her in sympathy and seriousness, once she herself has begun to philosophize about her life commitments to science and democracy, to openly share her "faith" with Beth and seek common ground, to start a conversation. The aim is to direct Beth's contentiousness in a constructive direction, to initiate *her* also into the life of philosophy.

I fear this will not be a conversation that Jeff or Beth's other classmates or Mary Ann's superiors are likely to feel comfortable with (especially if it goes on too long during time allotted for biology). Jeff, like Mary Ann, may fear his ignorance, fear what may lie behind it. Beth's other classmates, like many of Mary Ann's superiors, may resist anything beyond a perfunctory movement outside of Pieper's world of work (after all, there are, in all probability, achievement tests to be taken at the end of the year!). Given the concrete situation Mary Ann and her class are in I fear that after an initial attempt to react philosophically in class to Beth's concerns it *may* ultimately be best for Mary Ann to approach Beth outside of class, in private, and offer her friendship and conversation in *that* context. After all, don't these two have a good deal in common? Aren't both restricted by others as to what is to be taught in schools and how it is to be taught? Perhaps the entire group can (if Mary Ann picks her spots well) be initiated into more philosophy as time goes by.

Thus I imagine Mary Ann and Beth, after the limits of philosophy in their classroom situation have been reached, as partners in a further, ongoing conversation ("hidden away," away from a queasy school board, dogmatically unphilosophical parents, and "achievement" oriented classmates, in the catacombs, so to speak, like the first Christians!). What beliefs and values is Mary Ann committed to and why? What about Beth? How consistent is each? What kind of depth is found in each? (And what difference, I'm sure Beth will ask, do consistency and depth make?) What is science? What is democracy and democratic education? What is religion and religious belief? How do science (scientific reason) and religion (revelation) as supposed sources of knowledge compare to each other and to other supposed sources (e.g., poetry, art, history, even philosophy itself)? Do, for example, Scripture, Genesis, and science conflict? When, if ever, can they possibly conflict (Augustine on Scripture and science: "The Bible tells us how to get to heaven, not how heaven goes.")? Can they ever complement each other? How? The most important thing to remember in this conversation is that it is of no use to accept facile answers in order to accomplish something, in order to make philosophy too easily seem to meet the standards of the workaday world. The process, oddly enough, must in the end be welcomed as valuable in and of itself.

If I were Mary Ann (and I had been converted wholeheartedly to philosophy, and I felt that Beth had come to trust my sincerity and to understand the ways of philosophy to some extent also) I would ask her these questions also: How is it that so many who have been religious in the traditional sense of accepting Scripture as revealed have also welcomed reason, science, as an ally in faith? Anselm, Thomas Aquinas, more recently, John Henry Newman, as well as others, have done so. Faith seeking understanding. Might respect for reason be a duty of faith? Might the faith of a truly religious person require that he or she learn all there is to know about the latest science in order to clarify the nature and purpose of faith? Might this model of religious faith be worthy of Beth's consideration? After all, Mary Ann might ask her, If God created us and gave us brains, wouldn't he want us to use them? What fun it is to imagine Beth's response to questions such as these!

These questions ultimately point to philosophy understood as a habit of mind, a willingness and ability to compare the results of the various modes of knowing, to compare the many intellectual traditions in order to grasp a larger whole, a larger vision. Newman, in his classic *The Idea of the University*, suggests that only when this vantage point is reached can we speak of truly liberal knowledge. Surely this is the sort of knowledge with which liberal education must culminate. Surely it is the promise of such knowledge, the belief that it is possible and desirable, that ultimately motivates the enterprise of education in a democratic society. Ultimately this is the faith Mary Ann as a teacher must discern within herself and seek to pass on to her students. In Plato's *Meno* Socrates is said to express this kind of faith as follows:

> *I would contend at all costs both in work and deed as far as I could that we will be better men, brave and less idle, if we believe that one must search for the things one does not know, rather than if we believe that it is not possible to find out what we do not know and that we must not look for it.*[8]

If this is true of "things" in general, how much truer it must be of the things investigated by philosophers.

Notes

1. Whitehead is quoted in Josef Pieper, *In Defense of Philosophy* (San Francisco: Ignatius Books, 1992), p. 12.

2. Ibid., p. 13.

3. Michael Cader, ed., *Saturday Night Live: The First Twenty Years* (New York: Houghton Mifflin, 1994), p. 97.

4. For a careful discussion of the idea of science as a tradition of intellectual inquiry see Israel Scheffler's "Philosophical Models of Teaching" reprinted in his *Reason and Teaching* (Indianapolis: Bobbs-Merrill, 1973).

5. This idea of a paradigm is taken from Thomas Kuhn, *The Structure of Scientific Revolutions* (Chicago: University of Chicago Press, 1962).

6. Peirce's ideas on such matters are sympathetically yet critically discussed in Israel Scheffler, *Four Pragmatists: A Critical Introduction to Peirce, James, Mead and Dewey* (New York: Humanities Press, 1974).

7 For more on Dewey's ideas on science, critical thought, and democracy see Robert Westbrook, *John Dewey and American Democracy* (London: Cornell University Press, 1991).

8. Plato, *Meno,* in G. M. A. Grube, trans., *Five Dialogues* (Indianapolis: Hackett, 1981), p. 76.

Futher Reflections on "Faith and Truth"

Faith, Truth, and Philosophy: A Response to Alven Neiman

BY HARVEY SIEGEL

It is a pleasure to be able to continue this discussion with my colleague and friend Alven Neiman. Neiman makes several excellent points; we are essentially agreed. For example, Neiman insists, as I did in my first reaction to "Faith and Truth," that the teacher Mary Ann Massaro is best advised to engage in broad philosophical reflection concerning the issues raised by her student Beth's challenges to her (Mary Ann's) handling of the evolution/creationism controversy in her biology class and to help and encourage her students likewise to engage in such reflection. While Neiman's characterization of philosophy might be found by some to be controversial—after all, philosophers never agree about anything, even on what philosophy is—I agree with his claim that philosophy's apparent uselessness, and autonomy from the arena of practical concern, is what makes it in the end most useful and relevant to human life. I agree with Neiman that questions about the nature and value of science are fundamental dimensions of a liberal, democratic education; and I heartily applaud his use of Steve Martin's "Theodoric of York" skit as a device for raising such questions. (It is perhaps worth noting that Martin was himself a philosophy major as an undergraduate.) I agree as well that a decent science education must engage students in genuine inquiry and cannot simply present students with currently accepted scientific opinion, that such inquiry will lead inevitably to philosophical questions concerning the nature and value of scientific method, and therefore that philosophical reflection is a necessary part of a decent science education. Finally, I agree with Neiman that what he calls "paradigmatic commitments" in science are only misleadingly referred to as commitments of *faith,* as these commitments, unlike more traditional religious ones, are acknowledged by reflective scientists and philosophers to be provisional, testable, and fallible. On all this I think Neiman is exactly right.

Will all this deepen Beth's (or Mary Ann's for that matter) understanding of the issues she has raised concerning religion and science or concerning faith and truth? This depends on Mary Ann's success in her task, which Neiman characterizes well:

> *Mary Ann's job is to cultivate a habit of dialogue with Beth in order to befriend her in sympathy and seriousness, once she herself has begun to philosophize about her life commitments to science and democracy, to openly share her "faith" with Beth and seek common ground, to start a conversation. The aim is to direct Beth's contentiousness in a constructive direction, to initiate* her *also into the life of philosophy.*

Again, I think Neiman is right about this, but might not Beth (or her parents) charge that this valuing of philosophy and rationality is *itself* evidence that Mary Ann (and Neiman and I) are biased by a "faith" in, as Neiman says, "Enlightenment rationality"?

This is a deep philosophical question: Does a commitment to rationality enjoy any sort of cognitive or epistemic superiority with respect to alternative, rival commitments? Can such a commitment itself be justified, or is it as much a matter of unjustifiable faith as any other commitment? I won't try to answer this question here,[1] although I think that the provisional, testable, and fallible character of scientific commitments, which allow us to distinguish them from faith, are also characteristics of a reflective, philosophical commitment to rationality and equally allow us to distinguish a commitment to rationality from faith. I will rather simply point out that pursuing it requires an engagement with philosophy and that Beth needs to become engaged with philosophy as much as Mary Ann does if they wish either to defend, or simply to think more clearly about, their respective positions concerning faith and truth. Thus Neiman's depiction of "Mary Ann's job" is, again, exactly right.

The difficulties of pursuing this job—of "philosophizing the curriculum" if you like—are manifest, given the current climate of schooling (as Neiman points out). If I have any disagreement with Neiman, it is this: I think he is willing to give up too easily the effort to make Mary Ann's classroom the sort of place in which philosophy is routinely done and to allow Mary Ann and Beth to retreat too quickly to the privacy of "the catacombs." I would say, rather, that it is imperative that that conversation be carried on in the classroom, in public, and in ways that engage the entire class and school. Of course, saying that is easy; doing it, very difficult indeed. Nevertheless, that is what the commitment to philosophy requires.

Notes

1. I have tried to answer this question elsewhere. See my "Rationality and Ideology," *Educational Theory* 37 (1987): 153–67; and my *Why Be Rational? On Thinking Critically about Critical Thinking,* Institute for Critical Thinking Resource Publication, series 2, no. 1 (Montclair, NJ: Montclair State College, 1989), pp. 1–15.

A Reply to Harvey Siegel: Philosophy and Science in Education

BY ALVEN NEIMAN

Harvey Siegel's treatment of Mary Ann Massaro's problem consists of two major components. First of all, Harvey insists that in order to adequately respond to Beth's indictment Mary Ann must learn a good deal more about biology, creationism, and, most importantly, the philosophy of science. Second, he suggests that Mary Ann recognize certain moral imperatives that apply to her as a teacher in her present situation. I will begin my response to Harvey by discussing these components and then turn to a more general issue that I believe arises from a comparison between my earlier presentation and his paper.

What more of biology and philosophy must Mary Ann learn in order to adequately respond to Beth? According to Harvey, she must, first of all, become able to utilize, explain, and defend scientific method as a means of gaining knowledge. She also must be able to adequately discuss the nature of scientific knowledge. Finally, she must be able to show how, based on a critique of scientific method and knowledge, evolutionary theory and not creationism provides (to use my terminology and not Harvey's) the best "paradigm" now available for biological inquiry.

Here I would highlight, as Harvey does, that the knowledge Mary Ann needs is to an important extent *philosophical*. But I would go farther in this regard than he does. In my initial paper I implicitly laid out a kind of hierarchy of types of philosophical knowledge that Mary Ann should know something about. What types? First, I discussed a notion of philosophy as an examination of one's life, as a Socratic reflection upon one's own most basic beliefs and their interrelation. This sort of reflection includes the kind of knowledge Mary Ann should have concerning the nature and justification of her motivations and reasons for teaching in the first place. This is the sort of knowledge that every practitioner, in any line of work, needs in order to be reflective, where reflection signals a key aspect in the life of anyone who aspires to rational autonomy, or "self-rule." Beth's challenge initially provides Mary Ann some motivation to become philosophical in this sense, to become a "reflective practitioner." Given the crucial link between this kind of reflective autonomy and democratic citizenship, it is vital that Mary Ann engage in this kind of inquiry. For one of her basic obligations as a teacher in a society that aspires to democracy is to model such citizenship for students.

After this kind of Socratic philosophy comes the philosophical knowledge of one's discipline that is stressed by Harvey. Mary Ann must, once again, know something of the philosophy of her discipline, biological science. I think Harvey would agree that what is true in this regard for Mary Ann the biology teacher also goes for Jack the history teacher and Lorraine the social studies teacher. But would the same be true of Liz the English teacher and Art the home economics teacher? (Is there a philosophy of English? of home economics?) Instead of discussing these interesting questions I take up another point that is, by the way, meant to complement Harvey's account and add a third type of philosophical knowledge to my hierarchy.

My point here, boldly stated, is as follows: This second type of philosophy, in Mary Ann's case philosophy of science, is incomplete unless it becomes the type of philosophical knowledge that in my earlier paper I traced to the work of John Henry Newman. Briefly, Newman's philosophy is both a habit of mind and a vision ultimately meant to result from that habit. It is concerned with comparing and contrasting the claims the various putative modes of knowing make concerning one subject matter or another. Newman's claim is that unless we are philosophical in this broader sense it will be extremely difficult to be philosophical in a more specific disciplinary sense. In other words, Mary Ann's knowledge of the philosophy of science, and, hence, of the subject of biology, cannot be sufficient for her teaching unless she has become philosophical in Newman's sense.

Let me explain. I will make use of one of Newman's own examples, an example relevant to Mary Ann and Beth, the study of the human person. Many putative modes of knowing claim to speak of this subject: not only biology among sciences, but chemistry, physics, as well as the social sciences (a question for Newman's philosophy: Are these social sciences scientific in the same way natural sciences are?). Psychology aims to gain hold of the mind. Literature, poetry, and art aim to illustrate the human condition. Systems of rational metaphysics (another type of philosophy!) since Plato's time have aimed at knowledge of a "true" self beyond sensory appearance. And finally, theology, Scripture, revelation (these are similar but not the same—how so?). Each of these perspectives has its limits, but in an important sense we cannot understand the limits of any one without comparing it to all the rest. Without this wider view, distortion will likely result.

This problematic applies, I believe, not only to Beth but to all of us. To take the example of science and religion, it seems to me that much of what is wrong in the current debate over creationism in the schools results from the debaters' inadequate view of religion as well as science as putative modes of knowing. To understand the nature and limits of scientific knowledge of the self we need a clearer sense of the nature of claims made by other perspectives. In an important sense the claims of all significant modes of knowing the self must be compared and contrasted if we are to be clear about the status of any one mode and its claims. Modern science raises questions about human purpose, freedom, beauty, and goodness that seem, at least at face value, to call into doubt the legitimacy not only of religion but also literature and law, love and freedom. To adequately address such issues, Newman's habit of mind is a necessity. Until or unless this sort of philosophy is taught as a separate subject in high school or the university, teachers such as Mary Ann will be forced to shoulder this burden also.

Finally I wish to add one more type of philosophy to my hierarchy. Perhaps it is the culmination of all the rest. It is the kind of philosophy you are learning through the use of this book. It is the knowledge a teacher such as Mary Ann needs to understand in order to follow out the kind of ethical imperatives Harvey rightly applies to her case. Here all I would add to his fine discussion is a concern about his mode of presentation. Ethics, like the other subjects I've discussed (biology, Socratic philosophy, etc.), cannot simply be transmitted. Mary Ann must not simply be told what to do in this or that case. She must know how to decide what to do in whatever case comes along.

Here I can easily imagine the following complaint. So many complex kinds of philosophy, none simply transmitted, all involving difficult applications of general principle and law to specific instances such as the case of Beth and Mary Ann! But Mary Ann has to act now! What good is all this discussion of ideals? Has philosophy nothing of practical use to tell us? Must it always remain "up in the clouds"? The complaint can be put philosophically. As moral philosophers often insist, *ought* implies *can*. Mary Ann cannot be expected to do what isn't possible given the circumstances. She cannot be morally blamed for not flying like a bird! Can she be blamed for not learning all this philosophy in time to help Beth? An important distinction here is between what is adequate given the circumstances and what is ideal. Ideal accounts have their value. An idea of a perfect quarterback (or sedan or, in the case of Plato's *Republic*, just society) is valuable in evaluating lesser ones. Here I have been concerned to extend what I take to be the already somewhat idealized account of Mary Ann's problematic that is found in Harvey's original paper. I think that to a large extent the difference between our first papers stem, in fact, from the different relationship to the ideal found in each. In my earlier paper I was, in general, much more pessimistic than Harvey concerning Mary Ann's capacities and opportunities. Here, perhaps to rectify matters, I've assumed his rather ideal stand and extended it "to the limit."

How ideal is Mary Ann's situation? How much can we expect of her? The following questions are pertinent. First, what of Mary Ann herself? How much does she know? How good is her training as a biologist? How distant is she from a philosophical perspective with regard to biology and ethics? How easily could she (as Harvey asks her to do) master the creationist literature and grasp the (inevitably philosophical) issues related to Beth's challenge? Second, what of Mary Ann's broader environment? How much philosophy will Beth's classmates, their parents, the school board tolerate? (Remember those "achievement" tests! And, in this regard, do such tests measure ability to think biologically or simply to list currently held beliefs of biologists? Note how different answers to this question will affect what "achievement-oriented" students, parents, and school board members want in their classrooms.) How touchy will each of these groups become if and when Mary Ann discusses Scripture/revelation as a putative mode of knowing, even if the discussion is an intelligent one?[1] The list can be expanded. What advice is proper for Mary Ann depends not only on philosophy but on the answers to questions such as these. Perhaps a not unimportant imperative for the education of teachers as well as citizens in general is the creation of a society in which the discussion of the ideal is really much more to the point than it is now.

Notes

1. For a good defense of the value of responsible discussion of religion in school see Nel Noddings, *Educating for Intelligent Belief or Unbelief* (New York: Teachers College Press,

1993). If Noddings and Newman are correct, important ramifications follow concerning the failure of public schools to provide adequate teaching not only of science but also religion. Can it be that private schools that are open to the discussion (and hence *possibly* the responsible discussion) of religion/revelation are in a better position at least insofar as what is possible in this regard?

Discussion

Harvey Siegel and Alven Neiman agree that Mary Ann needs to confront Beth Knopf's challenges. They also agree on the basic way to confront the challenges—through philosophy. (What else are a couple philosophers going to say?!) While Neiman shows how "philosophy" might mean several somewhat different things and Siegel notes controversy about what "philosophy" is, they agree that philosophy is basically about a critical and self-reflective "habit of mind" and to that degree is similar to science. (I'll say more about philosophy in the next chapter.) And what's the payoff of these philosophical investigations? Mary Ann and Beth and maybe other students will be better able to get things right regarding the natural world, religion and science, and what education and life are all about. (I'm not saying that Siegel and Neiman make truth an end in itself. For them, philosophy is about developing a good life, not just finding truth. Yet I think it's fair to say they believe there is an issue whether lives are truly good or not.)

The possibility of getting things right, of achieving truth, is a central question here. For Neiman and Siegel it is central to understanding the issue of religious freedom, which is so prominent in the case. But the question of truth extends beyond this particular case. Lurking in the background of all we have done in this book is the issue of truth in ethics. Which of our writers have the truth on the ethical situations and issues with which we have grappled? Is truth even possible in these matters? Siegel and Neiman provide some valuable groundwork for our thinking about these questions.

In this discussion I will pose two main questions. First, Is "truth" a legitimate idea? Neiman and Siegel answer yes. This merits a careful look, however, for there are reasons for doubt. Another question also needs to be asked. Is "truth" an ideal that educators should pursue? Even if we decide "truth" is a legitimate idea, it does not follow that it should be an aim for educators. Neiman and Siegel argue that it is a proper aim, but, as we had with the questions we raised about autonomy in Chapter 6, might we have grounds for foregoing or curtailing the pursuit of truth? Might the pursuit of truth conflict with other more desirable aims, such as diversity or caring for students?

Is "Truth" a Legitimate Idea?

Many people these days are suspicious of claims to truth. In a world that is culturally plural, and where putative truths have been used to justify the most horrible oppression, doubts about truth have their appeal. Michel Foucault stresses how truth can be thought of as a product and weapon of power, particularly power geared to suppression of differences.[1] In our case, is the community majority using "truth" merely as a political weapon to marginalize the religious fundamentalists? There seems to be a good deal of hostility toward them, if Jan Wallace is representative.

There are two issues here. One is the misuse of truth. No doubt, truths can be misused, and some things that are called "true" do not deserve to be. In the quotes I shared in Chapter 2, Rorty focuses on the misuse of "truth." But the second issue is the legitimacy of the notion of "truth" itself. Much of Foucault's criticism is not so much that truth is misused but that "truth," in the sense of something that is no mere assertion of power, is not a legitimate idea in the first place. We should not confuse the two issues. From the fact of the misuse of truth it does not follow that truth is a false or useless idea.

Whatever their other differences, Beth, Neiman, and Siegel agree that truth is a legitimate idea. The issue is what the idea means. One thing that comes out of Neiman's and Siegel's discussion is that religious faith may be a way to pursue truth. As much as they criticize some of Beth's ideas about the place of faith in the search for truth, they do not say faith has no place. There was a time when many people believed science to be the one genuine road to truth. (Perhaps that belief lingers on even now with some people.) Recently, though, philosophers have questioned the superiority of science. A good deal of recent scholarship on the nature of knowledge and knowing has tried to expand our understanding of those things to make them more hospitable to a range of legitimate ways of seeking knowledge and truth. (Siegel raises the issue of superiority in his second essay. He, perhaps more than Neiman, would seem prepared to assert the superiority of methods of critical rationality for seeking truth. In Neiman's account of Cardinal Newman's notion of philosophy a hierarchy of "modes of knowing" is less evident. What might Noddings and Laird say? What do you think about the issue?)

Still, to be appropriately hospitable is not to be uncritically accepting. While Siegel and Neiman grant a place to faith, they are also very concerned about what place it should have. Particularly, they deny Beth's claim that because science is just another form of faith, faith should have a place equal to science. Neiman and Siegel agree that a key difference between science and faith is that scientific truths are held to be fallible and revisable. This assertion might seem odd at first blush. For if a claim might be mistaken, why should we call it a "truth"? It might help to distinguish their *fallibilist* conception of truth from an *absolutist* conception. In the latter view, a truth is true everywhere, for all time, for all people. On that view, the idea of a "fallible truth" really is an oxymoron. But there are dangers when people believe they have the absolute truth. History is full of horrors people have perpetrated on others when they believe they possess the absolute truth.[2] Fallibilism is an ethically important stance.

If that's the case, however, rather than speak of a different sort of truth, why not just stop making claims to possessing "truth"? Why not, as some people suggest, talk in terms of "justified beliefs"? That would permit judgments that some beliefs are more justified than others, while also emphasizing that these are just "beliefs" and not truths. However, are all claims "just beliefs"? If a man looks out the window and sees that it is raining, he does not typically think that he has a "justified belief" that it is raining; it is simply a fact that it is raining. Or again, is it just a "justified belief" that innocent people should not be tortured? At some level people know they might be mistaken about such things. (Unbeknownst to them, a movie crew might be producing artificial rain outside the window. Perhaps it is possible that the notion that torture is wrong is just a prejudice of a liberal democratic heritage.) However, as Bronowski explains it, this does not mean we are constantly uncertain. We can be certain, even though this is always within a "zone of tolerance."[3] In the case of torture, this zone is quite small. People who say torturing innocent people is wrong have little, if any, reason to believe they are mistaken. At any rate, the fact is, we use (explicitly or implicitly) the idea of truth quite competently when making claims about rain, torture, and many other things. That does not mean this practice cannot be mistaken. Yet by the same token, the success of the practice is weighty evidence for its legitimacy.

Supposing we do grant to Siegel and Neiman the idea of fallible truth, that still does not answer the question about whether science gets closer to the truth about the origin of species than religion does. Neiman and Siegel say science's success has something to do with its methods. Good scientists do not claim they are infallible. What they have sought are methods for checking their errors and biases; as Siegel says, science aims to be self-correcting. But then the issue becomes what sort of "check" is available to scientists. This has been a major issue for philosophy of science recently.

Earlier in this century philosophy of science was dominated by what has been called a *foundationalist* epistemology. The idea is that there must be some indubitable foundation to provide the needed scientific checks. Even if scientists cannot be absolutely sure about the truth of their theories, what they can be sure about, at least in principle, are certain facts (and perhaps other things, such as whether scientists have violated principles of logic in their thinking). Even if scientists disagree in their explanations of a certain fact, there *is* a "fact." This attention to facts was taken to distinguish science from other things (such as religion and philosophy).

The problem is that recent philosophy of science has challenged this foundationalist view. Thomas Kuhn, whom Neiman mentions, has been a very influential and controversial figure in this. Kuhn argues that "facts" do not provide the sort of foundation commonly thought. We do not just see phenomena but rather see phenomena *as* something. Depending on the "paradigm" in which they work, scientists may see the same phenomenon differently. Recall Neiman's comments about "seeing" sunrises. Why haven't people always "seen" that the sun, and not the Earth, is the center of the solar system? It is not that people were simply stupid or lacking in technology, Kuhn says. They could not "see" sunrises differently until they had Copernicus's theory to enable them to see how it could possibly be reasonable to see the phenomenon differently. This indeterminacy in facts is a place where Beth's charge of faith in science might gain a toehold.

Neiman's response is that Kuhn shows that "faith" has a role in science if that means that a significant amount of scientific work is not aimed at challenging one's paradigm but rather assumes the authority of the paradigm. But Neiman also emphasizes that scientists' ultimate aim is to revise and improve their paradigms. They do this while operating within some paradigm. This does not mean they cannot be appropriately objective, although it has to be said that this objectivity is not the sort a foundationalist believes necessary. There is growing acceptance of a *contextualist* (rather than foundationalist) view here. The contextualist idea is that science progresses by testing claims against a background of other beliefs that are not themselves questioned at the time (hence the importance of context), but which are open to question and revision in other circumstances. The idea is not that scientific claims cannot be objectively questioned but that they cannot be questioned all at once from some completely neutral foundation.

In what way is this objective? Kuhn insists that even though scientists subscribe to differing paradigms, they still share standards for holding to, or changing, their views, concepts such as accuracy, simplicity, fruitfulness, and the other things Siegel and Neiman cite. Scientists may disagree about which theories are most fruitful and accurate, say, or about how important fruitfulness is in relation to accuracy, but they still are obliged to justify their preferred theories in relation to those criteria. They need to provide reasons, and those reasons must be of a sort appropriate to scientific inquiry. And while the truth of scientific claims cannot be tested straightforwardly against "the world," that does not mean the world can be properly understood in just any old way. In technical terms, while a simple *correspondence* view of truth (in which claims are tested more or less directly via their correspondence with the world) is untenable because there is no theory-independent way to see the world, we are not compelled to fall back to a simple *coherence* view of truth (in which claims are tested merely for how well they fit or cohere to a particular paradigmatic view). Scientific claims are tested against *both* the world *and* particular standards and paradigms. For Kuhn, this does not mean science will arrive eventually at the final Truth about the world. However, even if we cannot know whether we are progressing *toward* the final Truth, we can know whether we are progressing *from* where we were. Science is interested in truth in the sense of achieving better understandings of the world.

A concrete example might help here. When it comes to evolution, scientists disagree whether evidence shows evolution occurs gradually and more or less continuously or whether it occurs in fits and starts. Creationists sometimes use this disagreement to suggest the hopeless difficulties of evolutionary theory. However, these scientists do not dispute evolution as the shared basis of their work. Indeed, Stephen Jay Gould, a proponent of the "episodic" or "punctualist" theory that challenges the traditional Darwinian "gradualist" view claims that evolution is a fact.[4] Debate may go on at the *theoretical* level, the level at which scientists debate the *explanation* of the facts, but that does not mean that there isn't a shared view of the facts that need to be explained and what those facts are. These are not "brute facts," self-evident and impervious to question. But if the facts are to be disputed it is up to critics to show why. (Hence Siegel's "burden of proof" point.)

Creationists might not dispute "the facts." However, they argue that their "paradigm" provides adequate explanations. Although the case does not specify what is in Beth's pamphlet, we might guess at what it contains. Consider some creationist claims regarding the Earth's age.[5] Creationists claim that because helium is constantly being produced by uranium decay, the small amount of helium in the atmosphere shows the Earth is young. However, helium escapes into space, and large amounts cannot accumulate in the atmosphere. Or again, creationists say that calculating from the rate of decay of the Earth's magnetism leads to the conclusion that the Earth is just 10,000 years old. The problem with this claim is that the Earth's magnetism not only decays but is renewed cyclically because of motion in the Earth's core. A last example is that creationists claim the unreliability of Carbon-14 dating. It is true that this technique can produce false results when used improperly. However, that does not invalidate the technique. In sum, while creationists and evolutionists can agree on some of the facts, creationists (at least the ones cited here) ignore other facts. Scientific truth is determined in part by how well the various aspects of a paradigm fit together. But some "fits" simply are better, more complete, more comprehensive.

To summarize the point of all this, I refer back to a distinction made toward the end of the last chapter. Evidence and scientific standards and arguments *under*determine scientific theory. However, this does not mean that theory is *un*determined. Some explanations of the natural world simply are not justified. In other words, science is pluralistic in the way I suggested for ethics in the previous chapter.[6]

This pluralism suggests a similarity between science and philosophy. What about the question of *philosophical* truth? Is truth possible in Neiman's grand discussion of "what it is all about"? Oftentimes, people make a sharp distinction between science and philosophy regarding the objectivity of each—science is objective, but philosophy is subjective. If we grant the conception of scientific truth just presented, however, we have reason to think that philosophical truths are possible in much the same way scientific truths are. Empirical evidence has a place even for philosophical questions. For example, how about the question "Is a religious life good?" Certainly there are observable and testable consequences of religion upon individuals and cultures that would inform the response to the question, for example, that religion sometimes helps people be ethically good. One might press and ask why being ethically good is good. That sounds like a candidate for a "just because" answer. Does that sort of reason mean a religious life must be just a subjective commitment? No. Like the contextualist view of scientific truth, the truth of philosophical beliefs can be based on other beliefs that are unquestioned but that *can* be questioned. The value of being ethically good can be questioned. We have been doing that in this book. Thus, if scientific beliefs are not mere matters of faith, neither are philosophical beliefs, even if they are not exactly the same as scientific beliefs.

So, is "truth" in science and philosophy a legitimate idea? Our answer depends at least in part on what we expect the "truth" to be. If nothing short of an absolutist or foundationalist conception of truth counts as truth, then science and philosophy do not yield truth; but neither do they claim to yield that sort of truth (contrary to what some critics contend). On the other hand, we have reason to think that fallibilist and contextualist conceptions of truth may be more defensible and desirable than the absolutist and foundationalist alternatives.

Is "Truth" an Educational Ideal?

Granting that truth is a legitimate idea, there is the further question of its ethical and educational priority. Siegel and Neiman contend that it is very important. Neiman closes his second essay by pointing to some of the practical difficulties of pursuing his ideal. (What do you think about that issue?) Still, pursuing truth through philosophical inquiry is the ideal. But why must an education for philosophical inquiry be the ideal? Why should Beth aspire to the liberal "rational autonomy, or 'self-rule'" that Neiman talks about, rather than whole-hearted submission to religious doctrine and divine revelation? Similar to the previous chapter, we have the issue of coercing Beth to face issues she might prefer to avoid. Let's look at this issue from the perspectives of the liberal views we discussed in the last chapter. (I won't consider a communitarian view. How might a communitarian respond?)

Comprehensive liberals could support Siegel and Neiman by saying that Beth simply is wrong, that an examined life really is better, regardless of what she happens to think. Furthermore, this project can coincide quite a bit with Beth's own desires and interests, even if she does not realize that now. Siegel asserts that philosophy could help Beth clarify and defend her views. Neiman shows how there is no necessary antagonism between religion and philosophy and that Beth has an interest beyond her religious views that can be served by philosophy, namely, her interest in figuring out what it's all about. (Recall how Professor Ray Torrey helped Arthur Brown understand "what it all means." Is an examined life a liberal concern only? How about Laird's ideas about moral development? How about the fact that Neiman uses Noddings to support his claims?) In short, Beth and Mary Ann may not be as far apart as first appears. As Neiman proposes, Beth may have a friend in Mary Ann with whom she can have a genuine meeting of minds and hearts.[7]

However, recall Galston's argument about valuing diversity. Even as democrats value autonomy and truth, they also need to value diversity, including religious diversity. As we have seen, some political liberals would be skeptical of the claim that the pursuit of truth is good for Beth, not because that claim is false necessarily, but because it is not the proper ground for deciding public school policy. Deciding what's good for Beth is not the business of the public school. At least, its interest in her good does not extend beyond what's required for democratic citizenship. Siegel and Neiman relate their claims for philosophy to democratic citizenship, so they recognize the importance of this sort of argument. Nevertheless, the question political liberals would ask is Can Neiman's and Siegel's recommendations be shown to be genuine requirements of citizenship in a liberal democracy, or do they actually (and illegitimately) go beyond those requirements?

Some political liberals might encourage the restraint we see in Siegel and Neiman. For instance, far from joining Neiman in criticizing Siegel for not carrying his philosophizing far enough, they would see virtue in keeping the philosophizing confined to issues of disciplinary adequacy in science. Mary Ann's first reaction to stay away from "philosophical" questions may have been on the right track. Similarly, contrary to Siegel, Neiman's idea of conducting the discussion "in the catacombs" might be endorsed just because it would occur outside of the school and not have the status of official school curriculum. They might encourage Neiman's suggestion that private schools are in a better position—practically, philosophically, and politically—to deal with these issues.

On the other hand, other political liberals would join Siegel and Neiman in encouraging "reflective autonomy" in public schools, because that may indeed be required for democratic citizenship. Again, the idea is that when entering the public arena of democratic politics, anyone must be prepared to critically examine and adapt his or her commitments to the extent required by justice and democratic living in a pluralistic society. If citizenship in a liberal democracy requires that people be able to appreciate the reasonableness of views that differ from their own, then public schools have reason to counter people who say that their ways of life are the only legitimate ones. This argument is taken to have particular force in the case of Christian fundamentalists who, unlike other religious groups such as the Amish, often aim to take a very active role in the public arena. Political liberals acknowledge that fundamentalists may be burdened in some way(s) by this policy. But they deny that the burden is unreasonable. As Stephen Macedo contends, "We will sometimes accommodate dissenting groups, but we must remind fundamentalists and others that they must pay a price for living in a free pluralistic society."[8]

However, before trying to settle this dispute we should consider the teacher's role. For instance, if Mary Ann agreed to be neutral on the issues some political liberals might be more willing to endorse philosophical discussions. There is a difference between Mary Ann—as a representative of the state—asserting a position on the issues and simply facilitating the discussion. Noddings, who argues for the political relevance of critical inquiry, also argues for a form of teacher neutrality:

> *Teachers committed to pedagogical neutrality will not say to students whose parents have taught them that the world is only a few thousand years old, "That's wrong." Rather they will acknowledge the fact that some people believe this, and they will lay out what most scientists believe. In doing this, they should admit that there are several conflicting stories within evolution theory itself. . . . [T]eachers need not say, "This is true," or "I believe that. . . ." They need only refer to beliefs clearly stated by others and let students weigh the evidence or decide consciously to reject it in favor of faith.*[9]

This sort of neutral stance is commonly believed to be the proper one. (Is Noddings talking about conversation here? Persuasion? Argument?) But is that belief correct? Siegel and Stephen Jay Gould might say Mary Ann *should* be prepared to say "That's wrong." Siegel is careful about when such a statement is justified and how it should be made, but he also says that Mary Ann has an ethical obligation to make the scientific inadequacy of creationism clear to students and not simply leave it up to them to decide. In regard to the existence of conflicting stories within evolution theory, recall Gould's distinction between evolution as fact and theory. He could say that it is simply false that the world is a few thousand years old, even though scientists dispute the "stories" of what happened during the billions of years since the Earth's formation.

What might motivate Noddings's hesitancy? It might be a manifestation of her caring approach to ethics. Is it caring to tell students they are wrong? Siegel might argue that it is. He puts truth telling on an ethical footing by linking it to respect. Do we care for people when hedging on the truth, by refraining from (respectfully) confronting them on issues about which they are in error? (In his appeal to respect, and in other ways, Siegel can be located with nonconsequentialists of a Kantian sort. How might Noddings respond? Siegel approves of Neiman's idea about befriending Beth. What might that mean here? How about consequentialist concerns regarding Siegel's and Neiman's proposed actions; consequences for Jeff, say? How about for Mary Ann's self-interest? Do Siegel and Neiman give enough thought to those?)

Noddings cites another reason for restraint. She notes that saying "That's wrong" can stop discussion. That is an important issue for people interested in democracy. Amy Gutmann, who, as we have seen, is a strong advocate of the political relevance of critical inquiry also stresses that democracy is not just about pursuing the truth; it's also about participation.[10] Do we do democracy a favor by driving religious fundamentalists out of public schools and to that extent discouraging participation in public debate about education? And, if we do have a legitimate interest in changing fundamentalists' ideas about democracy and schooling, Gutmann points out that much of civic education happens *through* participation. (What sort of politics is appropriate here?)

Even more, if we are interested in truth, and if we accept the contextualist conception of truth, truth is not something people can pursue while isolated from each other. Truth is pursued through argument with other people, through the clash of differing and perhaps competing ideas and perspectives. This does not mean we are never justified in excluding some views from the dialogue. (Must we really take seriously the racist views of neo-Nazis? Is it even possible to hear every view?) But we must carefully consider actions that might damage chances for dialogue. Rather than press for truth here, should Mary Ann and her school board look for ways to accommodate and compromise in the hope of encouraging participation? (Are accommodation and compromise desirable in this case? Are they possible? What form might they take?)

So, yes, appeal to truth can be used to close down dialogue, to silence dissenting voices. We may not want to pursue truth always. However, the matter does not end there. The pursuit of genuine truth is a defense against spurious "truths." It can be put to the service of people who are silenced and oppressed.[11] Rather than close down dialogue, the claim "This is true" invites dialogue and debate. As Thomas McCarthy puts it, "We can and typically do make contextually conditioned and fallible claims to unconditional truth (as I have just done). It is this moment of unconditionality that opens us up to criticism from other points of view."[12] By *unconditionality*

McCarthy means that truth claims are presented as applicable to other people and situations. When I say "I speak the truth" I am not just speaking for me but purporting to speak for others, too. This may seem the height of arrogance. And indeed there may be times when it is arrogant and unwarranted to claim to speak the truth. Yet if we understand our ethical task as one of struggling for a shared ethical world rather than a mere confederation of parochial enclaves or individuals, attempting to speak the truth becomes an ethical obligation.

On the other hand, truth claims invite responses (argument? conversation?) in a way that "This is just my opinion" does not. If ethical claims are just opinions, an "I'll-take-it-or-leave-it" attitude on the part of recipients is not unjustified. There is little if any sense of accountability to others' "opinions." However, we are accountable to others' truth claims in a much stronger way. In a sense, they claim to be speaking for me, for all of us. I cannot just take them or leave them as I wish. I can still disagree and aim to show they are wrong. They may in fact be wrong. But as truth claims they merit an argument, and not just "Well, my opinion is different." People on the receiving end of a claim to truth have an obligation to respond (which is not to say they always must respond).

Conclusion

So, is truth an educational ideal? That is a question to treat with care. On the one hand, "truth" itself is a difficult notion. However, we do have grounds for thinking it is a legitimate and worthy idea in both science and philosophy. On the other hand, truth is not the only thing ethical teachers need to be concerned about, as this and our other chapters have amply shown.

I close by suggesting that the question is more *how* truth should be pursued in a liberal democracy than *whether* it should be pursued. We may have reasons for curtailing the pursuit of truth, or even suspending it altogether, under some circumstances. However, even philosophers such as Galston can and do argue for the truth of some values that public institutions in a democracy are justified in expounding; for example, democracy itself. There are fallible and revisable ethical truths to guide teachers' work. The point is not to dispense with the pursuit of ethical truth, but to be wise about it. (And can't there be a truth regarding whether someone acted wisely or not?)

Perhaps you are unconvinced by these claims. You will have to think whether they are justified by the evidence and arguments (conversations?) in this book. Do our writers speak the truth? Do they claim to speak the truth? Are their recommendations any less forceful if we consider them justified beliefs rather than truth claims? Is education ethically better if we see it aimed at truth than if we do not?

With this chapter we conclude our series of cases. We have confronted (wallowed in?) a great many complicated, and likely frustrating, questions and issues. What sense, if any, can we make of all this? It is time to try to take stock of where we stand regarding the question of ethical judgment in teaching. The next chapter offers some closing thoughts for you to consider.

Notes

1. See Michel Foucault, "Truth and Power," in *The Foucault Reader*, ed. Paul Rabinow (New York: Pantheon, 1984), pp. 51–75.

2. For a moving account, see Jacob Bronowski's chapter "Knowledge or Certainty?" in his *The Ascent of Man* (Boston: Little, Brown and Company, 1973), pp. 353–77.

3. Ibid.

4. Stephen Jay Gould, "Evolution as Fact and Theory," in *Science and Creationism*, ed. Ashley Montagu (Oxford: Oxford University Press, 1984), pp. 117–25.

5. These examples and the responses are taken from Tim M. Berra, *Evolution and the Myth of Creationism* (Stanford: Stanford University Press, 1990), pp. 126–27.

6. Harvey Siegel has severely criticized Kuhn, therefore he might not endorse the contextualist view I have sketched. However, he advocates a pluralism that is similar (if I understand it correctly) to what I propose. See his *Relativism Refuted* (Boston: Reidel Publishing, 1987).

7. A "friendship" may not seem possible here. But Neiman is not saying that Beth and Mary Ann should be "buddies." He reminds me of Gadamer's idea of friendship based on a shared aim of seeking what is right. It is that commonality, not love, that is essential. See Hans-Georg Gadamer, *Truth and Method*, 2nd rev. ed., trans. Joel Weinsheimer and Donald G. Marshall (New York: Crossroad, 1989), p. 323. Gadamer goes so far as to say that *only* such friends can advise each other on "questions of conscience." What do you think of that claim?

8. Stephen Macedo, "Liberal Civic Education and Religious Fundamentalism: The Case of God v. John Rawls," *Ethics* 105 (1995): 496.

9. Nel Noddings, *Educating for Intelligent Belief or Unbelief* (New York: Teachers College Press, 1993), pp. 133–34. Macedo (p. 476) takes a similar stance, asserting that public authorities should not take "a position on the question of how—or whether—God fits into the whole business" of creation.

10. See her *Democratic Education* (Princeton: Princeton University Press, 1987).

11. Benjamin Barber, *An Aristocracy of Everyone* (New York: Ballantine Books, 1992).

12. Thomas McCarthy, *Ideals and Illusions* (Cambridge: MIT Press, 1991), p. 33.

8

Of Cables and Cobwebs
Some Closing Thoughts on Ethical Judgment in Teaching

I don't know about you, but I myself have an acute sense that it is well nigh impossible to do justice to all the issues this book presents. Perhaps we should begin by admitting that any remarks I make here will continue the dialogue we have begun, not finish it. Still, I think we have gotten somewhere in our task of understanding ethical judgment in teaching. Perhaps we have not come upon final answers to our questions (are there final answers to be had?), but we may at least understand the questions better. This aspect of articulateness about ethics is very important for teachers to have. Teachers are constantly bombarded with demands to be precise and decisive in their goals for education. Precision and decisiveness have value, to be sure; but perhaps this book shows that they can be unreasonable and undesirable demands, at least if we are seriously interested in doing the ethically right things for students and others. Perhaps an informed understanding of the complexity of ethics can help teachers be articulate respondents to demands for simple answers. (And let's face it, a lot of the calls for ethics in education are pretty simplistic.) Often, this understanding will be shown by posing questions for people, just as our writers do to each other and as I have done to them. To some people this questioning might be evidence of confusion and ignorance. But as Gadamer suggests, "the important thing is knowledge that one does not know."[1] Think about it. If someone who read one of our cases said to you, "No doubt about it; I know exactly what to do," would you think that person was very knowledgeable about the ethics of teaching? If, as we have gone along, your stock of good questions has grown, your sense that you don't know has become even greater, then you've learned a lot!

However, we don't have questions only. We can make defensible judgments about our cases, and some general conclusions about ethics in teaching can be drawn from our discussions, or so I'd like to say, anyway. Even if there aren't conclusions, perhaps we can at least do a bit to organize the questions that persist; having questions is not the same as being confused or chaotic. In the Introduction I posed a number of issues for you to keep in mind as you went through this book. By way of closing thoughts I'll return to those and think about what we might conclude about them at this point.

Why Ethics?

Let's start with a big issue: Why ethics? Early on I stated that this book was not for people who see no point in being ethical. But why would good people need ethics? I believe that it's safe to say that even good people need to try to better their understanding of what is good and right. I started off with two questions ethical people might ask. The first concerned neutrality. From our discussions we can draw two senses of neutrality. One is the neutrality of not taking partisan stances on certain ethical issues (which may or may not be justified). The other sort of neutrality is a much broader reluctance to engage with ethical situations. I said that this book would show you how everyday teaching situations call for ethical judgment. Perhaps our cases are similar enough to cases that you know that the claim seems plausible to you. Therefore, neutrality in the latter sense is quite troublesome. Yet, how often do teachers really encounter such crises? How "everyday" are these? (What's your experience?) Our writers show (despite the limitations of the case study format), that ethical concerns pervade teachers' everyday world outside of crises. Suppose in Connie Nakamura's classroom there had been no Steven to create an obvious problem. Would that mean her spelling program was fine, ethically? Would that mean the ethical growth of her students should not concern her? Suppose there were no Beth Knopf in Mary Ann Massaro's classroom to put her on the spot. Would that mean there are no institutional and political issues for Mary Ann to confront ethically, no need for her to engage herself and her students in philosophy? Do conditions for dialogue exist so that teachers can meaningfully confront crises when they arise? "Freedom and Discipline" prompts us to ask that question. In response to the question "Why ethics?" our writers would appear to say that it is unavoidable for conscientious teachers.

But this gets us into the second question: Are there times when being ethical might not be the best thing? We considered instances where that might be true. Recall James Griffin's point about saving one's life even if that means failing morally. Perhaps such an action is the right thing to do; moral considerations may not be overriding in all cases. Yet such behavior has an ethical cost. An ethical life is not impossible after such a "failure," but it will never be quite the same as it was before. An ethical life would show itself when the person acknowledges and feels the cost. It would show itself when the person tries to redeem him- or herself. Even if saving one's life is an ethical failure, that action does not constitute a turning away from ethics.[2] Ethics need not, and probably should not, always be at the forefront of teachers' minds. But it persists as the background project, as teachers are continually searching for, and being responsible to, what is ethically right and good. It is in this sense that teaching is fundamentally an ethical activity, not a technical one. Sure, teachers need to be guided by certain pedagogical concerns—the content of their academic discipline, say—but those always operate against an implicit or explicit ethical background.

The other issue wrapped up in this discussion was what "ethics" means in the first place. In several places we confronted Weber's idea of ethics as some sort of blend of concern for ideals and practicalities, intention and responsibility, principles and consequences. Ethical judgment is a matter of practical wisdom. That seems to me to be a sound stance. (Would all of our writers agree?) But I would like to offer a way of sharpening the issue a bit. As our writers point out many times with many issues, we should avoid simple "either/or" stances toward pairs such as principles and consequences. However, that does not mean that any old "both/and" approach is as good as another. For example, an ethically sound politics of teaching does not relate ends and means by holding that the end justifies the means. In that sense, principles (such as not betraying trust) need to come before consequences; our vision of the good cannot be so important to us that we use practicalities as an excuse to violate basic moral requirements. In other words, what is right is prior to what is good. On the other hand (have you noticed how often I say that?), there is also a way in which what is good is prior to what is right. This is the sense in which one's principles and duties are meaningful only against a broader horizon of what is significant, a vision of the good that those principles and duties are meant to serve.[3] Why is trust so important? What is the image of human flourishing that trust serves, and that enables us to know how to trust or not trust wisely? It was in this sense that I wanted to resist reducing ethics to "morality." A sound politics of teaching does not lose sight of a vision of the good.

This conception might help us understand the relationship between perspectives such as the ethic of duty and the ethic of care and liberalism and communitarianism. These perspectives do not line up clearly with the right/good distinction. Noddings and Laird have ideas about what is right, as do communitarians, and Kantians have ideas about what is good. Yet it is fair to say that they have different emphases regarding the right and the good. Perhaps recognizing the role for both the right and the good helps us see how the perspectives we've discussed can contribute to judgment, what their strengths and limitations might be. However, recognition of these roles does not tell us when the good or the right should come first; that's a matter of judgment. But it does highlight the need for a dialectic between right and good, rather than a simplistic choice of the one or the other.

Ethical Judgment

Now what about judgment in ethics? What can we conclude about it? In the Introduction I warned that we should be careful about judgment, and nothing in the book prompts a different conclusion. We need to be careful about being judgmental. We considered the effects this can have on people, as when we thought about arbitration and adjudication, conversation and argument, relativism and truth. As we saw, there is reason to think that each member of these pairs has a place, but that is not because there are times when we shouldn't be concerned about our relationships with other people. We need to rethink the common claim that adjudication, debate, and the pursuit of truth are always destructive of human relationships. Adjudication need not be punitive or dictatorial. Argument can actually bring people together. Truth can serve people who are oppressed. Even those of our writers who emphasize conversation, arbitration and related notions show (perhaps to a greater or lesser extent) an explicit or implicit belief that there are better and worse ways of doing things and that it is not just up to individuals to decide that for themselves.

My claim in the Introduction was that the cases required judgment. Our writers engaged in the sorts of things I identified with judgment—determining salient features, thinking about how various concerns should be served, handling conflicts between those concerns. None of our writers offered a formula for thinking about these things. But perhaps that is no surprise. It is likely that the knottier issues revolve around the questions of what good ethical judgments look like or whether there is any way of saying what a good judgment is. What can we conclude about those questions?

Our writers' reflections are quite varied, and not just because the cases were different in their content. Some essays are relatively long; others quite short. Apparently there are differences in judgment about how much discussion particular cases require. Noddings begins by setting out quite specific courses of action and working from there. Others, such as Neiman, start out with a "big idea" (in Neiman's case, philosophy) and never do get very far into the details of action, at least not in the way Noddings does. Sichel's essay seems to present her thought process much as it actually unfolded. Other essays are more clearly reconstructions of the process that do not necessarily mirror judgment as it actually happened. Thus, the form of the writers' judgments also appears to be different. Our writers place themselves differently in regard to their cases as well. Some put themselves in the protagonists' places. Williams even puts this on a very personal level. Others always maintain an "outsider's" perspective. Related to this, did you note the differences in how writers addressed each other—by first name or by title such as "Dr." or "Professor"? In ethical judgment, are certain images of one's partners more helpful than others? Our writers draw from a range of resources to help their judgment. Katz, Siegel, and others cite some philosophical works; Burbules does not mention any. Some writers want to identify themselves pretty clearly with a particular philosophical perspective; Farber explicitly argues against emphasizing one perspective. Robertson thinks of her experiences in her own home town. Brown remembers some of his old teachers. Sichel, Laird, and Pendlebury bring in their memories of literature. Some want to know a lot of the details in the case. Others are not so concerned about that. Thus, there are differences in opinion regarding the amount and nature of information and other background needed for ethical judgment. No doubt there are other differences we could mention. (Do any others occur to you?)

But what does all this mean? The complexity does not mean that there cannot be better and worse judgments. As you read and discussed, perhaps you concluded that some of the essays showed better judgment than others. Certainly, neither I nor the contributors would contend that the essays are perfect. Except for some editing for length and wording, I tried to present the essays pretty much as they came from the authors. The idea was not to present perfect models of ethical reflection but examples as they happened. In the real world, after all, judgment is a process that has an extension in time. We wanted to show people engaged in that process, which couldn't happen if all the stumbling and revision occurred behind the scenes. Still, it seems that good judgment is not a singular thing. It may take some number of legitimate forms. Good judgment is itself a matter of judgment.

However, that fact does not imply that good judgment is just anything. For example, could it be that the many agreements we see in the essays are evidence that our writers are converging on genuinely good judgments? There are at least two sorts of agreement. One is agreement on what to do in the case, which occurs even when writers disagree about the reasons for the recommendation. Thus, Williams and Noddings agree to a great extent on what Lucy should do even as they disagree on whether honoring community wishes is a good reason for doing it. Our writers did not always reach agreement on action. Burbules and Sichel differed in their recommendations for Andre, for instance. But there we see a second sort of agreement, agreement on the sorts of values that should guide Andre's judgment. This agreement allows for some variation in recommendations, yet it still constrains them. The point is that even though our writers have some fundamental differences and disagreements, their judgments are not wildly divergent. Judgment carefully exercised does not lead just anywhere. That thoughtful people arrive at similar conclusions certainly is some evidence for the good quality of their judgments.

However, we should be careful not to conclude too much from agreement. If a bunch of neo-Nazis were asked to comment on the cases we might get a good deal of agreement among them, but we would have reason to question whether that was any indication of good judgment. Our writers are not neo-Nazis, but we still need to be cautious about what their agreements show. Do they show convergence on truths, or at least justified beliefs, or do they simply show that our writers are like-minded? (I cannot say that our writers represent all possible philosophical perspectives, although I did try to recruit people who I thought differed in outlook. Frankly, I was surprised at the extent of agreement. Either I was wrong in my assessment of their differences or else they really did connect across their differences. What do you think?) Perhaps the extent of agreement at least shows we should not exaggerate the ethical differences that exist. Often people seem to think that our ethical world is hopelessly rent by insuperable differences. Obviously there are deep differences. But are they all insuperable? Even if some of them are, does that show that the aim of achieving some fusion of horizons through dialogue, or some understanding and compromise through conversation and compassion, is hopeless?

On the other hand, there is something about the content and outcome of the essays that speaks to their legitimacy. Unlike neo-Nazis, our writers are concerned about tolerance, equality, and compassion, and it is likely that we have some intuitive feeling that their recommendations are on the right track. We need to be careful about what our intuitions tell us, however. For example, when some teachers I know read Noddings's essays they found it difficult to agree with her. (Did you have a similar reaction?) Noddings might be wrong. Noddings herself invites us to challenge her. So, my point is not that those teachers' conclusion is wrong. Yet if we are to have knowledge of these matters we must be open to challenges to our intuitions. As Gadamer puts it, we must conceive of possibilities *as possibilities*.[4] We need to struggle to see challenges to our intuitions as genuine possibilities for us. We have to try to meet them on their ground. We need to question our intuitions.

Such a caution does not mean that we should automatically discount our intuitions, however. A contextualist view of ethics holds that we must judge against some particular ethical values. We cannot doubt them all at once. Indeed, we cannot be rational about these matters unless we have some substantive vision to judge them against. Now there is a modern prejudice against this idea. Supposedly, we cannot be rational about ethical values. But that has not always been the view.[5] And I think our discussions give us reason to question it. People can and do share "common meanings." The presence of these in people's judgment is an indicator of the good quality of that judgment. Some conclusions are supported by those values, and some are not. That might be a tough call at times; it is a matter of judgment after all. It may be difficult to articulate what makes the judgment a good one. It might be a case of "I know one when I see one."

Such a conclusion might seem very unsatisfactory. But here, too, we run into a modern prejudice. It is often said that a belief is justified only if we can articulate good reasons for having it. But that claim has been challenged recently by Thomas Kuhn, for example.[6] Part of Kuhn's notion of paradigm is that paradigms provide exemplary models for solving problems. Why they are good ways of solving problems cannot be entirely captured in explicit rules. That's part of the reason why examples are needed. Kuhn refers to this knowledge as "intuition" or "tacit knowledge." Through learning these models—which have a history of test and success; they don't come from nowhere—we are able to make judgments, but we cannot always state all the reasons why our judgments are justified. At some point it may be legitimate to say "I just know." It isn't that these intuitions are forever impervious to scrutiny. The point is that they need not all be scrutinized in order to justify judgments. This is part of what is behind my claims about the "inside-out" flow of judgment. We can examine and criticize our writers' reflections, but good reasons for believing them need not be fully identified and justified beforehand. Moreover, although we may disagree with some of our writers they may still make contact with many of our ethical intuitions (although some of our authors also try to challenge some of our intuitions). The reasons they present for their positions are the sorts of reasons we can recognize, even if we are not convinced by them. The way the substance of their reflections does or does not fit our ethical intuitions is legitimate evidence for judging the quality of those reflections and their conclusions.

Of course, we need to be careful here as well. We must be willing to criticize, revise, and even abandon some of our intuitions, our "paradigms," as needed. Such willingness is another central feature in our writers' essays. There is an unmistakable readiness to confront challenges, and this readiness is not a simple waiting for others to raise challenges; the writers raise the challenges against themselves. Just a few examples: in the midst of her first essay Sichel imagines how "Scott chimes in" with outrage at how she describes him; Noddings presents Kant as a challenge to her views; Siegel confronts the charge of Enlightenment bias. It is true that Sichel, Noddings, and Siegel raise these challenges in order to criticize them. But opponents are given a voice in the dialogue. They are introduced to us rather than hidden away so that we won't know about them. They are treated as meriting a response. On the other hand, the criticism we see is not destructive only. Siegel criticizes Beth quite strongly, yet he also makes it clear that Beth was right about some things. Even when their point is not to show that others are right, the writers attempt to understand what others say and help readers understand, too. Noddings explains Kant's view. Farber criticizes Connie yet still tries to understand how her actions might make sense, given her institutional context. In short, the writers try to see others' views as possibilities. (Do they always try hard enough?)

All these things happened in first essays. We see similar responses in the second essays. In all of those essays the writers try to connect with their partners. This connection often takes the form of agreement. All of the writers note where their views coincide with their partner's. It is significant to remember that even though people disagree, they should look for common ground. Besides noting agreements, the writers sometimes explain in what way their partner's view on something is better. The exchange is not viewed as a competition. The writers do criticize each other, at least in most instances. But this is not just to score points. Even in criticism, a main concern is to understand what the other person is saying. There are several examples in which someone takes significant time to restate the partner's case. These are restated, not to put words in someone's mouth, but to show that the partner is understood, or at least that the writer is trying to understand him or her. The authors do not want their differences to rest simply on misunderstanding. Sometimes views are restated so that the critic can find something to agree with in what the partner says. Sometimes it is the differences that are highlighted, but often the further point is to show how both views can work together, or at least that the dispute needs to stay open. Sometimes the point is, indeed, to say that the other person is wrong, but the aim is, universally, to keep the discussion going. Disagreement is pinpointed and put on the table for more discussion. The critic gives reasons for the criticism. The partner's position is explained. The critic uses the partner's claims to elaborate on or restate her or his position. This does not all occur to the same extent in all the essays, of course, but, in general, the writers are open and attempt to understand and learn, to advance the dialogue.

This certainly contributes to our belief that these judgments are good. The writers explore more than one side of the issues. They consider possible weaknesses in their positions. They defend their views, to be sure, but it is not a propagandist's defense. Even if we cannot agree with their views, we at least (I hope!) have found the writers to be people worth talking to. They will hear our views and respond carefully. They will be swayed by good arguments.

What I am identifying here is the fusion horizons I described in the Introduction. Good judgment is not judged only by the particular values that go into it or by the conclusions that emerge, important as those elements are. The process itself is important, too. (More important?) Our writers' views may not have been radically changed in their exchange with their partner. Even so, they show how it is possible (but not always inevitable or desirable) to take others' views seriously, to respond to them, and by so doing better to understand one's own beliefs, others' beliefs, and the issues at stake.

The Role for Philosophy

Our writers are all philosophers of education. Obviously, my belief is that the writers' philosophical expertise speaks to the credibility of their judgment and that philosophy offers something important for your own ability to exercise good ethical judgment and be articulate about ethical issues. I am hoping you will engage in a philosophical fusion of horizons. We should think about that further, however.

Some educators are quite ready to agree with Neiman that philosophy is a useless activity, although without the complimentary spin he gives to it. Often, the uselessness of philosophy is contrasted with the usefulness of empirical research. Empirical educational research is useful because it deals with actual classrooms, it yields concrete recommendations, unlike philosophical research.

By no means do I want to say that empirical research is useless. Yet if the argument in this book is correct, the usefulness of empirical research is limited; it needs to be supplemented by ethical knowledge and inquiry. Empirical research into language arts teaching might have given Andre Taylor ammunition for criticizing Roger and Scott. Empirical research into various negotiation techniques might have suggested effective ways to get Scott and Roger to change their minds. But should Andre try to get them to change their minds? Should he criticize them? Empirical research might help us understand the impact various policies have on people and schools, but what impacts should be sought and which should be avoided? Ethical inquiry helps us ask and answer such questions and is thus eminently practical and useful.

On the other hand, as Neiman and Siegel suggest, that may be the wrong argument. The virtue of philosophy may be its uselessness. Neiman meant this somewhat ironically, but there is something important to consider here. Neiman attributes the "uselessness" of philosophy to its distance from "ordinary desires and needs." The idea is to "reflect on the most basic aspects of things, . . . those things we explicitly or implicitly value most of all." In other words, with this sort of philosophy we delve into our most fundamental ideals. If the argument of this book is correct, philosophy of this sort is no luxury for teachers. If done well it is central to teachers' work, for it provides the ethical backdrop for participating meaningfully and responsibly in ethical judgment in teaching. While in this book we have been cautious about the role of ideals in teaching, Weber's point, once again, is that concern for the practicalities of "ordinary needs and desires" must be complemented by the vision provided by ideals. Neiman's point is that we fail to appreciate the complementarity if we don't distance ourselves from practicalities now and again. Our writers' (legitimate) concern about the importance of context in the cases they write about does not alter that point. Teachers must be sensitive to the details of their situations if they are to know how or whether their ideals should be enacted, but they also must have a sense of which ideals are worthwhile. Understanding ideals requires applying them in particular situations, just as Gadamer contends, but this application does not deny Neiman's "useless" philosophy; it simply means that such philosophy is not sufficient in itself.

It is true that philosophy in this sense does not provide concrete directions for actions (yet at least some of our writers do offer recommendations that are pretty specific). But that is not its role. Gadamer says an ideal, or "utopia" as he calls it,

> *is not the projection of aims for action. Rather the characteristic element of utopia is that it does not lead precisely to the moment of action, the "setting one's hand to a job here and now." A utopia is defined by the fact that . . . it is a form of suggestiveness from afar. It is not primarily a project of action but a critique of the present.*[7]

Thus ideals can have a practical role in judgment. They are a way to critique the status quo "from afar." They suggest certain principles for action, just as our writers' ideals do for them. These are *principles*, so they do not dictate courses of action. But perhaps that is just as it should be. As Whitehead proposes: "In a sense, knowledge shrinks as wisdom grows: for details are swallowed up in principles. The details of knowledge which are important will be picked up *ad hoc* in each avocation of life, but the habit of the active utilisation of well-understood principles is the final possession of wisdom."[8] If it is wisdom we are after in ethics, we need principles and not simply details. Whitehead does not say that details are unimportant. He writes about learning principles through close attention to details. But that activity takes place in his stage of precision. The task in the further stage of generalization is to actively apply those principles. I am not suggesting practicing teachers should be in the stage of generalization only. As Whitehead conceives it, people may be in several different stages because they are learning new things. It is not as if at some point good teachers can dispense with conscious attention to details. Still, if Whitehead is right (is he?), at times teachers need to turn away from "knowledge" in the sense of accumulating details, to acquisition of principles that make sense of those details, even if those principles do not straightforwardly provide prescriptions for practice.

Of Cables and Cobwebs

In sum, I'm arguing that we can make sense of ethical judgment in teaching. We need to be careful about how much we should expect by way of guides for judgment. But there are principles—principles regarding substantive values of freedom, excellence, unity, interpersonal relationships, self-interest, and so on; and principles regarding the procedures of judgment, such as seeking challenges—that can be discerned and that are helpful practically. (What other principles do you believe are important?) That still might not be clear to you. Even if it is clear, and especially if it is not, I feel the need to offer you some explanation of my activities in this book, for it might seem to you that I have been trying very hard to thwart you in your attempts at sense making. Every time we get close to reaching some sensible conclusions, in my discussions I bring up some alternative view, some "on the other hand," to upset things. I should explain myself.

First, we should note that my challenges do not always challenge our writers' conclusions, at least not all of them, or not radically. Criticism need not imply disagreement on all things. Still, the challenges are not gratuitous or insignificant. My claim is that we need to be careful about resting with less than the whole story. The implications of the challenges I present may not appear in the case at hand, but they might be significant in another. (Did you find that to be the case when you considered additional circumstances and cases?)

Okay, let's say that you buy that, but then how can we make sense of the notion that we can pull some principles out of all this? For all my talk about objectivity, argument, and truth it may seem we have ended up with an incoherent crazy quilt of views. The various contending views I present to you may give the impression of a cobweb. The fibers between and within consequentialism, virtue, caring, duty, liberalism, communitarianism, equality, diversity, politics, and all the others may appear willy-nilly, crisscrossing, moving off into all sorts of directions, without any rhyme or reason. But I think that conception is mistaken.

The metaphor is more properly a cable than a cobweb. So far as our positions on the ethics of teaching, I think we should do as Charles S. Peirce advises: "trust . . . to the multitude and variety of its arguments than to the conclusiveness of any one. Its reasoning should not form a chain which is no stronger than its weakest link, but a cable whose fibers may be ever so slender, provided they are sufficiently numerous and intimately connected."[9] We've been weaving cables. Our principles are cables. Our "equality" principle, say, is a cable constituted by "equality" strands, "excellence" strands, "nonconsequentialist" strands, "caring" strands, and so on. The fibers are interwoven but still distinguishable. They don't melt into one homogeneous mass. Indeed, the cable metaphor suggests that we do not want an "alloy." The strands need to maintain their integrity. Won't their difference weaken the cable, though? Might their mutual "repulsion" actually tear the mass apart? There is tension, certainly. Focusing on the tension certainly prompts more anxiety than if we were to simply ignore the conflict. Ignorance is bliss, after all. In ethical matters, however, some amount of instability is desirable; we need to be open to change. But, further, the strength of the cable comes from the challenges. With the challenges comes a corresponding strength. If our cable's fibers are never tested and improved, will they be strong enough when real challenges appear? Some of our fibers may fail. They may not be as strong as we thought. But that does not doom us. If we put all our faith in an ethic of duty, say, we would be at a loss if it were to fail. If we see how it can be interwoven with other possibilities, we will be in a position to proceed as that fiber is repaired and refined.

The cable metaphor suggests the possibility of a direction and coherence that includes complexity. The fibers are not woven haphazardly. Yet the metaphor also suggests the possibility of connections with other cables. It fits with the pluralist view of ethics I have argued for. Many different cables can share some common sources even if they branch apart down the line somewhere. It might be difficult to trace things back to the source, the fibers might need to be carefully teased apart to uncover the common core; but it may still be there.

This may be a nice image, but a clever metaphor is not an argument. What evidence do we have that things can and should work this way? To find some evidence we need look no further than our writers. Here we have people who have been able to make sense of the complexity. They have pulled it together somehow. They don't claim to have done it perfectly. They don't claim that their cables are completed. But they do make a start. The possibility of error amidst all the complexity should not stop us from trying to pull things together. As Francis Bacon said, "Truth emerges more readily from error than from confusion."

Our writers have commitments. They have direction. They have principles for action. They make good judgments and recommend defensible actions. And they do this while embracing ethical complexity. They interweave challenges into their thoughts and beliefs. This has not destroyed them. It makes them stronger. It makes them sensitive to the possibility and desirability of new weavings. They are able to make connections with people who disagree with them and to support each others' efforts at ethical understanding.

We could have made things a good deal easier for you if we had emphasized the "outside-in" model of judgment. I could have asked the writers to stick to a particular clear framework of issues and principles. But is the real world of ethical judgment like that? I think this book gives us reasons to question whether it is.

The Ethical Teacher

So what does all this mean for teachers? Well, for one thing it means developing a sound ethical vision of what life and education are all about. At work in our writers' essays are explicit and/or implicit images of what is worthwhile. These images, while importantly personal, are not mere subjective preferences. Some ideals simply are inappropriate to teaching, even if they are good. Like Pendlebury, I am inclined to see teaching as a practice, and, according to Gadamer, "Practice consists of choosing, of deciding for something and against something else."[10] Ethical teaching is not just anything; teachers who wholeheartedly embrace the practice will have to choose against other things. And not just because there isn't enough time in the day to do everything. The musician who is devoted to her or his own skill and performance can lead a good and admirable life. Virtuosos need that sort of commitment. But these virtues are not the virtues of a teacher, which are tied to the interests of students (among other things). One of the most important judgments teachers or prospective teachers need to make is whether teaching is right for them.[11]

We need to be careful, however, not to think that ethical teaching can be reduced to a list of virtues or principles. Honesty is important in teaching. But does that mean a person who cheated once on a test in college cannot be a good teacher? What about someone who once tried to buy alcohol with a fake ID? While we need not ignore such things, neither do we want to be moralistic. Even good people make mistakes. Perhaps to have failed ethically and learned from it is better than never having failed at all.

While our discussion suggests the importance of substantive virtues and principles, it also emphasizes another aspect of an ethical educator. Burbules gets at it when he writes of an ethical teacher as an experimentalist, someone who doesn't aim to settle things once and for all. This echoes Dewey's view that I shared in the Introduction: Ethics involves "severe inquiry and serious consideration of alternative aims." As I warned then, we need to be careful about that claim. Yet while inquiry is not the only ethical aim, it is an essential one. It may only lurk in the background oftentimes, but it is still there as a reminder that the pursuit of the good is an ongoing task. We need to revisit our aims and think whether alternative aims are better.

The ethical life of teaching is continually, even if not constantly, a challenge to teachers' ethical understanding. This belief does not require that you agree with my claim about the possibility of ethical truth. Even if ethics is no more than a struggle for improvement and justified belief (and that has a lot going for it), dialogue and argument still play a central role. In either view, essential to ethical educational practice is openness to the complexity of the ethical world. Integrity is essential, too. Yet ethical teachers are open to, and actively seek, dialogue and exploration. Ethical character is not judged by the passion with which one holds dogmatically to some ideal. It is from such stuff that human misery is made.

All this represents a major undertaking for teachers, particularly if it is true (as I think it too often is) that teachers are not given the opportunity—either in their pre-service or their in-service experience—to conceive their teaching in ethical terms, to dialogue with each other and other people about ethics, to seriously engage in teaching as an ethical practice. Perhaps that means that a first ethical task is to engage in the politics of achieving those conditions. This is not just for the benefit of teachers. If conditions for ethical dialogue and action do not exist for teachers, it is likely that they do not exist for students and others either. My hope is that your experience with this text will help you be a wise, articulate, and respected participant in the ethical project of education. Keep up the dialogue.

Notes

1. Hans-Georg Gadamer, *Truth and Method*, 2nd rev. ed., trans. Joel Weinsheimer and Donald S. Marshall (New York: Crossroad, 1989), p. 365.

2. For an argument of this sort see Robert Louden, "Can We Be Too Moral?" *Ethics* 98 (1988): 361–78.

3. Charles Taylor, *Sources of the Self* (Cambridge: Harvard University Press, 1989), p. 89.

4. Gadamer, p. 365.

5. See Taylor, p. 86.

6. See Thomas Kuhn, *The Structure of Scientific Revolutions*, 2nd ed. (Chicago: University of Chicago Press, 1970), pp. 191–98.

7. Hans-Georg Gadamer, *Reason in the Age of Science*, trans. Frederick G. Lawrence (Cambridge: MIT Press, 1981), p. 80.

8. Alfred North Whitehead, *The Aims of Education and Other Essays* (New York: Macmillan, 1929), p. 58.

9. Quoted in Richard J. Bernstein, *The New Constellation* (Cambridge: MIT Press, 1991), p. 327.

10 Gadamer, *Reason in the Age of Science*, p. 81.

11. Margret Buchmann, "Role over Person: Morality and Authenticity in Teaching" *Teachers College Record* 87 (1986): 530.

9

Additional Circumstance and Cases

Additional Circumstances

To what extent are the contents and outcomes of ethical judgments dependent upon the particular circumstances of the situation faced? Think once again about each of the main cases in the text, and consider what your judgment would be if the conditions below existed. Perhaps you can think of other circumstances to consider as well.

Freedom and Discipline

Think about what you would recommend to Andre if his situation were changed in the following ways.

1. Roger is a woman, Rhoda. Scott is a woman, Sonia. Andre is a woman, Angela.
2. A parent group comes to Andre demanding that he take immediate action on the situation.
3. Roger's and Scott's students come from severely disadvantaged circumstances. The students do not come from such circumstances.
4. Scott begins to criticize Andre in front of other teachers. Roger begins to criticize Andre.
5. Roger declines to play any major part in discussion of the language arts curriculum, citing the many commitments he already has, but Scott agrees to join in. Scott declines for similar reasons, but Roger agrees. They both decline.
6. Roger and Scott participate in language arts discussions but openly show their hostility to one another.

7. Roger has a mild heart attack and blames it on the stress Scott has caused him. He will need to recuperate for several weeks and Andre must recommend a substitute. He could recommend a substitute who more or less conforms to Scott's manner of teaching, one who is similar to Roger, or one who takes a position somewhere in between.
8. Scott requests a transfer to a school that does not feed into Roger's junior high. Roger requests a transfer to a school that does not receive students from Scott's school.
9. Scott asks Andre for a letter of reference for his application to another school district. Roger asks Andre for such a letter. Andre must make a recommendation on Scott's application for tenure.
10. Andre's superintendent criticizes his handling of the situation. She demands immediate action. Andre is a candidate for superintendent at another school district and needs a good reference from his superintendent.

Self and Others

Think about what you would recommend to Lucy if her situation were changed in the following ways.

1. She has no children. Her children encourage her to protest the testing policy. She is a single parent. She is a beginning teacher.
2. Her principal is a man, Carl Carter. Lucy and Carole are both white. One is white, and the other black.
3. Sweetwater is an affluent, middle-class suburban town. It is a poor, rural town.
4. Carole is in full and enthusiastic agreement with the board's new program.
5. Several of her teacher colleagues come to Lucy and say they will follow if she takes the lead in resisting the board's program. Only one approaches her. Many approach her. An untenured colleague says that he or she will take the lead in resisting if Lucy also takes part. This person is a tenured colleague.
6. Students come to Lucy to complain about the new program.
7. Some of the parents who voted against the plan approach Lucy for advice and/or leadership.
8. Along with the new program of testing, the school budget is increased. The budget is decreased.
9. In the next several years it's found that while the new program has been in effect the average of students' scores on the achievement tests rise and the "extras" aren't sacrificed. There appears to be no difference in test scores. The "extras" are sacrificed.
10. Tests scores rise, but it's found that those students who fail the eighth grade or twelfth grade tests tend to drop out of school at higher rates than previously.

Communities Near and Far

Think about what you would recommend to Stan if his situation were changed in the following ways.

1. Stan is an experienced, tenured teacher.
2. At the last minute, the parents who threatened to keep their children from participating in the field trips change their minds and allow their children to go.
3. The parents who are critical of Stan's plan gain the support of other parents so that a majority of Stan's students will not be making the trips. Some of these students ask to come along anyway.
4. Parents who oppose Stan's project plan fund-raising activities for the same days and times as Stan's trips. They plan to use the money collected to start a scholarship fund for students in the school.
5. The relief agency releases Stan from his commitment to act as district coordinator and finds someone to replace him. A replacement isn't found.
6. Famine in Africa becomes even worse.
7. The week before the first trip to the suburbs, one of Stan's students is shot in a drive-by shooting.
8. Stan's students do well on their standardized achievement tests. They do poorly.
9. Stan's principal and superintendent become involved, supporting the parents and teachers against Stan. The principal and superintendent support Stan.
10. The social studies teachers end their meetings without developing a new curriculum plan, feeling they can make no progress without more involvement and support from Stan. The principal and superintendent express their annoyance with the whole social studies team. The social studies teachers complete their meetings and recommend a curriculum plan to the principal and superintendent but without Stan's approval. The principal and superintendent accept the plan and press for implementation.

Excellence and Equality

Think about what you would recommend to Connie if her situation were changed in the following ways.

1. Steven is a girl, Stephanie. Steven is from a minority ethnic group. Steven is severely physically handicapped.
2. Connie ends her spelling competitions. On the spelling section of their national achievement test, the scores for her brightest students stay the same while the scores of her students who have trouble academically drop. The first group's scores go down and the others' goes up. The scores for each group go up. The scores for each go down.

3. Connie keeps the spelling competition. Steven begins to get perfect scores again and other students stop being upset. They get even more upset. Steven continues to do poorly.
4. A popular annual ritual is a city-wide spelling bee. Several students in the city have gone to the state and national competitions. No students from the city have ever made it to the state or national spelling bees.
5. After students in the class talk it over with Connie, the majority want a change in the spelling program. The majority do not want a change in the spelling program.
6. In the student vote, the students who do well in spelling do not want to change, but the students who do poorly do want to change. The opinions are just the reverse.
7. Ed Shapiro is strongly opposed to a change in his arrangement with Connie. He is somewhat opposed. He is opposed because it would be too much trouble to change. He is opposed because he does not believe it would be helpful for his students.
8. Connie polls the parents of her students. The large majority of parents want to keep the spelling program the way it is, although they do not have strong feelings about it; a few parents strongly support a change in the spelling program. The opinions are just the reverse.
9. Connie's principal encourages her to maintain her program. Her principal encourages her to change.
10. The school board decides to make a major investment in education for the gifted. The board decides to cut back funding for gifted education.

Unity and Diversity

Think about what you would recommend to Sally if her situation were changed in the following ways.

1. The identity of Cathy's group is different. This is a group of African American families who want to maintain an Afrocentric culture and ask for more representation of African and African American history in the school curriculum. This is a group of homosexual couples and their children who want gay and lesbian issues covered in the school curriculum. This is a group of white separatists. This is a group of Native American families. This is some other cultural group.
2. The Vietnamese decide to sue the school district.
3. In school there are fights between the Vietnamese and other students. Things continue to be peaceful.
4. Sally starts receiving threatening phone calls because of her support for the Vietnamese.
5. Cathy Tran asks Sally to help her be more accepted by the majority students. Cathy runs away from home.

6. Dr. Tran asks Sally to help him encourage Cathy to be more a part of the Vietnamese community.
7. After serious discussions between the community groups, the consensus is to leave things as they are. The consensus is to pursue a more robust sense of community. Opinion is divided: one group or the other prefers the status quo while the other desires more interaction.
8. The state legislature mandates that all schools have a multicultural curriculum. Sally is asked to chair her school's committee to develop a multicultural curriculum.
9. The state legislature passes a bill proclaiming English as the official language.
10. The Vietnamese decide to sell their home and move away from Smithville.

Faith and Truth

Think about what you would recommend to Mary Ann if her situation were changed in the following ways.

1. Mary Ann knows ahead of time that Beth plans to distribute her pamphlets.
2. Jeff is not in Mary Ann's class. Jeff reacts very strongly and emotionally against what he perceives as attacks upon his religion.
3. Beth is not articulate and forceful about the issue. Beth is harassed outside of school.
4. Beth approaches Mary Ann to talk more about the issue. Mary Ann approaches Beth, but Beth rejects her overtures.
5. The majority of students in Mary Ann's class do not want to continue the evolution/creation debate. The majority want to continue it. In each case, Beth and Jeff are not part of the majority. They are part of the majority.
6. The policy on equal time for creationism is approved.
7. The school board decides that neither creationism nor evolution should be taught.
8. The parents who support the equal time policy decide to drop it and pull their children out of the public schools.
9. Mary Ann's own parents are very religious and do not like her position on creation.
10. Mary Ann believes creationist theory.

Additional Cases

How might the various concepts, values, and perspectives we have explored be applied in other cases? What do these other cases show about the merit and limits of these concepts, values, and perspectives? Do other ideas need to be considered that we have not explored? Keep these questions in mind as you think about the cases below.

Student Teachers

Lorraine Kidwell couldn't believe her ears. John Meyers, her principal, had called Lorraine to his office to discuss placements of student teachers from Central State University with science faculty at their school, Randolph High. Lorraine was science department chairperson. John always consulted department chairs about these placements. John began by telling Lorraine to stay calm and then went on to say that the professor in charge of secondary science placements at the university, Mark Burgess, had asked to place three student teachers at Randolph and requested that Lois Henry in biology, Ralph Smith in chemistry, and Charlotte Nye in earth science be the faculty to get them. This news surprised Lorraine. First, never before had the university identified specific faculty in this way and, second, Lorraine was not on the list! She had had student teachers every year for the past eleven years. What was going on here?!

John said he understood Lorraine's surprise. He himself had been somewhat taken aback by Dr. Burgess's request. This was the first time that Dr. Burgess was in charge of placements, and John figured he simply did not know what the routine was. John therefore explained to him over the phone that in previous years Randolph chairpersons made the final decision about which faculty would get student teachers and that as a matter of courtesy if nothing else, Lorraine should not be excluded this way. Dr. Burgess replied that he knew what the traditional practice had been but he wanted to change things nevertheless. He said that he meant no disrespect to anyone but that, frankly, he was concerned about quality control and wanted to be sure his student teachers had experience with the best teachers. Regarding Lorraine Kidwell specifically, again he meant no disrespect, but he did not want his students placed with her. If his proposal was unacceptable to Randolph High faculty he would understand, but then he would have to place his students in other schools in the city. John ended the conversation by telling Dr. Burgess that he would have to discuss this with his faculty and get back to him.

As John spoke, Lorraine's surprise abated (even as her indignation swelled). Of course Mark Burgess would think this way. Lorraine had come to know Dr. Burgess a bit during the four years he had been at the university. Although Ben Wunderlich had been the senior science education faculty member at the university and coordinator of student teacher placements, she had interacted a little with Dr. Burgess as he was often at Randolph observing student teachers and consulting with their supervising teachers. It was not difficult to see that Dr. Burgess had little regard for some of the science teachers at Randolph. Some supervising teachers he worked with had told Lorraine that Dr. Burgess was not bashful about criticizing their teaching to their faces and in front of the student teachers and about making unfavorable comparisons between their teaching and that of other teachers in the school, such as Lois Henry, Ralph Smith, and Charlotte Nye, all of whom, as it happened, were past or present students of Dr. Burgess's. Now Ben Wunderlich had retired, and Dr. Burgess had taken over as the senior science education faculty member. Apparently, his criticism of some of the Randolph science teachers was taking an even more dramatic form.

Lorraine herself did not believe that all the science faculty were equally good. Yet it had been her policy to "spread around" student teachers among all the science faculty who wanted them. She did not want faculty to get into a competition over who would get student teachers. Plus, none of the faculty were so awful that student teachers couldn't learn something good from them. Yes, Priscilla Schultz, the other chemistry teacher, was pretty set in her ways, but her enthusiasm was infectious. No one could get quite as excited as Priscilla when it came time to study sweet-smelling esters, for instance. Barney Adams, the other biology teacher, was nearing retirement, and he *did* tend to teach too much from the text alone, but he had a marvelous sense of humor and a sincere love for young people. And Arthur Mason, the earth science teacher, had been for many years a field geologist for an oil company before he became a teacher. He had many wonderful stories of the delight, danger, and drudgery of earth science in real-life applications. Their cardinal sin, Lorraine supposed, was that they did not whole-heartedly subscribe to the "constructivist" approach to teaching that Dr. Burgess stressed. While Lorraine herself could see some merit in this approach for her own field of physics, she had a hard time getting excited about it. It seemed to her that Lois, Ralph, and Charlotte did too much to credit students' "constructing their own knowledge" and not enough to credit established knowledge and teacher-led activities. She guessed these views of hers were the reason she was left off Dr. Burgess's list.

John listened silently as Lorraine expressed these thoughts. After she finished he sat for a minute collecting his thoughts. He then began by saying he was not pleased about the stance Dr. Burgess was taking, yet he did not want to tell Dr. Burgess to take a hike, either. People at the university had told John that Mark Burgess was a "rising star" who was beginning to establish a national reputation in science education. He was applying for a large grant to establish a "professional development school" at one of the city's three high schools. John's university contacts seemed to think that Dr. Burgess had a very good chance of getting such a grant, if not this time then in the near future. John said that Randolph could benefit if it was part of Dr. Burgess's project. Among the three high schools it did the most to serve the lower-income students of the city. Unlike the other schools, they did not have a wealthy PTA to buy extra lab equipment and other materials. Grant money could be used for such purchases. Dr. Burgess talked big about going to other schools, but it would be a hard sell for him to convince grant-giving agencies to pour money into schools that already were well off. In fact, it could be that he needed them more than they needed him. He asked Lorraine to think about this and speak with her faculty.

Lorraine called a meeting of all the science faculty. She explained the situation and the thoughts she and John had shared. There was an uneasy silence for ten or fifteen seconds. The group had never really tackled an issue like this before.They had avoided, as much as possible, any direct or prolonged confrontation over their differing views on teaching. Finally, Priscilla said that they should do what was best for the students and that it sounded like going along with Dr. Burgess's wishes was the way to do that. Arthur, who was clearly upset, said that they didn't need an "ivory-tower type" holding them hostage. Yes, their students didn't have all the best equipment, but they were getting a good education. Besides all this talk of grants was just that—talk.

After another uncomfortable pause, Lorraine turned to Lois, Ralph, and Charlotte and asked them what they thought. Lois said she was embarrassed by the whole business. She said she didn't see herself as superior to her colleagues. Charlotte broke in and said it wasn't a matter of superior and inferior but that Dr. Burgess was trying to establish a coherent, focused program with a clear set of goals. He didn't want his student teachers getting mixed messages. Ralph said he believed it was a matter of inferior and superior. He said he believed the approach Dr. Burgess advocated had solid research support. He said the other teachers needed to incorporate this approach into their teaching.

At that point Lorraine turned to Barney and asked for his view. Barney said he wouldn't be at the school for more than another year or two. He said he'd go along with whatever the younger folks wanted.

Lorraine asked for a show of hands on whether to accept Dr. Burgess's plan. Charlotte, Ralph, and Priscilla voted to accept it, and Barney joined them. Arthur, Lois, and Lorraine voted not to accept it.

Lorraine was not happy about the results of the vote. What are her responsibilities now? Should the vote stand? Should the conversation be continued? Should she now support the faculty vote when she reports to John? Should she continue to resist? Is a compromise plan possible? desirable?

The Faculty Advisor

It was Monday morning at Middleway High. After the football game the Friday before, Barry Lyons, a junior at Middleway, had been beaten up by several students from Brockton, where Middleway was playing that evening. Barry had been with three other male students from Brockton. They are all homosexuals. No one tried to deny that the students were beaten up because they were gay. The Saturday and Sunday editions of the town newspaper were full of comments from Brockton and Middleway students. Their explanations boiled down to: "Some people just don't like queers." Apparently, no Middleway students participated in the attack. Still, some (who weren't identified by name) were quoted in the papers as saying that while they didn't condone the attack, they understood the feelings of the attackers. For example, some said that homosexuals should keep their sexual orientation private. The boys who were attacked "were asking for it" because they were flaunting their homosexuality.

If asked, most Middleway students would have said they did not know that Barry Lyons was gay; neither Barry nor anyone else ever made an issue of it. But it was difficult to avoid it now, what with Barry coming to school with his face swollen and bruised and his hand bandaged. As she stood outside her classroom door, Lisa Campbell, Barry's history teacher, saw that at one end of the hallway Barry was surrounded by apparently sympathetic students, while at the other end ten or twelve students were laughing as they watched what appeared to be a reenactment of the attack, provided by several boys. Lisa felt they were being cruel and insensitive, especially because Barry could easily see what they were doing. She walked down the hallway and broke up the group, telling them that they were making too much noise and needed to get to class.

Lisa's classes went on more or less as usual; no one brought up the fight, not even in Barry's class. By the end of the day she had put the incident out of her mind. But as she sat at her desk after school grading some papers, Frances Eastman, one of the English teachers, came into Lisa's room, shut the door behind her, and asked Lisa if she could spare a few minutes to talk with her. Lisa said sure, but she groaned inside. She didn't like Frances. Lisa had clashed with Frances over school policies and other issues several times. Once in the teachers' lounge Lisa had made a casual comment about her boyfriend wanting her to quit her job if they got married, and Frances jumped on her about standing up for her rights as a woman. Lisa considered Frances to be too liberal and too strident and opinionated in her beliefs. Lisa knew Frances considered her to be too conservative and complacent. Frances had never approached Lisa to talk in private like this. What could she possibly want?

Frances got right to the point. She told Lisa that Barry and four other homosexual Middleway students had come to her to ask for her help in establishing a school-sponsored gay and lesbian literature study group. Any school-sponsored extracurricular group such as this had to have a faculty sponsor. Frances wanted to know if Lisa would be willing to be faculty sponsor for the group. Lisa was completely dumbfounded. Her first thought was "Why me?"

Frances explained that the group needed someone who had credibility in the community, which was decidedly conservative. The more conservative members of the faculty would never agree to sponsor the group. The faculty who were sympathetic to the gay and lesbian students were already viewed with some suspicion by many community members. Any cause they were associated with could be too easily dismissed as left-wing and radical. What these gay and lesbian students needed was someone who could not be so easily dismissed and so could help them gain sympathy and respect. Frances said she thought Lisa was such a person.

Many thoughts were swirling through Lisa's mind. Frances really had caught her by surprise. Her initial thoughts were that this was not a good idea at all. Yes, she was sympathetic to these students. She did not believe they should be hurt or humiliated because of their homosexuality. But was school the proper place for the proposed support group? Why did it have to be school-sponsored?

Frances replied that it wasn't just a support group. Because it would be a literature study group it would have an educational aim. It would be open to any interested students. Thus, it was appropriate as a school-sponsored activity, just as the math club and science club were. The school sponsorship was vital as a symbol that the school would support these students and be a model of tolerance in an intolerant community.

This literature could be presented in established English classes, Lisa said. Frances responded that she already did include some of this literature in her classes but more was needed. If she tried to do more in a for-credit course, the community would not stand for it. An extra-curricular activity was different, however.

Lisa said she wasn't sure that schools should start taking sides on the issue of homosexuality, especially since many people in the community considered it sinful. She confessed that she herself was not comfortable with it. Frances's reply was that this group was not trying to force beliefs about homosexuality on anyone. But even more than that, shouldn't the school take sides on the issue to the extent of standing up for tolerance?

Lisa wasn't convinced, but she took another tack: She was a history teacher; she didn't know anything about gay and lesbian literature. Frances said that didn't matter. The students would take the lead in identifying books and articles and in leading discussions. Lisa didn't even have to participate actively if she didn't want to. All she had to do was be present at the meetings.

Lisa asked Frances if she had spoken to their principal Sandra Collins. Frances said that she had, briefly, and that Sandra would support them, although Sandra also said that there would be considerable opposition (which hardly needed saying). Still, Sandra felt the group would have a good chance of overcoming the opposition; she was willing to give it a try.

Lisa and Frances sat looking at each other for a few seconds. Then Frances spoke again. She said she realized that this was asking a lot of Lisa. Lisa and she had disagreed pretty strongly in the past. Yet she always believed Lisa to be a sincere and caring teacher; that's why she had come to her. What she was asking was for the students, not just for a "cause" or to make a point.

Lisa wanted to tell Frances to leave her alone; she didn't like how Frances was pressing her. Instead, she said that she'd have to think about it. Frances got up to leave. On the way out she suggested that Lisa talk to Sandra and some of the gay and lesbian students before she made up her mind, and she thanked Lisa for her time.

Lisa didn't talk to Sandra or any students. She wasn't in the mood for any more arm twisting, so she drove straight home. One part of her said that she should agree to be the sponsor. She didn't know who the other gay and lesbian students might be, but she did like Barry and was concerned about him. She had to admire their courage in wanting to stand up to the hostility. And she did not like the intolerance being shown by some students and community members. On the other hand, she was not keen on the idea of being in the middle of a big controversy. She had to live in this community. She had grown up in a town not far away, and her parents and brother still lived there. She did not want to have to leave the area. Anyway, why should this be her fight? Wasn't it a fight for Frances and the other teachers who were always so vocal on these issues? Her boyfriend said it was, when Lisa talked to him about it. Even so, Lisa was nagged by the thought that it really wasn't as easy as that.

Around seven o'clock that evening Sandra called. Frances had told her that she had spoken to Lisa. Sandra asked Lisa if she would come to her office before school tomorrow to talk about the study group. She apologized for calling Lisa at home but explained that the situation was serious and that she wanted to start thinking about what to do. Sandra reassured her that she wasn't asking Lisa for a decision about being advisor for the group; she just wanted to talk about it. Lisa agreed to meet with her in the morning.

What should Lisa do? What should she say to Sandra?

Politics of the Lunchroom

Annie Johnson and the other teachers of the fifth-and-sixth–grade team—Margaret Henning, Fred Sawyer, and Mark Carlson—agreed that they should be proud of their students. Their experiment in democracy was a success. The teachers had given their students the chance to make a change in their school day. The students suggested and debated some options. Some of these the teachers considered a bit shaky, for example that there should be no more homework. But the team agreed that they should not veto such things out of hand. They were very concerned about the students' cynicism; when the idea of the vote was first suggested they had been disturbed but not particularly surprised at the number of students who rolled their eyes and questioned whether the teachers really meant this seriously. Believing themselves to be part of the community, the teachers had offered their views on the differing options and had pointed out how doing away with homework might not be a good idea, but in the end that was one of the options voted on. However, that had gotten only a few votes. The idea that won was for there to be free seating at lunch. The present procedure was that students sit down at the tables in the multipurpose room in the order they came in. Thus, they did not always get to sit with their friends. Even if they stood together in line, they could get separated if one got the hot lunch while the others who brought their own lunch were seated. The students wanted the freedom to sit where they wanted. This seemed quite reasonable to the teachers, and it was something the great majority of students felt very strongly about. To Annie and her team, it seemed that the students had learned something important about their power and responsibility as citizens in a democracy.

As team leader, Annie had the job of sharing the voting results with the school principal, Al Rosenzweig. Al had been very supportive of the teachers' experiment. He sat in on the discussions and shared his views. He was pleased by the results that Annie shared with him. His only concern, which he had mentioned to the students before, was that the students might take too much time eating if they were sitting with friends. Students had to be out of the multipurpose in time for the room to be prepared for a physical education class. He didn't think this would be a big problem, though.

And he was right, at least right about *that* problem. The students had heard Mr. Rosenzweig's concern and were quite good about finishing their lunch in time. There were some laggards, but that was always a problem anyway. Toward the end of the first week, when Annie asked her students about the new lunchroom plan, they said they were very happy about it. The rest of her team reported hearing the same thing from their students.

As Annie passed Al's office on her way into the building the Friday morning of that week, Al asked her to come in for a minute. After Al had closed the door he told her that he wanted to warn her that Monday morning he would tell the fifth- and sixth-grade students that he was ending the free seating plan and returning to the previous lunchroom arrangement. He said that he had noticed students saving spaces for their friends, turning away other classmates who tried to sit down. He also saw students avoiding sitting by certain of their classmates. In short, he feared that some students' feelings were being hurt. He admitted that you can't make people like each other by making them sit together, but at least he did not have to give students the chance to exhibit their dislike so clearly. He wanted Annie to be in the lunchroom that day so that she could see that he was not mistaken about this.

As Al talked, the burning in Annie's face gradually subsided. Her initial anger at Al's abrupt and unilateral decision eased somewhat as she comprehended his concerns. Still, even as Al talked, vivid in her mind was the look on her students' faces when they would hear this announcement Monday morning: some showed shock; others showed an "I-knew-this-would-happen" smirk. What would happen to their trust in her and the other adults in the school? What would be their attitude about democratic decision making? On the other hand, perhaps they would react the way she did. After initial surprise and anger they might recognize the force of Al's reasons and agree that a change was needed. But then again, maybe they wouldn't.

She asked Al for some time to discuss this with her team and the students. Al refused. He had to follow his conscience on this, he said. He could not allow students to be hurt. He conceded that this would look dictatorial to some. He could live with that. Besides, one of the prime concerns of constitutional democracy, he reminded her, was protection of the minority against oppression by the majority. We recognize the power of the executive and judicial branches of our government to veto decisions made by voters and their representatives. He was simply exercising his executive prerogative. Opening this up to discussion would take time and would likely cause the issue to become bigger than it already was, putting even more focus on the students at risk of being hurt by the rejection of their classmates. Because school was about to start Annie couldn't take time to talk more with Al. On her way out of the office she told him she'd observe the lunchroom that day.

What she saw in the lunchroom that day seemed to confirm what Al had said. Some students were saving seats, and some students sat alone. Annie could have guessed ahead of time who they would be; they were the couple kids who didn't have many friends. Still, the other students weren't outwardly mean to these students. They simply avoided them. Wasn't that OK? The students had plenty of opportunities to work together, and, in general, they did that quite well. They didn't all like each other particularly, but isn't that just part of life? So many of the other kids were obviously having a good time.

Annie felt she needed to talk things over with her team members. When she went into the lounge to eat her own lunch she called her team together. She didn't usually eat with these teachers. While they worked together well enough, they were not friends. Besides, Fred's conversation was usually about his out-of-school real estate business, which bored Annie to death; Margaret had an annoying habit of chewing with her mouth open; and Mark preferred to spend his time reading. But they pulled together now. All were upset by Annie's report of her talk with Al and felt they had to do something. Fred wanted them to confront Al as a group and demand time to think things over and work things out with the kids rather than simply dictate to them. Mark and Margaret were unsure of the wisdom of a confrontational strategy. They thought Al could be reasoned with. Margaret agreed with Fred, though, that they had to be prepared to hold the line against Al; his proposal would destroy what they had begun.

She was concerned about the couple students who might be hurt by continuing the free seating policy. But had they complained to anyone, or was this just Al's problem? That was something to find out. If they were having trouble, there might be ways of dealing with it other than vetoing the majority's wishes. Mark was more inclined to say that while he didn't like Al's action, it wouldn't be a disaster either. They could go through the debate and voting process again. The students would understand.

The lunch period was nearly over by now. Annie suggested they meet after school or during the weekend in order to talk more. But for one reason or another, people's schedules didn't allow it. Fred told Annie that he would support her in whatever plan she came up with. He had trust in her judgment, and, as team leader, she had to be able to speak for the group without them second-guessing her. Margaret and Mark agreed.

While Annie appreciated her colleagues' confidence, she thought that they needed to make a team decision about this. But it seemed that she had little choice. They needed to make some sort of response to Al. What should that be?

The Flute Trio

Mr. Marx got a cup of coffee from the teacher's lounge and retreated to his office. He had conducted try outs for flute section leader that morning and competition for the coveted first chair was positively fierce. That his high school's band boasted three solid flutists was turning into something of a mixed blessing.

Before Mr. Marx, on his desk, lay one more manifestation of his problem, the entry form for district music contest, which had to be sent in the next day. According to contest rules, each school was limited to two solo entries for each instrument. Each of the three flute players—Julie, Jodie, and Mary—wanted to enter a flute solo in the competition. None of them had gone to the contest before and were anxious to have a chance to perform. All had chosen their music. All had spent hours practicing and preparing. All were capable and likely to represent the band and the school well in competition. Mr. Marx knew he had to make a decision that favored two of the three girls and simultaneously inflicted real pain on the third. He sipped the last of his coffee and once again considered the three, each in turn.

Julie was a fine student flutist. Though only a sophomore, she had an impressive talent along with a healthy dose of ambition as well. Well, maybe not so healthy. In addition, she had the advantage of parents who not only supported her ambition but also contributed actively to its fulfillment. Julie's affluent parents purchased a very expensive, high-quality flute for her and had consistently provided for private study with a fine flute teacher. Julie, fully supported by her parents, was a very competitive person who worked hard and expected to enjoy the fruits of her labor regardless of what others might think. While her skill certainly contributed to the flute section and the band, Mr. Marx felt that this contribution was tempered somewhat by the strife she caused among other members. Julie seemed to care little for the flute section as a cohesive unit within the band. She set a good example by attending all rehearsals, submitting to rehearsal discipline, and consistently performing her part well. On the other hand, she barely spoke to the other flute players and rarely offered help or encouragement. She clearly believed she was the best flutist and deserved to be first chair and chosen to compete in the music contest.

The second member of the flute triad was Jodie. The junior flutist was little problem to Mr. Marx. While she lacked the financial and parental support enjoyed by Julie, she nearly compensated by working very hard to become a more competent musician. She cooperated with other students to make the flute section a cohesive unit that blended well with the other sections in the band. She appeared to be an excellent leader whose talent, while not as prodigious as Julie's, seemed more compatible with achieving group goals. Jodie's only problem seemed to be Julie. She had stated unequivocally that Julie was clearly out of line in expecting to vault into the coveted first chair as a sophomore. Although she normally was quite malleable, willing to do whatever was best for the band, she drew the line at allowing a sophomore to lead the section or compete in the contest.

That left the third member of the trio, Mary, a senior. Mary was probably the weakest flute player of the three. However, she was a proven leader, was well-respected by other students, and had been a loyal band member. Mr. Marx wasn't certain what Mary's reaction would be if she weren't chosen to play her solo in the contest. He had, however, observed Mary's antipathy for Julie firsthand. Mary was ambitious herself and shared Jodie's belief in seniority. However, the real problem with Mary was her mother. Mr. Marx might be able to get by without complaint if he chose Jodie to be section leader over Mary, but Mary's mother was certain to make trouble if her daughter was passed over for the contest—especially if the student he chose in her place was a sophomore. Mary's mother had a reputation among the other teachers for complaining whenever she felt her children had been slighted or mistreated in any way. On the other hand, if she liked a teacher, she could be a tremendous help. She seemed to like Mr. Marx for some reason, and other faculty members occasionally expressed envy at his relationship with her. He had often asked for and received help in fitting uniforms, fund raising, rides to activities, and the like. Although it seemed to Mr. Marx to be pretty weak, maybe even unethical, it also seemed obvious that his best interests would be served by remaining on the good side of Mary's mother.

Mr. Marx wasn't crazy about the competitive aspects of his band program. He believed that students were pushed to compete in too many phases of school life. Sure, he knew competition prepared students for a life that is, after all, certainly competitive in many ways. In addition, healthy competition can be a great motivator. Mr. Marx was well aware that competition for chairs had contributed to the overall competence of the players in nearly every section of his band. On the other hand, he also believed that band should foster an attitude of cooperation and teamwork in students. Any successful musical organization should be a cohesive unit working toward a common goal. Skill and willingness to work cooperatively with others in spite of differences is also a valued trait for adults in society. Perhaps if we weren't all so concerned with getting ahead of someone else our society would be a better one. In light of this thinking, perhaps the student who was the best at flute playing alone shouldn't necessarily be the section leader, nor should she necessarily be rewarded with the contest solo opportunity.

Looking at the situation this way seemed to raise more questions than it answered. There seemed to be other considerations as well. What about the question of Julie's moral development? Shouldn't learning to work well and cooperatively with others be a part of the education of more gifted students? Should Julie expect to be rewarded wholly for her talent without regard to her leadership contributions? Might important social relationships with other students be strengthened if she could be made to understand the other girls' perspective? On the other hand, should Mary and Jodie expect to receive preferential treatment simply by virtue of their seniority? Clearly they believed that to be the case. To be sure, Julie would have other opportunities to compete in the music contest while this year represented Mary's last chance. Would it be just to deprive Mary of this opportunity that she arguably deserved? Perhaps the seniority argument should carry some weight.

Mr. Marx had called the contest director and asked her to relax the two solo rule for once. She refused to do that. That hadn't bothered Mr. Marx too much, since he knew that even if he had been allowed to enter all three flutists, that would not have solved the section leader problem. He had discussed his problem with the school administrator, who advised him to have an independent judge hear the three performers and choose the best two players, disregarding other factors. Clearly, the principal hadn't given him a directive but merely advice. The trouble was, Mr. Marx was pretty sure the outcome would not be much better than if he were the judge. Mr. Marx thought about simply refusing to choose a first chair flutist or to send anyone to the contest. But none of these options seemed right. Mr. Marx really believed that the three girls' long-term welfare could be enhanced by working through the problem. To take the easy way out would be leaving the dispute unsolved.

Mr. Marx approached Julie, Jodie, and Mary individually to share his dilemma with them. He hadn't been sure what he hoped would happen, but as things turned out, no progress was made. Each student stuck to the position she had taken all along. While it didn't seem that any of them would hold a grudge against Mr. Marx if he chose against her, it was also quite clear that each would be very upset if things did not go her way.

Mr. Marx wished that he had more time to work on this problem, but he had to act immediately, at least on the choice of soloists. What should he do?

What to Do about Ron?

Milt Solon is the counselor at Branched Oak High, the one high school in Branched Oak, a predominantly blue-collar town of about 25,000 people. One afternoon in early October he was thinking about Ron Miller. Ron is a 15-year-old who enrolled as a freshman at Branched Oak High that fall. In August Milt had put together a class schedule for Ron. He had looked through Ron's school records, which had been forwarded by his previous school, Bentley Junior High, and he had talked by phone with the counselor and principal at that school. He had also talked with Ron in his office. He had expected his parents to come, too, but they did not. Rather than reschedule the appointment, he met with Ron alone. What emerged was a picture of a tragic situation, and at that time Milt had felt utterly at a loss about what to do for Ron.

Ron's family moved into town over the summer from Bentley, another small town a couple hours' drive away. Ron's father had been unemployed for about 16 months. Although a good worker when sober, he had trouble keeping jobs because of frequent absences. Bouts of heavy drinking and generally poor health contributed to that. Nevertheless, during the summer he and Ron's mother had both found jobs at Branched Oak's meat-packing plant.

Ron had done poorly in his academic work in the past. Presently, he performed at about the fourth grade level in reading and math. He had repeated the eighth grade and was constantly in danger of failing his classes. His IQ was around 90, and he had no identified learning disabilities. The principal and counselor at Bentley reported that when the Millers lived in Bentley the police had been sent to their house several times by neighbors complaining of shouting in the Miller home. Apparently, Ron's domineering father frequently abused him and his mother verbally. It is suspected that they had been abused physically, too, although the police and the school had not been able to prove that, and Ron and his mother had not been willing to press charges against Mr. Miller. Ron had told people that a poor report card is one thing that made his father "upset."

Ron told Milt none of this. He did tell him that he was a poor student and that he was not looking forward to coming to Branched Oak. He told him that he was planning to drop out when he turned 16 in November. The one time he was animated was when he talked about art. Ron enjoyed art and worked hard at it. The counselor at Bentley had confirmed this, although she also said that Ron did not have exceptional talent. Ron said that he had been hired part-time (two hours a night, three days a week) to do graphic art work at a printing shop in Branched Oak. The owner of the shop told Ron that she would be interested in hiring Ron full-time if he would first get some more and varied art training, especially in computer graphics. Ron was very excited about this job. He had made friends among the shop workers in a way he had been unable to do among other students. Plus, his father and mother had encouraged him to work so that he can contribute some income to the family.

Branched Oak High offers some elective art classes that could provide some of the art training the shop owner wants Ron to have. It also has a policy that students must have satisfactory academic standing (a grade average of C) in core subjects of reading, composition, math, history, and science in order to take elective courses. Ron has a D average in each of these subjects. The policy states that in such a case the student must be placed in basic sections of core subjects, and, during elective periods, work in the remedial-learning center.

Milt was not crazy about this policy. It had been instituted before he came to Branched Oak. And in Ron's case, he was not at all sure it prescribed the right curriculum. He could foresee Ron being completely turned off and just going through the motions until he could drop out of school. Milt felt it was imperative to keep Ron in school. Dropping out might result in some short-term benefits for Ron, but his long-term interests would be better served if he were helped through his academic troubles. Who could know if his art job would still be there in a few years? How could he manage day-to-day activities without some basics skills in language and math? Art classes might very well provide the incentive for him to stay in school.

But when Milt suggested to his principal, Dale Hawkins, that Ron be exempted from the policy, Dale was sympathetic but very hesitant. Dale reminded Milt that the policy was very popular with the community and faculty and that it had worked well. It really did appear to give students an incentive to "get their act together." Besides, if they started making exceptions to the policy, where would it end? Dale did say that they could stretch the policy to the extent of enrolling Ron in one art class at the start of the school year but that if he didn't make satisfactory progress in his other subjects he would be pulled out of the class.

Milt thought about Dale's suggestion as he walked back to his office. It might be worth a try, but it really wasn't the best plan. What if Ron was pulled out of the art class? He'd probably drop out. He might be motivated to work hard, but it might very well be that his problem was not lack of hard work. His home life alone surely was a big obstacle to his concentrating on academic work. Plus, the threat of losing the art might be an unhelpful extra pressure rather than an encouragement.

Milt had one other idea. He called the print shop where Ron worked and talked to the owner. Milt explained his situation and asked the owner whether she could give Ron some on-the-job training. The owner said she could to some extent and, in fact, had already done so. She knew some of Ron's situation and wanted to help him. But she could only do so much. She herself was operating close to the margin. If she was to stay in business she needed employees who could be productive. She couldn't afford to spend a lot of employee time training and supervising someone like Ron. Ron had learned a bit just by being in the shop, but Ron was far from being able to do a regular employee's work. In fact, the owner was not sure how long she could afford to pay Ron even the little bit she was. Ron was welcome to be at the shop all he wanted, of course, but Ron had told her that his father was already impatient about him not earning enough. If he was not going to be in school he was going to have to work for a regular wage.

By this time, it seemed to Milt that Dale's proposal was the best that could be done, given the circumstances, but he wasn't at all happy about it. He wanted to talk to Ron about it. Rather than call Ron at his home (he felt it best to bypass Ron's parents), Milt talked to him at the print shop, and he agreed to meet Milt in his office the next day. When Ron came in Milt explained the plan about having him in an art class contingent on his progress in other classes. Milt probed for his feelings about the plan, but Ron revealed little. Milt tried to stress to him that he and the teachers were there to help him all they could. Ron said thank you and left.

In early October when Milt checked on Ron's progress in his classes, he found what he feared he would. Ron was doing reasonably well in his art class—a B—but his average in his other classes was a D+. Dale just told Milt to pull Ron out of the art class. What should Milt do?

How Much Help Is Too Much?

Dieter Thomas was feeling good as he passed back his sophomore students' papers on Walt Whitman. As a class they had done a great job, and he was reveling in the students' accomplishment. Even Donna, who always had to struggle, had turned in a solid B paper. Donna wasn't in class that day, but Dieter wanted her (and the other students) to hear about her success. So, knowing Donna's friend Tammy would probably talk to her that evening, as he returned Tammy's paper to her he remarked, "Tell Donna she did a really nice job on her paper."

Tammy smiled and said loud enough for everyone to hear, "Yeah, well, Dave wrote it for her." Dieter knew his surprise showed in his face despite his best attempt to appear nonchalant. Clearly, the students were expecting some response from him; this was the sort of thing teachers were supposed to get upset about. They looked to Tammy and then to him. But after what he hoped was an indiscernible pause he continued passing out the papers, giving praise to the other students, but saying nothing in response to Tammy. The bell rang, the students picked up their books and left the classroom, and Dieter sat down at his desk to think about what to do.

Dieter was no fool. He had dealt with plagiarism in his classes several times during his teaching career. But Donna presented a particularly difficult case. She had been diagnosed as having an attention deficit disorder and mild to moderate dyslexia. She had always been a hard worker, though, receptive to help, and mostly able to maintain a positive attitude in spite of her difficulties. Most of her grades in Dieter's class and others were in the low C range. But Dieter thought B work was within Donna's capability at times, so he hadn't been taken aback by the quality of Donna's paper. The possibility of plagiarism hadn't crossed his mind because of what he knew about Donna and because the paper hadn't read like a plagiarized paper. It wasn't as if Donna's paper was copied from somewhere. Enough of the class material and discussion had been integrated into the paper that Dieter felt sure Donna had had some hand in its composition.

Plus, it wasn't as if some other student had done the paper. The "Dave" Tammy referred to was Dave Lewis, Donna's adoptive father. Dieter knew Dave quite well. Dave often was at the school asking about Donna's progress and asking for advice about what he could do at home to help Donna. Dieter encouraged him to work with Donna. Perhaps Tammy was exaggerating Dave's role in writing the paper. Nevertheless, Dieter thought he needed to talk to Dave about this. If for no other reason, he needed to be able to explain to Tammy and the rest of the class the truth of the situation. He knew he could talk to Dave. He was an honest, reasonable person.

When Dieter called after school Dave answered the phone, having just gotten home from work. Dieter said he and his class had missed Donna and asked if she was ill. Dave replied that Donna had a touch of the flu but that it wasn't serious but would probably keep her out of school another couple of days. He commented about how nice it was that Dieter called to ask; he said he'd tell Donna. Dieter said he had another reason for calling; he wanted to ask about a paper Donna did for his class. Dave asked if he meant the Walt Whitman paper. Before Dieter could say anything

Dave said how hard he and Donna had worked on the paper and how proud they both were of the final product.

Dieter hesitated a few seconds. He thought of telling Dave that he called to say how good the paper was and leaving things at that. Instead, he heard himself asking Dave how much he had helped Donna. When Dave asked why he was asking, he told him what Tammy had said in class that afternoon.

It was Dave's turn to hesitate. Dieter could hear him struggling for composure, and before Dieter could say something reassuring Dave began, his voice cracking, to pour out his soul for nearly ten uninterrupted minutes.

First he criticized Tammy for making the comment. This was Tammy's way of further alienating Donna from the other students and so making Donna more dependent on Tammy. Tammy was a controller, and Donna was vulnerable. Dave had been trying to keep Donna away from Tammy but without much success. Tammy was no genuine friend to Donna, but she was one of the few students willing to spend any time at all with Donna.

Yes, Dave said, he had spent a great deal of time working with Donna on the paper. Donna had read the Whitman material aloud and Dave helped her with her decoding and comprehension. Together they discussed the material and what they should write. Together they composed the paper sentence by sentence. Donna suggested what should be written and Dave helped her decide on the best wording. Perhaps one could say that he had written the paper for Donna if that meant the final wording was largely Dave's rather than Donna's. But Donna was there the whole way through, participating and learning. Donna told him that she had learned more than she ever had before.

More than the learning, the project had helped reestablish their father-daughter bond, Dave said. Establishing that bond had seemed impossible seven years before when Donna first came to him as a foster child. Yet with time and the commitment of adoption the bond had been forged. But now, with adolescent self-doubts and the influence of people like Tammy, Donna had been growing distant again. Things weren't helped by the fact that Dave's wife, to whom Donna had been quite attached, wanted a divorce. Donna had blamed Dave for driving her away. But when they finished this paper Donna had given Dave a kiss, which she hadn't done for a long time. Could Dieter imagine what that meant to him?

By this time Dave was sobbing heavily. He apologized to Dieter for losing control. Dieter tried to console him and told him not to worry, that he wouldn't do anything to hurt Donna. He said that he accepted Dave's explanation and, as far as he was concerned, that was the end of the matter. Dave thanked him, and he hung up the phone.

When he first hung up, Dieter wasn't sure that he hadn't promised Dave too much, that he hadn't been too quick because of his concern to ease his mind. But as he thought more about it, he felt that he had made the right decision. It seemed to him that this was not a case of plagiarism but of some honest help of the sort Donna needed. Besides, it was right to respond to Dave's cry for understanding. In fact, he felt like a jerk because he had only called because of the paper and not from genuine concern for Donna's well-being. His question about her illness had only been the obligatory preliminary to the business he was really concerned about.

By next morning Dieter had decided that when he met with his class he was going to deal with Tammy's comment although he did not know exactly how. She was not going to get away with hurting Donna or with putting him on the spot in front of the class. He was still thinking about this during the before-school faculty meeting and he didn't catch much of what his principal was talking about. Until, that is, the principal made the announcement that he and the school district had been named as defendants in a suit brought by parents who claimed their son had been allowed to graduate without adequate basic skills. He explained to the faculty that his hands were tied if faculty gave students passing grades that they didn't deserve. It is better to honestly acknowledge students' academic difficulties so that they can get the help needed, he said. All the schools in the district, but their school particularly, would be closely scrutinized in the next weeks and months. He asked for the faculty's help in meeting this challenge.

Dieter was no longer sure about the wisdom of his promise to Dave. What would be in Donna's best interest? How would people interpret his actions? Didn't he have to follow through on his promise to Dave? What should he do?

Notes on Contributors

Arthur Brown is Professor of Theoretical and Behavioral Foundations of Education at Wayne State University. He was instrumental in the establishment of the Center for Academic Ethics at Wayne State, and from 1989 to 1996 served as its director. He has been very active in University Governance. On two occasions he was given the Educator of the Year Award by the Phi Delta Kappa chapter at Wayne State. He has served as President of the John Dewey Society, The Society of Professors of Education, and the Midwest Philosophy of Education Society. Professor Brown's principal professional interests are in ethics, political philosophy, and organizational theory, especially but not exclusively as they relate to education.

Nicholas C. Burbules is a professor in the Department of Educational Policy Studies at the University of Illinois, Urbana/Champaign. His central interests are the philosophy of education, educational policy, and technology and education. He is currently the editor of the journal *Educational Theory.* His most recent publications include *Dialogue in Teaching: Theory and Practice* (Teachers College Press, 1993); "Reasonable Doubt: Toward a Postmodern Defense of Reason as an Educational Aim," in Wendy Kohli, ed., *Critical Conversations in Philosophy of Education (*Routledge, 1995); and "Authority and the Tragic Dimension of Teaching," in James W. Garrison and Anthony G. Rud, Jr., eds., *The Educational Conversation: Closing the Gap* (SUNY Press, 1995).

Paul Farber is an associate professor in the Department of Education and Professional Development at Western Michigan University. Following several years of teaching in the public schools, he entered the field of philosophy of education and is now engaged in teacher education,with responsibilities centered on the social and philosophical foundations of education. At Western Michigan he serves on the executive board of the Center for the Study of Ethics in Society. His scholarly work has focused principally on the ethics and politics of education, teacher education, and the political culture and context of schooling. In addition to articles in a number of different journals, he coedited the book *Schooling in the Light of*

Popular Culture (SUNY Press, 1994), coedits the State University of New York Press series *Culture and Education,* and serves as coeditor of *The Philosophy of Education Newsletter.*

Karl Hostetler taught in public and private schools for eight years. He worked in a rural school and in schools in Chicago and New York City. He also taught in Venezuela. He is presently an associate professor in the Center for Curriculum and Instruction at the University of Nebraska-Lincoln, where he teaches philosophy of education. His primary research interests are the ethics and politics of schooling.

Michael S. Katz is an associate professor of Education at San Jose State University. His primary research interests focus on ethical issues in teaching. He has taught at the American University, the University of Nebraska at Omaha, and San Francisco State University.

Susan Laird teaches women's studies and philosophy of education at the University of Oklahoma, where she serves as coordinator of the Social and Cultural Foundations of Education program and as an associate professor of Educational Leadership and Policy Studies and of Women's Studies. Philosophical articles she has written have appeared in various journals and edited books. Much of this scholarly work has been motivated by concerns that arose directly from her practical experiences as a teacher in several different settings, including teaching English in a public senior high school. Most especially, she is concerned that educators know and think about women's contributions to educational thought and that we learn to think beyond the concept of teaching taken for granted as "standard" and beyond the careless notions of coeducation now complicit both in "how schools shortchange girls" (American Association of University Women, 1992) and in the well-documented "chilly" campus climate for women. After earning her Ph.D. at Cornell University, she taught for four years at the University of Maine and returns there every summer as a visiting scholar.

Alven Neiman is an assistant dean and concurrent associate professor in the College of Arts and Letters, the University of Notre Dame. As an assistant dean he directs the College's Core Course, a year-long interdisciplinary seminar required of all sophomores. As a philosopher of education he has written and published a number of pieces concerned with the nature and state of higher education in the United States.

Nel Noddings is Lee L. Jacks Professor of Child Education at Stanford University. Her area of special interest is philosophy of education and, within that, ethics, moral education, and mathematics education. She is a past president of the national Philosophy of Education Society and President of the John Dewey Society. She was a Phi Beta Kappa Visiting Scholar for the year 1989–1990. In addition to nine books—among them, *Caring: A Feminine Approach to Ethics and Moral Education, Women and Evil, The Challenge to Care in Schools,* and *Philosophy of Education*—she is the author of more than one hundred articles and chapters on various topics ranging from the ethics of caring to mathematical problem solving.

Shirley Pendlebury is the director of Teacher Education and an associate professor in the Department of Education at the University of the Witwatersrand in Johannesburg, South Africa, where she teaches courses in Philosophy of Education, Curriculum, and Teacher Development. In the early 1990s, she served as a coordinator of the Teacher Education Research Group of the National Educational Policy Initiative, established to advise policy-makers on the transformation of education in a post-apartheid South Africa. She is the author of several articles and chapters on teaching, luck, and wise practice. She is also the editor of the Southern African journal *Perspectives in Education.*

Emily Robertson is a dual associate professor of Education and Philosophy and chair of the Department of Cultural Foundations of Education at Syracuse University. Her research interprets the aims of education in relationship to moral, political, and social ideals and to theories of knowledge.

Betty Sichel holds a Ph.D. in philosophy of education from New York University, is a professor emerita of Education at Long Island University, and is a visiting researcher in the Department of Educational Leadership and Cultural Studies, University of Houston. During 1995–1996 she served as president of the Philosophy of Education Society. She has published articles on a variety of topics, including feminist ethics, moral education, professional ethics, and the educational ideas of classical Greek philosophy. She is author of *Moral Education: Ideals, Community, and Character* (Temple University Press, 1988). Her college teaching has always involved the education and professional development of teachers. During the last few years, she developed an innovative graduate teacher education program in collaboration with middle school principals and teachers.

Harvey Siegel is a professor of Philosophy at the University of Miami, Florida. His primary interests are in epistemology, philosophy of science, and philosophy of education. He is a past president of the Philosophy of Education Society. He is the author of many papers in these areas, and of two books: *Relativism Refuted: A Critique of Contemporary Epistemological Relativism* (D. Reidel, 1987) and *Educating Reason: Rationality, Critical Thinking, and Education* (Routledge, 1988). He also edited the anthology *Reason and Education: Essays in Honor of Israel Scheffler* (Kluwer, 1995).

Dilafruz Williams teaches foundations courses in teacher education and administrative licensure programs. She has received a grant from the Spencer Foundation for her study of the contemporary relevance of Gandhi's educational philosophy. She has also received an Outstanding Junior Faculty Award at Portland State University. For three years she has been the president of the Holistic Education Group, American Educational Research Association. She also serves on the editorial and review boards of *Holistic Education Review* and *Research in Middle Level Education.* Being grounded in practice, she is primarily interested in examining the nature and formation of communities in urban schools. Her publications cover a wide range of topics in education: ecology, inclusion, cooperative learning, middle-level education, and nonviolence.